THE STRANGE WORKS OF
TARO YOKO

The Strange Works of Taro Yoko: From Drakengard to NieR: Automata
by Nicolas Turcev
Published by Third Éditions
32 rue d'Alsace-Lorraine, 31000 TOULOUSE
contact@thirdeditions.com
www.thirdeditions.com/en

Follow us:
 : @Third_Editions
 : Facebook.com/ThirdEditions
 : Third Éditions
 : Third Éditions

Edited by: Nicolas Courcier and Mehdi El Kanafi
Editorial assistants: Damien Mecheri and Clovis Salvat
Texts: Nicolas Turcev
Proofreading: Claire Choisy, Jean-Baptiste Guglielmi et Zoé Sofer
Layout: Pierre Le Guennec
Classic cover: Bruno Wagner
Collector's edition cover: Johann Blais
Translated from French by: Shona Carceles Stuart Smith (ITC Traductions)

This educational work is Third Éditions' tribute to Taro Yoko's video games.
In this unique collection, the author retraces a chapter in the history of Taro Yoko's games by identifying the inspirations, background and contents of these games through original reflection and analysis.
Drakengard and *NieR* are registered trademarks of Square Enix. All rights reserved.
Cover art is inspired by Taro Yoko's games.

English edition, copyright 2018, Third Éditions.
All rights reserved.
ISBN 978-2-37784-048-9
Printed in the European Union by TypoLibris.

Nicolas Turcev

Foreword by Taro Yoko

THE STRANGE WORKS OF
TARO YOKO
From Drakengard to NieR: Automata

03rd | THIRD
éditions

PUBLISHER DISCLAIMER

We chose to use the written form "Taro Yoko" to put an end to the confusion surrounding this creator's name, often written "Yoko Taro," which suggests that Taro is his last name, whereas it is his first name.

In Japan, name order is different from the West. In the Japanese archipelago, as in China or Korea, the last name is placed before the first name. Indeed, "Yoko Taro" is correct in the Japanese sense, since Yoko is his last name. However, this is not the commonly used order applied by Western press or specialized publishers. We do not read about Miyamoto Shigeru or Kojima Hideo, but Shigeru Miyamoto and Hideo Kojima.

Nevertheless, the confusion surrounding Taro Yoko is driven by various factors. The first is none other than the games themselves, whose credits specify "Yoko Taro." Also, the creator enjoys casting doubt on this, even on social media (Yoko Taro on Twitter, Taro Yoko on Facebook). Finally, Yoko is a common Japanese first name—the difference being that it is in fact a female first name. This last point is probably what caused the initial confusion.

By choosing to write Taro Yoko, we simply comply with the traditional Western approach, which places the first name before the last name. However, we are bending the rules of Japanese to English transcription, which would result in "Tarô Yokoo"—but since even the official game credits spell it without a circumflex accent and with only one o, we will stick to Taro Yoko. The names of Japanese toponyms and Taro Yoko's collaborators are however written with their accents in accordance with Third Éditions' typographical methods.

CONTENTS

THE STRANGE WORKS OF
TARO YOKO
From Drakengard to NieR:Automata

FOREWORD

Hello, this is Taro Yoko.

I've been asked to introduce myself, so... How should I put it? I am the person who made the games which are (perhaps) presented in this book.

"Perhaps" because I have not read the book yet. Who knows? Maybe the author had fun writing things which have absolutely nothing to do with gaming and are solely focused on "*kawaii*" culture or the otaku trend in Japan, for instance. Either way, I like both. And in any case, only insane people take an interest in such cultures.

In short, it is obviously a great honor for my team and I to have our games featured like this in such a faraway country as France.

However, I cannot help but think that a book on such a subject is very likely to end up being an unprofitable venture. I worry about the author, but also tend to think that he must be somewhat crazy as well to come up with such a subject. Oh well, it does not matter.

Besides, I just thought of something. The person reading these lines must have played titles such as *Drakengard* or *NieR*–or at least have an interest in them–and is probably not the only one. They too must inevitably be strange people to read a book striving to describe such odd games coming from a remote archipelago like mine. In the end, we find ourselves in the following situation: some eccentric wrote a book on games designed by another eccentric and played by people who are equally eccentric.

Frankly, I worry about the future of our planet.

However, when I see crazy people all over the world getting excited with knives, rifles or missiles in front of cameras, when I hear about all these deaths on the news or, worse, when I watch these businessmen in suits holding a Starbucks coffee and getting excited about the stock exchange price instead of worrying about those dying that they see on the news, I suddenly find us much less eccentric. And to think that these businessmen are considered "normal" by society...

Who knows? Our world may have already gone completely mad.

With that,

Taro Yoko

THE STRANGE WORKS OF
TARO YOKO
From Drakengard to NieR : Automata

PREFACE

G ames have been more than just games for several millennia. The ancient Egyptians saw the game 58 Holes (ancestor of the Game of the Goose) as a spiritual vehicle on which the divine will was imprinted[1]. Long before Jean-Jacques Rousseau explained through *Emile* that games teach children the reality they will face as adults, mankind had already sensed that this entertainment allowed them to duplicate, play with and manipulate their environment and thus symbolize the world. But also to take part in it and, by a fair return, be influenced by the games' symbolism. Playing cops and robbers already represents a view on society (repressive), it conveys a message (complying with the law) and internalizes it through performance. Thus, games represent the world just as well as the world represents itself, better at times, since they reduce it, break it up and paint it to isolate the meaning of the background noises that interfere with understanding. Incidentally, games, like any other medium, are valuable indicators of how we try to represent our interaction with the world and define its value system.

Hence, we can have legitimate concerns about the deep feelings spreading through our civilizations, when the majority of the most popular video games suggest the use of a firearm as the main means of action. The success of the *Call of Duty* shooting game series, for example, is enough to diagnose the ultra-militarized state of Western nations and the prevalence of the feeling of perpetual war in public opinion. Of course, nobody waited around for the FPS genre before they started to "play war"; chess and the game of Go have century-old traditions. But yesterday's world, in the 10th and 15th centuries when these hobbies were invented, was essentially the theater of large battlefields. On the other hand, we are currently living in an unprecedented time of peace in history. A respite concurrent with the incredible multiplicity of game forms allowed by the advent of video games and microcomputers. Yet, violence still seems to be at the heart of the global entertainment project. It is in part this strange situation, to say the least, which inspires the titles of the Japanese director Taro Yoko.

---

1. Players threw sticks or jacks whose final position reflected the will of the gods.

Throughout his career, the image of mankind depicted by most big-budget video games has led this Nagoya native to despair. While games grant us the ability to understand each other and build bridges by allowing the player to experience different worlds than his own, the majority of the industry has chosen not to exploit this ability and instead suggests that we beat and dominate each other, by any means possible: crowbars, guns, punches, decapitations, tanks, the list goes on. Video games, in short, prefer to do business by glorifying violence rather than taking advantage of its interaction abilities in order to strengthen human bonds.

Through his works, from *Drakengard* to *NieR: Automata*, Yoko attempts to explore the reasons behind this strange fascination with conflict. Are men so vicious that they must triumph, discriminate, hurt and kill even for entertainment? In order to answer this question, throughout his approach the creator analyzes mankind's dark sides: madness, war, perversion, suicide, among others. Consequently, his games, themselves particularly violent, are rarely viewed at first glance as channels through which human flaws are called into question. Since Yoko's method is subversive, he appropriates the subjects that challenge him to better emphasize contradictions, false pretenses and a somewhat short logic. But the creator is by no means provocative or pointing fingers to shortcomings. In reality, we are dealing with an otaku full of kindness and curious about the world. Mischievous, intrigued, sometimes a little naive, slightly perverse and occasionally rebellious, Taro Yoko is above all endowed with an incredible ability to divert conventions in order to inject strangeness. He always positions himself one or even several steps apart, juggling with all sorts of unnatural alliances that generate the character of his games. Indeed, they combine, with an unusual majesty, the carefree melancholy of the entertainment practice with the story of mankind slowly perishing in long agony, because in the huge devastated battleground of mankind's war against mankind, Yoko perceives entertainment as a hope, a horizon, a bulwark against evil. The director's great altruistic project is part of the portrayed opposition between games and nihilism. By creating video games, Taro Yoko is not just experimenting. He wants to save the world.

NICOLAS TURCEV

Journalist specialized in pop culture, he has contributed to the following magazines: *Chronic'Art*, *Carbone*, *Games* and *Gamekult*, and occasionally participates in the video game analysis site *Merlanfrit*. He is also the author of several articles of the *Level Up* collection at Third Éditions.

THE STRANGE WORKS OF
TARO YOKO
From Drakengard to NieR:Automata

CHAPTER I — CREATION

D uring the 2000s, a trend towards consolidation and centralization emerged in the Japanese video game industry. In just three years, from 2003 to 2005, three of the world's largest conglomerates were created: Square Enix (then Square Enix Holdings Co.), born from the merger between Square Co. and Enix; SEGA Sammy Holdings, the outcome of the joint takeover of the developer and publisher SEGA by Sammy, a pachislot and pachinko[1] manufacturer; and Namco Bandai Holdings (later renamed Bandai Namco Holdings), an entity created through the merger between Namco and Bandai Co, two major players in the entertainment industry. This massive reorganization thus claimed to address a twofold problem, both domestic and global.

On a local level, Japan's technology industries were weakened following the Lost Decade and the deflationary spiral that followed the bursting of the Japanese speculation bubble–the abrupt stop of The Glorious Thirty's[2] Japanese economic miracle. Combined with, at times clumsy, business strategies the difficult economic times prevented these video game leaders from stabilizing their profits, which were overly subjected to headwinds. The numerous mergers thus offset a structural need for consolidation induced by a dangerous climate. SEGA, according to Sammy's CEO Hajime Satomi's[3] own admission, had been in the red for at least ten years on the day of the merger in 2004, partly because of the lack of solidification and uniformity in the company's organization chart. Similarly, Square warded off the curse cast by the box office flop of its first computer-animated movie, *Final Fantasy: The Spirits Within*, by establishing a partnership with Enix. For the publisher, who favored in-house productions and generally assumed all risks, the merger ensured more flexibility in order to absorb this kind of impact. In addition to the economic slump, Japan's video game industry was also facing a demographic dilemma: the extraordinary aging of the

---

1. Crossover between a slot machine and a pinball game.
2. A strong economic growth period in the country from the early 1960s to the 1980s, corresponding to Japan's entry into mass production-driven capitalism.
3. https://www.gamespot.com/articles/sammy-reveals-new-logo-changes-at-sega/1100-6099624/

population. The phenomenon was abrupt. In a matter of about twenty years, from the late 1980s to the beginning of the new millennium, people aged sixty-five or older who represented one tenth of the total population now accounted for over one quarter. According to the OECD (Organisation for Economic Co-operation and Development), the birth rate of 1.8 children per woman in 1980 dropped to 1.3 in 1999 and is just beginning to recover today. The share of young people aged fifteen and under fell by eight points between 1983, the NES's launch date in Japan, and the year 2000, to come crashing down at 14.6% of the population. Set at 12.9% in 2013, this rate remains the lowest of the OECD in years. Teenagers, the beloved targets of video game communicators, especially in Japan where the industry was built upon the presence of consoles within the family unit, were becoming scarce. In the joint press release following the announcement of their merger, Bandai and Namco also noted the impact of the "drop in numbers of children" on their respective activities. Hence, in part, the need to acquire more striking power to win the favors of an increasingly smaller audience.

On the global level, the emergence of these small video game empires initiated the preparation of hostilities against international competition. Even though these Japanese *holdings[4] were obviously in competition with each other, they were doubly so with the rising Western majors* threatening to invade their console gaming territory. Yôichi Wada, appointed president of Square Enix at the time, was right: "This is an offensive merger, in order to survive[5]," he declared in 2002. The first item on the counter-offensive list, common to all these new entities, was the pooling of production costs. The AAA titles or blockbuster budgets, even adjusted for inflation, had increased significantly as the mobilized teams had grown, sometimes reaching or even exceeding the size of Hollywood teams. The cost of labor was indeed becoming difficult to reduce, largely because of the vacancies related to 3D development (Motion-Designer, CG Designer, Shader Artist). This inevitably drove video games industry players to group and create synergies with their respective talents in order to save precious financial resources. This symbiotic spirit can be found in the new strategic complementarities that emerged from these mergers. Taking advantage of acquired rights on a large number of well-known Japanese animation characters, Bandai could for example insert strong licenses (*Naruto, Digimon*, etc.) from the in-house catalog into Namco's games and thus strengthen its sphere of influence. Through such partnerships, these new major entertainment groups were seeking to take over the market with their flagship brands, using all possible

---

4. A company that incorporates shares in other companies and generally sets the course for the strategy of the group it represents.
5. http://www.ign.com/articles/2002/11/25/square-and-enix-merge

channels and no longer being solely limited to the video games' channel. Yôichi Wada named this tactic the "business model of polymorphic content." "It's very difficult to hit the jackpot, as it were. Once we've hit it, we have to get all the juice possible out of it," he explained in 2008 to justify his theory[6].

With the birth of these conglomerates, Japanese publishers also found themselves in a position whereby they could foster and structure the country's productive fabric around themselves and beyond. Enix, which already had a tradition of delegating design to a small *pool* of loyal studios (tri-Ace, Quintet, ChunSoft, etc.) amplified the process after the merger with Square. A plethora of spin-offs based on *Dragon Quest* or *Final Fantasy*, their two flagship licenses, but also other unpublished projects were entrusted to specialized studios whose orders were increasingly multiplying, driven by a strong subcontracting demand from major publishers. Three of these are of interest to us: Cavia, Access Games and PlatinumGames. Like many of their counterparts, their history and the history of the *Drakengard* and *NieR* games design are inextricably linked to the configuration of Japan's industry and the ups and downs of its leaders.

DRAKENGARD
Cavia's birth

It all started with a drink. In 1999, Takamasa Shiba and Takuya Iwasaki met in a bar. The former was a producer at Enix, and the latter a jack-of-all-trades at Namco, who had recently been put in charge of the military flight game *Ace Combat 3: Electrosphere*'s development. Iwasaki took advantage of this meeting to make a proposal to his colleague: what if the player wielded a dragon instead of *Ace Combat*'s fighter planes? In no time at all, the two men laid the foundations for the future *Drakengard* (*Drag-on Dragoon* in Japan): a dragon flight simulator taking place in a medieval fantasy-type universe. At the time, negotiations between Square and Enix had not yet begun, and Enix, mainly a publisher, could not count on its main partner studios to handle the design, as it was busy with the production of the next iterations of *Torneko*, *Dragon Quest* or *Star Ocean*. Iwasaki resigned from Namco and founded Cavia in March 2000 to begin the development of the title, with Enix's support. A large portion of the employees then emigrated from Namco, since they mainly came from teams that had worked on *Ace Combat*, *Ridge Racer* and the *Resident Evil* and *Crisis* franchises. At the same time, the modest structure opted to subcontract in order

6. http://www.gamesindustry.biz/articles/square-dance

to fill its order book. Created in the midst of the Japanese animation boom, Cavia chose to position itself in the games' niche linked to licenses that spread the otaku subculture throughout the archipelago. At the same time as *Drakengard*, it launched the production of a Game Boy Advance game bearing the name *One Piece* and the *Resident Evil: Dead Aim* spin-off on PlayStation 2. It was also during this period that Taro Yoko, barely thirty years old and a confirmed otaku, stepped in.

Beneath the mask

Nowadays, most of the players who have heard of Taro Yoko do not associate his name to any particular face. Inconvenienced by public appearances, the director systematically equipped himself with a device to cover his face during meetings with the press, at least since the creation of *NieR*. Shortly before the announcement of *NieR: Automata* at the E3 2015, Yoko even had a mask made, based on the character Emil, by a plastic artist from PlatinumGames for a mere four hundred euros. Since then, he has worn it every time he is in the presence of photo and video cameras. His persistence in hiding his face under this thick layer of plastic naturally arouses curiosity. One might be led to believe that this is a communication strategy or the eccentricity of an enigmatic creator. Nevertheless, the visual anonymity of the director is in no way a means to nurture the mystery of his personality. Far from comparing himself to the likes of Banksy (a famous street artist and statement maker, who prefers to remain anonymous), Yoko just prefers to let his games speak for themselves. In fact, ask him, and he will answer with no difficulty that he grew up in Nagoya, in the Japanese prefecture of Aichi. Restaurant managers (izakayas, ramens, tempuras, etc.), his parents flitted from one restaurant opening to the next and entrusted their son's education to his grandmother. These were the 1970s and the standard Japanese family unit still encompassed three generations. When he started high school in the 1980s, young Yoko discovered the otaku culture, the result of strolls through amusement arcades and muggy afternoons spent watching loads of *anime*. "Dark and unattractive" according to his own description, Yoko did not belong to the small circle of popular boys at the time—he would secretly curse his friends when they went to the beach to have fun with a few girls. Furthermore, the situation would not improve during his years at Kobe Design University: he had by then become a true otaku and girls always avoided him. The "ladies" as he calls them, were not part of his youth. Yoko, like a perfect metronome, always comes back to this subject during public statements. Sometimes as a joke, though more often to try, visibly, to revisit a key moment of his past. At this point in his life, Yoko was aware that he was on the losing side of the human lottery–or rather of the symbolic relationships of dominance during puberty. So it is probably no coincidence that his later works show so much fascination for the harmful effects of pitting people against each other.

The video game which made him want to become a designer was from the shoot them up genre: *Gradius*. Amazed by the deluge of bullets, endless possibilities seemed to present themselves to him: "You just have to take a black screen and put a few dots on it, and that's it, you can really feel that space," he raved. The potential of the medium seemed infinite, capable of expressing poetry as well as cinema. At the end of his studies, he began his career at Namco as a CG[7] Designer, then joined Sony Computer Entertainment, from which he was dismissed, before finally landing at Cavia in 2001, where they wanted to make him the artistic director of *Drakengard*, before granting him the reins of development.

Project Dragonsphere

Indeed, overwhelmed by his work as director on *Resident Evil: Dead Aim* and his numerous contributions to other titles[8], Takuya Iwasaki rapidly promoted Taro Yoko by granting him the project leadership role in his place, and settling for a co-producer role with Takamasa Shiba. Scriptwriter Sawako Natori tackled the writing process with Yoko, while the rest of the main team revolved around them, including character designer Kimihiko Fujisaka, executive producer Yôsuke Saitô (Square Enix), composer Nobuyoshi Sano and head designer Akira Yasui. Most of them will be involved, at different levels, in future sequels. Together, they started bringing Iwasaki's original dragon flight simulator idea to life. Code name: "Project Dragonsphere." But Enix intervened after some time. The publisher was impressed by the success[9] of the beat 'em up *Dynasty Warriors 2* game (the *Musou* series in Japan), which involved saturating the screen with enemies to allow the player to wreak havoc. Shiba therefore pressured Cavia into incorporating hack'n'slash[10] combat phases into the game in order to broaden the target audience. It was also, at the time, a means of innovation. For the producer, *Drakengard* was an opportunity to push back the boundaries of RPGs, action games and flight simulations by mixing the codes of these genres. "All three modes merge into one very interesting game," he declared to the European press

7. For Computer Graphics.
8. From 2000 to 2003, when *Drakengard* was being created, Takuya Iwasaki appeared on the credits of no less than five games, including *Kingdom Hearts* (as character designer).
9. One hundred eighty-five thousand sales over the first week following its release.
10. Literally "hacking and slashing," the hack'n'slash video game genre enables the player to fight against hordes of monsters usually in a repetitive way.

in 2004, after the release of the game. "So one could argue that the overall effect is like an orchestra, where a cello or a violin doesn't exist individually, rather they are merged into one harmony." Shiba's vision, which differed somewhat from the original project, belonged to a system hybridization trend, popular among major publishers who sought to fill their games with varied content in order to satisfy the appetites of the most hardcore players. In order to influence Cavia and raise the teams' awareness of the *Dynasty Warriors* style, Shiba gathered the team in a corner of the office and made them watch DVDs of epic movies saturated with massive battle scenes: *The Mummy*, *The Scorpion King*, *Gladiator* and so on. The aim was to transpose the feeling of power in the face of adversity from these scenes into the game. But according to Yoko, this shift generated, above all, an uproar in the studio: everything, or almost, had to be redone.

At that moment, Cavia, a small studio cut out for relatively modest projects, found itself wading out of its depth. From a flight simulation game, the project had transformed into a medium-sized action-RPG, draining the work force of just over a hundred people within a relatively narrow structure. The first drafts of the game not being calibrated for the beat 'em up genre, Cavia resolved to rework the skeleton of *Drakengard* itself. New problems arose. How could they display a mass of characters, and model a map big enough to make it look like the fight is taking place on a real battlefield without ruining performance? How could they adapt the camera and controls to ensure smooth transitions between ground combat and flight phases? In addition to these programmer headaches, the new specifications included the appearance of magic spells with saved animations, which were both classy and expensive. But there was no other choice: they were part of the essential prerequisites for the heroic fantasy orientation claimed by Enix, and later Square Enix. In light of these technical challenges, Yoko planned to make *Drakengard* fit on two discs, but production refused. Obviously lacking human and technical resources, Cavia could not deliver a properly finished product. The jump mechanism, since it could not be debugged in time, does not appear in the final version. The camera, tight and difficult to handle in the Japanese version, was reworked in the American and European versions, together with the removal of the rather flagrant bugs. But it was still not enough. Unsurprisingly, during its release in the West in 2004, *Drakengard* was criticized by the press and critics for its mechanical and technical shortcomings. The graphics engine hiccupped as soon as the screen was even remotely overloaded, the display distance was fair at best, the ground environments were, most of the time, dramatically empty and dull, the modeling of enemy infantry units and their animations were hardly credible, and the beat 'em up action in particular, even for the time, drastically lacked originality and variety. The movements of

Caim, the hero, were limited to a handful of takes, often similar and extremely repetitive, in addition to being slow. In Japan, the euphemism *"slow action"* is used to define this general failure. Later, when *Drakengard 3*[11] was released, Shiba implicitly acknowledged a distribution error. Primarily specialized in the creation of Namco arcade games, Cavia did not have the necessary expertise to refine and adjust the action aspect set by Enix. However, the teams did offer something new by overlaying the *Ace Combat* structure on the role-playing one.

Ace Combat's heir

Many have seen *Drakengard* as an attempt to reinterpret Team Andromeda's *Panzer Dragoon* rail shooter series, which itself made an attempt at role-playing games with the *Panzer Dragoon Saga* installment. But *Drakengard*'s essence, like many of its ideas, in truth inherited Iwasaki's work on *Ace Combat 3*. Several of the series' recurring motifs which contributed to its success and identity came from Namco's game. We can naturally begin by mentioning the third-person flight mode and free-moving camera, the *"Strafe Mode,"* in which the red dragon Angelus, controlled by the player, can burn the battlefield from the air. The family lineage was probably concealed by the press due to the catastrophic Western porting of *Ace Combat 3*, which deprived it of many of its assets. Among the elements cut during localization were six possible endings and different storylines that depended on the player's performance during the main missions. The original version was widely staged and also contained long radio communication sessions between the main characters as well as cartoon scenes, all of which were fully dubbed. Many elements cut from the version sold to Europeans and Americans were added to *Drakengard*'s structure.

Divided into thirteen chapters, themselves subdivided into sub-chapters available from a map menu, *Drakengard* contained three types of missions: airborne missions, ground missions, and a hybrid type of mission where the player could alternate between the two. In addition to the main campaign, various side quests offered to revisit previous areas in order to collect additional weapons and treasures. Nothing more common, in short. This became more complicated once the player had finished the game for the first time and had to navigate between sub-chapters to try and reach the additional endings. In accordance with the arcade philosophy that permeates its programmers, Cavia hid part of the storyline behind performance conditions. The stories of the supporting characters, in particular, were only available after finishing specific parts within a certain time limit. But the craziest challenge, in the sense of

11. https://www.youtube.com/watch?v=D5Q7J7rHts0

insane, remained the collection of every single weapon, necessary to reach the fifth and final ending, called "ending E."

In addition to non-linear storylines and multiple endings, *Drakengard* actually introduced a mechanism that would be replicated in all the other games of the series[12] : the weapons collection and enhancement mechanism. There were sixty-five in the first installment, divided into several categories (sword, pole axes, etc.), which had their own statistics and combos. The more a weapon was used to kill, the more experience points it would gain, and would therefore be able to level up, three times at most. In addition to the change in appearance that accompanied this power increase, each level up revealed a small part of the weapon's history, almost always incredibly tragic. And as in its sequels (with the exception of *NieR: Automata*), *Drakengard* required the player to collect the entire arsenal in order to access the final ending. An almost impossible task to accomplish without the use of a guide, given their at times preposterous acquisition conditions[13]. Just as eccentric, the ending E teleported the player into modern Tokyo. A "joke" according to Yoko, inspired by the alien easter eggs of *Silent Hill*[14]. Actually more than a joke, this was the culmination of a strategic demarcation process undertaken by Cavia during the design phase.

Operation Distinction

The dilemma was: how could *Drakengard* set itself apart from the competition? The stakes were crucial as the market in which the game had to position itself was saturated, both by the annual presence of *Dynasty Warriors* and the flood of titles. Between 2001 and 2003, over a hundred Japanese role-playing games appeared solely on the PlayStation 2[15]. Shiba's insistence on using heroic fantasy codes with a *Dungeons & Dragons'* approach in this game did not help find a solution: this kind of universe was already all over the stalls of video game stores. All the same, Yoko was asked to design a fantasy universe close to *Final Fantasy* or *Dragon Quest*. Knowing that he had no chance of overthrowing these two leading lights on their own turf, the director preferred to follow a different path. He set the action in European medieval folklore (notably Celtic myths). He then tried to introduce real country names to bring a sense of reality at odds

---

12. The weapons' design was almost identical in each game for financial reasons.
13. One of the worst involves making enemies appear by following an arbitrary path consisting of six bends in a tortuous castle.
14. Except for *Silent Hill 4: The Room* and *Silent Hill: Downpour*, all games in the series contained an absurd hidden ending in connection with an alien invasion.
15. According to the specialized site *Legendra.com*.

with the fantasy genre: France, Germany, etc.[16] But production objected to this, and forced him to use more generic and less realistic names: "Land of forest", "Land of mountains" and so on, and since he could not differentiate himself with an original universe, Yoko chose to change the tone. Taking the opposite approach to the Japanese RPGs for teenagers, often bright and good-natured, he intentionally turned towards darker, even taboo themes. The game theme was based on immorality. The strong presence of hack'n'slash elements would serve as a foundation for this orientation. In Yoko's mind, it was indeed the perfect opportunity to reflect upon the tendency that video game heroes had towards killing without shame, without the slightest trace of moral distress. At the time, *Dynasty Warriors* was ironically the most obvious example, since the series had built its reputation on the scale of carnage it produced on screen. Surely, Yoko thought, the characters participating in such atrocities must actually go mad and should not deserve a happy ending. Madness thus became the leitmotif of the first *Drakengard*, whose characters suffered all more or less from insanity, in one form or another: incest, pedophilia, cannibalism, blood lust, the overstatement was intentional and exaggerated[17], but not totally meaningless—both on the marketing and the artistic levels. For the director, displeased with the inclusion of ground action phases, reviewing the beat'em up genre with a narrative overlay allowed him to distance this violence imposed on him and to deploy an atmosphere original enough to be noticed.

To accompany and underline this tacky atmosphere, Nobuyoshi Sano (*Tekken 3*, *Ridge Racer*) composed a chaotic orchestration soundtrack elaborated from extracts of popular classical music (Dvorak, Debussy, Mozart, Wagner, etc.), twisted and distorted to the extreme. The request came from Takamasa Shiba, the producer. The latter asked Denji Sano, the musical director, for something "classically sophisticated" with a dark madness element. The team in charge of sound then theorized a method to obtain *"otodama,"* meaning "mystical sounds" or "spirit sounds." Takayuki Aihara, co-composer, selected the greatest classical music phrases that would serve as raw material. These were orchestrated, then digitally reconstructed. They were then superimposed, mixed and cut using a computer, as if a madman had put them in a shaker, with no real will to harmonize times and atmospheres. Sano used the entire technological arsenal to break down and rearrange tracks: loops, reverse playback *e tutti quanti*. Altered through techno music technology, the initial classical music extracts no longer resembled anything recognizable, other than a long contorted incantation or a never-ending tainted

---

16. *Drakengard*'s map is a reversed map of Europe.

17. Some of these themes were somewhat reduced by censorship when the game was released in Europe and the United States in 2004, such as Leonard's pedophilia or revenge against God. Only five years after the Columbine killing, video games were still perceived as a morally suspicious object.

trance. This allowed the composer to corrupt anything familiar, to bring out the agony, echoing the mental cacophony of the characters and the horrors of the battlefield. The effect was so striking for Sano that he felt like he had perverted history. At the time, the soundtrack's deconstructionist approach did not really please the critics or the players. Too cacophonous, too loudly ahead of its time. Accustomed to more melodious and harmonious compositions typical of Japanese RPGs, fans of the genre were disconcerted. However, *Drakengard*'s soundtrack remains one of the most interesting attempts of mixing the use of noise and the expressionist approach with a large variety of classical music in video games. The very fact that it could exist was a feat, as progressive rock or lively scores were standard at the time. But for the producer Iwasaki, this musical orientation was obvious, as he would explain in the booklet accompanying the soundtrack reissue[18]: "*Drakengard* depicts the pitiable madness of those people who have been brainwashed. The player acting this out needs an accompaniment that makes him experience those negative feelings." Iwasaki concluded by rejoicing that *Drakengard*'s music worked as "a hallucinogen inducing a nightmare that will not end", a sign that any compromise on this subject was rejected in favor of radical experimentation. But Taro Yoko is the best person to talk about this strange musical object. We cannot resist the urge to share his entire analysis with you, also released with the soundtrack reissue in 2011. Bittersweet and poetically naturalist, it sheds light on both the game and the personality of the person who designed it.

"It would be difficult to explain the music of *Drakengard* in a single paragraph. I want you to imagine the following: on a morning without school or work, a carefully selected egg has been lying on the table since the previous night at room temperature. You lightly pluck the egg off of the table and crack it over a bowl filled with cooked *koshihikari*[19] rice, adding a dash of *katsuhobushi*[20], finely grated on a wood block. To top it off, and here you need to be careful, you add a few drops of light-colored soy sauce. You take your time to lightly stir in these ingredients. Filtered amidst the grains of cooked rice, part of the egg cooks, and part remains raw. It must not be mixed in too thoroughly. If it is possible, it is best to leave two to three clumps of white rice completely untouched by the egg, sitting like clumps of marble. Combined with the raw egg, this rice, which is as hot as possible, will make the perfect temperature. We calmly debate the merits of our respective ingredients as all of this spreads inside your mouth and fills your empty stomach. Then, we consider the song as we kill each other."

18. Https://web.archive.org/web/20140222144620/ http://www.squareenixmusic.com/features/liners/ Drakengard.shtml Japanese to English translation by Ben Schweitzer.
19. A very popular rice variety in Japan.
20. A fermented and dried bonito fish preparation.

A real gourmet, Yoko is also, as has been said, an experienced otaku. To nurture the deviance of his protagonists and the repulsive climate of his game, he will draw his inspiration from *seinens*, the name of adult mangas with usually more complex and morally ambiguous themes than mangas for teenagers. The *Berserk* manga and *Neon Genesis Evangelion* animated series were taken as reference points. The former for its dark fantasy atmosphere and the character Guts on which Caim was later modeled, the latter for its gloomy ambiance and its casting of tortured teenagers on which Yoko and Iwasaki intensely based themselves to create *Drakengard*'s climate. The director also took this opportunity to settle his scores with some Japanese animation stereotypes which he found questionable. In addition to the violent failings of video games, his deconstruction initiative targeted the animation series *Sister Princess* and its fetishism of the perfect little sister cliché. Released as a manga, on television and in video games in the form of an *eroge[21]*, *Sister Princess* tells the story of twelve sisters who idolize their only older brother. A popular example of the abounding harem literature[22] in Japan; Yoko offered an acid satire through the character of Furiae and her incestuous desires towards her big brother Caim. The ending B, in which Furiae transforms into a monster and multiplies endlessly, is devised as an illustration of these sisters' superficiality and cruelty.

Although these examples are aimed at illustrating the room for maneuver that Yoko had in order to impose his vision, the truth is a little more nuanced. Throughout development, the director had to fight to ensure that his ideas prevailed. The increasing accumulation of small trifling details irritated Yoko to such an extent that he gave up directing *Drakengard 2*. First, he was asked to color the sky blue instead of the red and gray hues used to give the game its surrealistic cachet. Then, to adopt a new nomenclature full of gibberish invented for the game when it could be based on existing mythologies. Above all, producers had to intervene before the characters became too dark. For example, the actions of Leonard, the pedophile priest, were supposed to be further explored.

Cavia restructures itself

When *Drakengard* was released, it won the support of a large number of players from Japan and the West. In the archipelago, the game sold twenty-two thousand copies during the first week and rose to the top of the sales rankings.

21. For *erotic game*, a Japanese video game genre containing erotic scenes. In specific terms, this is a *bishôjo* game for young heterosexual men, where the *gameplay* focuses on interacting with pretty girls. The player's aim is to create a relationship with one of them.
22. Type of situation in Japanese animation where the hero or heroine is surrounded by a multitude of admirers that he or she must or can seduce.

This number had doubled by the end of 2003. In Europe, the game sold a little over a hundred thousand copies during the first year following its release, a fair result given the time and the targeted niche market. This success was enough for Square Enix to give the green light for the development of a sequel. Yoko then proposed a concept that would reconnect with Cavia's arcade roots: a space shooter with dragons. But his idea was rejected fairly quickly. Instead, *Drakengard 2*, designed by the same creative executives with the exception of Yoko, essentially took the hybrid beat 'em up formula of its predecessor and tried to improve upon it. The action theoretically takes place[23] eighteen years after *Drakengard*'s ending A, when Angelus, the red dragon, becomes the Goddess of the Seal after Furiae's disappearance. Some of the original characters, including Caim, Seere and Manah, cross paths with the hero, Nowe, one of the knights in charge of protecting the Seal. Directed by Akira Yasui, head designer of the first installment, this second creation fell in line with Japanese RPG standards and offered a much more colorful, lively and teenage world than its predecessor. Square Enix sought to soften the tone so that *Drakengard* could convince a broader audience and thus become one of its flagship licenses. But this shift disappointed many early fans, who cherished the gloomy atmosphere of the original installment. In retrospect, Shiba will concede that his publisher's request had been a mistake[24], as critics had received this new episode more indifferently—this time, the more conventional universe and characters could not make up for the *gameplay*'s shortcomings, which remained virtually unchanged.

As for Yoko, busy with other priorities, he only intervened in the last design phase as video editor. His detachment from the project did not, however, prevent him from expressing his creative disagreements to Yasui, with whom he maintains what he calls a "love-hate" relationship. Their rivalry took on such proportions that it was immortalized in the game, through the history of the Kingsblood weapon. This story tells of the near fratricidal battle between two generals who were once friends, provoked by their identical covetousness for a unique sword. Quickly, the battle led to war. To defeat their opponent, one used sheer strength (Taro Yoko), whilst the other used strategic flexibility (Akira Yasui). It seemed they had reached a stalemate. The apologue ends with the comment of a villager on the battleground, who noted that the two generals were both brave warriors, and that the world would have been a happier place if they had cooperated instead of sowing destruction. As for the two programmers, on good terms outside the office, they never worked together again.

23. In truth, *Drakengard 2* is located in a different time branch disconnected from the storyline of *Drakengard*, but follows, in substance, the events of ending A.
24. http://www.shacknews.com/article/81558/*Drakengard3*-trying-to-avoid-formulaic-jrpg-tropes-with-its

Nevertheless, *Drakengard 2* sold well. Clearly well enough for Cavia, reassured by the good results of *Ghost in The Shell: Stand Alone Complex* and *Naruto: Uzumaki Chronicles*, to increase the scope of its operations. In October 2005, Cavia changed its name and became a holding company for studios: AQ Interactive. The former president (1984-1998) and founder of SEGA of Japan, Hayao Nakayama, taking over the chairmanship of the new company's board of directors, was behind this operation. The apple does not fall far from the tree, as AQ Interactive's structure replicated the structure of the blue hedgehog's firm before its acquisition by Sammy, namely gathering together several development units with low synergies[25]. This is no coincidence, since AQ Interactive placed under its protection subsidiaries formed or joined by SEGA defectors who left shortly before or after the merger with Sammy. We can mention Artoon, founded by Sonic Team character designer Naoto Oshima, followed into his exile by a large part of his team and that of Team Andromeda, including Yoji Ishii (*OutRun*, *Panzer Dragoon*) who would take on the CEO position of the holding company. Transformed by Microsoft Game Studio Japan into a support studio for the production of Mistwalker[26] games, including *Lost Odyssey*, the company Scarab, renamed Feelplus for the occasion, also fell into AQ Interactive's hands. Renamed Cavia Inc., the third and last subsidiary assembled the video game programming processes of the original company. The offensive announced by this reorganization was initiated during the holiday season: in December, each of the three studios announced the development of one or more titles for next-generation consoles.

Set up like a war machine taking the new consoles (Wii, Xbox 360, PlayStation 3) by storm, AQ Interactive followed the centralist trend, a feature of the Japanese industry at the time, aware of the Western landslide which was about to sweep in. Nevertheless, it stood out as it avoided directly absorbing production teams in a parent company and preferred maintaining relationships step-by-step. This applied not only to the cooperation between Feelplus and Mistwalker, but also between Mistwalker and Cavia Inc. for the creation of the *Cry On* RPG, Cavia's first major project using high definition consoles along with the extremely second-rate *Bullet Witch*. The action-RPG *Cry On,* of which little is actually known[27], would however be canceled by AQ Interactive at the end of

25. What we call "second party studios," which are generally granted greater independence, both financial and artistic. In the early 2000s, SEGA transformed most of its in-house studios, or first party studios, into second party studios. A decision buried during the merger with Sammy in 2004, which established more interdisciplinary "R&D Divisions."

26. Studio founded by the creator of *Final Fantasy*, Hironobu Sakaguchi, after his departure from Square caused by the box office failure of the computer-animated movie *Final Fantasy: The Spirits Within*.

27. Except that it was to be co-produced by Takuya Iwasaki, directed by Hironobu Sakaguchi himself (the emblematic director and producer of the *Final Fantasy* series, president of Mistwalker since he left Square), with the participation of Nobuo Uematsu, historic composer of the *Final Fantasy* music.

2008, three years after its disclosure, and more importantly only a few months after the American subprime[28] crisis, which did not spare the video game sector.

Cavia, which ended up with a big gap in its calendar, did not greatly benefit from AQ Interactive's contribution either, whose biggest mistake was probably to have partly focused its publishing activity on the Xbox 360. Not very popular in Japan, the American console never really managed to find its audience there. Many Japanese studios, including Mistwalker, which thought they were getting a head start on the Western market by offering exclusives, suffered a severe setback. Thus, *Bullet Witch* and *Tetris: The Grand Master Ace*, Cavia's two main titles published by AQ Interactive on Xbox 360, were a flop. Despite everything, the studio managed to keep up with its order activity by subcontracting for Capcom (*Resident Evil: The Umbrella Chronicles*), Bandai Namco (several games from the *Fate* series) and SEGA (the Wii adaptation of *Sega Bass Fishing*). But in the midst of the Japanese video game crisis[29], which was reinforced by a renewed economic recession in the country, Cavia's future became uncertain. Its next game, *NieR*, was to become its swan song.

NIER

At first, a yearning for magic

The first brainstorming sessions for *Drakengard*'s next episode began shortly after the release of the second installment, this time with Taro Yoko on the front line. However, Shiba warned his colleague that with the arrival of seventh generation consoles, AQ Interactive would not support a project on the PlayStation 2, which was sentenced to death. The game was therefore shifting to the next platforms. The Xbox 360 was initially considered. But little by little, what was to become *Drakengard 3* on paper mutated into something completely different. So much so that, internally, the name was abandoned and replaced by *NieR*. The first script drafts speak of a battle taking place in a world shaped by the imagination of picture books. We find the traces of this preliminary work in

---

28. In 2007, the burst of the American subprime financial bubble (toxic mortgage loans securitized into shares) caused a chain reaction: several major banks went bankrupt, the United States went into debt to save the banking system, and the global economy was seriously damaged.

29. Primarily concerning the console sector, our main focus. From the mid-2000s to the present day, the historical domestic market has experienced a sharp drop in turnover while revenues generated by mobile games are going through the roof. So much so that the two curves intersected at the turn of the decade and will no longer meet: in 2016, according to *Famitsu* magazine and analyst Yano, game and console sales represented 2.59 billion dollars (a 54% decrease compared to 2012), compared to 8 billion dollars for the mobile market.

the boss names of the future game, all inspired by popular tales like *Pinocchio* or *Hansel and Gretel*. But the magic approach was abandoned relatively soon in favor of a more fantasy and adult universe. *NieR* then evolved into a spin-off of the first *Drakengard*, and would later even be considered as its sequel, since it developed on the ending E. Although the creators did not express themselves publicly on the reasons for this shift, at least one reason can be easily identified. At the time, Square Enix showed interest in the project, and the publisher already owned a franchise exploiting the children's fables niche: *Kingdom Hearts*. Moreover, the birth of *Kingdom Hearts* embodies a turning point in the publisher's strategy, that of action-RPGs, which greatly influenced *NieR*'s positioning.

Square Enix's hesitations

Around the end of the 2000s, the firm noticed the exhaustion of the traditional turn-based formula of Japanese role-playing games. While the numbered episodes of *Final Fantasy* and *Dragon Quest* were still selling just as well, their secondary products based on this old model were increasingly struggling to convince. And at the company's headquarters in Shinjuku, it was clear that the increasing power of graphics processors announced a new era for video games, more resolutely focused on action. Thus, some of its flagship series such as *Final Fantasy VII* or *Final Fantasy: Crystal Chronicles* were put through the action-RPG mold[30]. This repositioning, ceremoniously initiated by the publisher with *Kingdom Hearts* and its collaboration with Disney, spread throughout the production chain and impacted the publisher's partner studios.

The behavior of Yôsuke Saitô, producer at Square Enix responsible for Cavia, perfectly illustrates this transformation. First in favor of Yoko steering *NieR* in the direction of an epic RPG in the same vein as *Final Fantasy* or *Star Ocean*, the executive changed his mind during development, instructing instead the director to produce a "truly action-based" game. Yoko only partly listened to him and delivered a traditional action-RPG in terms of its game mechanics, doing rightly so seeing that Cavia did not excel in the beat 'em up field. But Saitô's U-turn was not devoid of logic. Square Enix did not yet have an action-packed flagship game explicitly aimed at adults—in short, the equivalent of a *Kingdom Hearts* for the twenty-five to thirty-five age group. The stakes were high since, as indicated in the preamble, the audience was aging and the publisher was seeking to retain players who had grown up with the brand. Yôichi Wada, the CEO, was also aware that Japanese people in their thirties, today's working adults and yesterday's teenagers, no longer had the necessary time to immerse themselves in a

---

30. Respectively *Final Fantasy VII: Dirge of Cerberus* and *Final Fantasy Crystal Chronicles: Ring of Fates*.

grand adventure for hours on end. Action games, shorter by convention, could therefore offer an interesting solution to this problem[31]. More than an editorial epiphenomenon, *NieR* therefore represented an opportunity for Square Enix to fill a void in its catalog[32]. And although the vision conferred by Yoko did not fully meet its specifications, synergies still existed. At least the main conditions were met: hack'n'slash gameplay, dark universe, tragic plot, dialogs full of swearing, an abundant amount of blood... Although it did not get its own *Devil May Cry*, the crystal firm at least made sure it had its place on the starting line.

NieR is split in two

A few signatures later, Cavia was launched at full speed on the rails of a project that would last three years, generously assisted by Square Enix's teams (50% of the team on average) who heavily relied on the success of this new license—especially for export. This took place to such an extent that a close collaboration was established between the publisher's American offices and Cavia's management. During a presentation meeting in Los Angeles to gather Western opinions, Yoko and his producer were invited to give a presentation on the scenario: in a desolate world, a young warrior tries to save his little sister, Yonah, from a terrible disease thanks to his fighting skills. The Americans reacted strongly to this. Nier's character, sixteen, thin, androgynous, visibly fragile, almost feverish, did not meet the Western market's expectations. According to the decision makers, the fact that such a young man could wield enormous swords might look ridiculous. Everything was disrupted: the hero must change. Small side note: it is probably worth noting that this occurred in the midst of a video game dadification[33] trend. Yoko responded and worked on the development of a second protagonist, or rather a more westernized and mature version of the hero. Nier is no longer a brother, but a forty-year-old father built like a tank. Square Enix validated the marketing of two versions: one with the young character, the other with the old character—with (almost)[34] no

31. Square Enix's acquisition in 2009 of development studios Eidos, IO Interactive and Crystal Dynamics, all of which specialized in action games, was an attempt to partly overcome this situation on the international scene.

32. The major success of *NieR: Automata* in 2017, gladly presented as an action game during the promotional campaign, later proved this strategy right.

33. Literally "paternalization," refers to a recent trend in video games, which appeared with the seventh generation consoles and the emergence of independent games, highlighting father characters. Intended to reflect the new emotional experiences of aging creators within a rather young medium, this trend will particularly and absurdly result in the outrageous virilization of the male ideal. A few compelling examples: *The Last of Us, Dishonored, BioShock Infinite, Heavy Rain*.

34. A date and some minor dialogs, in addition, of course, to the necessary modifications to the hero's family status change.

other difference between the two. At the same time, a PlayStation 3 version was initiated to maximize chances of success. After a sharp cultural analysis, the company finally decided to only release the box containing the father version of Nier's adventure in Europe and America, published as *NieR* on Xbox 360 and PlayStation 3. While in Japan only, this variant would be named *NieR Gestalt*, and was released exclusively on the Microsoft console. As for the Japanese PlayStation 3, it received the young Nier in *NieR Replicant*. Child's play really. Except that the original version, the one contained in *NieR Replicant*, came close to not being released. During another gathering across the Pacific, Square Enix's US staff, concerned about the potential delays caused by the porting of the game on Sony's machine, proposed to cancel *NieR Replicant* and only keep *NieR Gestalt*. Yoko, outraged, successfully opposed the proposal by warning his management of the consequences of such a decision on the team's morale and of the inevitable drop in productivity which would certainly follow, condemning *NieR Gestalt* to suffer an even greater delay. A victory that felt like revenge for the creative director after his repeated struggles with production on *Drakengard*, but which, above all, underlined the great degree of freedom he enjoyed, confirming his author's position in a relatively sparse Japanese landscape in this respect.

Programming based on diversification

From the outset, Yoko rejected the idea of repeating *Drakengard*'s eccentricities and wanted his game to focus on more radiant themes such as friendship and effort. The director quickly got bored, though resting on his laurels was out of the question. Above all, he wanted to avoid struggling for the validation of his creative choices. "I thought, with *NieR*, that I would make a normal game. That's what I tried to make, a normal game,"[35] he recalled shortly after the announcement of *NieR: Automata*. But he was quickly forced to admit to himself that in reality, he "can't make anything but strange games," as he would later recognize in a long interview published in the *Grimoire NieR*[36]. So it was goodbye to the joys originally envisaged, and make way for the strange and uncomfortable.

Yoko drew *NieR*'s strangeness from the events of September 11, or rather from its direct consequence: the war on terrorism. The Iraqi conflict unsettled his feelings about murder and the domination desire. While he was convinced that you had to be crazy to slaughter tens, hundreds or thousands of people, as *Drakengard* tried to demonstrate, the vehemence of the Middle-Eastern conflict

---

35. https://www.gamespot.com/articles/new-nieR-will-stay-weird-but-this-time-with-platin/1100-6428 262/
36. Published shortly after the release of the game in Japan, this guide retraces and expands the story of *NieR*, and clarifies many parts of the plot.

persuaded him that, in reality, thinking that you are doing what is right or being convinced that you are within your rights was enough to kill. Influenced by this revelation, *NieR*, from the moment of its creation, undertook to play on points of view.

The pre-production fable, which was to serve as a script, told the adventure of a group of heroes trying to prevent villains from picture books from resurrecting their leader, a scientist. Classic. Except that the antagonists' intentions were not necessarily the ones we expected. In fact, they realized that in the fairy-tale world, the same story repeated itself ad infinitum and that, therefore, their destiny was to be forever evil and eternally punished. The scientist they are trying to resurrect once attempted to deliver them from this torment, before he was killed by the heroes, who once again hope to foil the villains' plans. Moral of the story: it is all a matter of perspective.

In the final version of the game, this desire to broaden the horizons of the unique perspective is reflected in the game mechanics of the New Game $+$[37]. Unlike *Drakengard*, it is no longer just a question of offering an alternative ending, but of changing the direction of the spotlight focused on a singular and unique reality. The decision to make the Shadows speak and the additional scenes scattered along the way to the second ending instilled doubt, and drastically rearranged the understanding of the initial script. A likelihood concern for Yoko, using this to accuse the vanity of our convictions. It is this same attention to reality that consciously drove him to leave a large part of the operation of the Gestalt Project's complex machinery unexplained. Jointly developed with Sawako Natori and Hana Kikuchi (his new script recruit), the aim of this element was only to control the action. The emotional arc of Nier and his sister or daughter was the priority. In short, a situation quite similar to the state of our world for Yoko; the reasons motivating the outbreak of one conflict or another being forever truncated, distorted, hidden under the ramifications of history.

Also equipped with the framing theme, the gameplay unfolds like a portfolio of video game genres, juggling with camera angles like so many lenses, diffracting the player's vision of the universe he is traveling through. The heart of the action mimics *God of War*–dantesque boss battles, beat 'em up jousting–and constitutes only one aspect of a multifaceted prism. The profusion of genres–

37. A term that designates a common mechanism in video games whereby players can start the game again with additional bonuses of various types (objects, experience, additional scenario, etc.) once they have finished it for the first time. For *NieR*, it is a "semi-new Game +," in the sense that the player starts again about halfway through the game.

visual novel[38], *danmaku*[39], platform, etc.–a protean tribute of Cavia's otaku to video games, was precisely born of Yoko's frustration with the limitations imposed by the genre, by the triumph of one classification over the other. As part of his great undertaking of decompartmentalizing points of view, with *NieR* the director sought to destroy the very concept of gender, break down walls, and blast foundations. Hence, the crazy idea of erasing the player's save during ending D.

The idea germinated quite early on in the director's mind, but fearing that production and the rest of the team would express their disagreement, he preferred to remain silent. However, when he finally revealed the functionality a little later, producer Yôsuke Saitô approved it and arranged for it to be included in the final product. Shortly after the release of the game, a torrent of traumatic testimonies abounded on Internet forums. The players shamelessly hailed him as either a genius or a criminal when their precious save was overwritten. Then, one particular detail aroused their curiosity. When launching a new game, it proved impossible to reuse the name of the character chosen in the lost save. This was in fact the legacy of a different game architecture, contemplated by Yoko in the event that the overwriting had not been approved. According to this plan, the player would have to complete the game no less than seven times before reaching the last ending. After the first three endings, A, B and C, the console would reserve the name given to the main character and the player would not have been able to reuse it. If the player once again reached these same endings (with another character), he would enter *The Lost World* short story (published in the *Grimoire NieR*). This particular story narrates Kaine's fight against the Forest of Myth machines and her internal struggle to remember Nier. At the end of the maneuver, the player would be able to enter the name of his first character, then access ending D. The game mechanics, as we understand, tried to allegorize the dichotomy between Kaine's oblivion and the player's memory.

Two-stage reception

Despite all its audacity (narrative, game mechanics, meta-entertainment[40]), *NieR* initially struggled to convince. The unanimous Western critics (a little less in Japan) tore it apart. A proper death blow brought about by the convergence of several elements. The first and most obvious factor was the release date.

38. A very particular genre of text-based video games. The player simply scrolls through texts on a colorful background, with choices about the following actions and the future of the character(s).
39. Literally "bullet curtain," sub-genre of the shoot them ups (game based on dodging projectiles) for experienced players, characterized by an intense torrent of projectiles on screen.
40. In other words, playing on rule systems and thus producing a reflective discourse on video games.

Scheduled to arrive barely a month and a half after the arrival of *Final Fantasy XIII* in American and European stores, *NieR* inevitably suffered from the graphic comparison. Two Square Enix titles, two quality standards: while the 2010 flagship RPG flattered the retina thanks to the capabilities of Crystal Tools (Square Enix's own game engine), Cavia's release displayed sadly empty and bland environments, with little depth and few saturated colors. The contrast between the performance of the two games was striking. However, if A is beautiful, does that mean that B should suffer the consequences? In the video game industry, and in 2010, the answer was yes. This element of comparison however only becomes meaningful when we take into account the dominant axiom of gaming critics during that period. Increasingly accustomed to the formula of blockbusters, which had managed to monopolize media space and players' gaming time during the seventh generation of consoles, critics had gradually shifted towards a product appraiser role based on the AAA standard—others will say that they had merely confirmed their original vocation[41].

Broaching the subject of *NieR* in its pages, *Playstation Official Magazine UK* thus castigated an action game that "does not live up to the standards we are entitled to expect[42] ." *Gamespot*, on the other hand, would have preferred to play "the hero in a grand adventure" rather than "an ugly errand boy with bad hair and a sick daughter[43] "—even though *NieR* never claimed to offer the first option. Moreover, the critic went on to describe the text sequences of *Lost Odyssey* as "far superior" to those of *NieR*, confining himself to a gratuitous analogy neglecting the analysis of their respective functions in the narrative. *NieR* was described as an "average" game by *9Lives[44]*, in reference to its relative position in the grand scheme of video games rather than the quality of the game itself. Thus, certainly far from being above reproach, *NieR* (like other Japanese video game outsiders released at that time[45]) owed its critical failure to it being at odds with conventions. Its gradual rise as an iconic game in the years following its release, the inextinguishable fervor of its community of players and its reissue by Square Enix—following the excitement generated by the announcement of its sequel *NieR: Automata*—would later confirm that this time, the press had it all wrong. Each time he is asked to theorize about the causes that led such a badly received title to acquire such an aura, Yoko systematically gives the same

41. Sites and magazines that will renew video game reviews, like *Polygon* and *KillScreen* in the United States or *Games* in France, will only appear a few years later.

42. June 2010 Issue, p. 105.

43. https://www.gamespot.com/reviews/nieR-review/1900-6 260 971/

44. http://ps3.9lives.be/games/nieR/reviews ?id=188 728

45. Such as the games of Hidetaka "Swery" Suehiro (*Deadly Premonition*, *D4*) or those of Goichi "Suda51" Suda (*Shadows of the Damned*, *Killer is Dead*) which experienced, in the same way as Taro Yoko's productions, a lukewarm critical reception, but managed to win many fans' sympathy.

answer: "*NieR* is like an abandoned puppy or a broken doll. It's cute in a way, but also disturbing, and you can't help but love it even if you can't put your finger on what's bothering you. " But unfortunately, the fans' love would not save Cavia.

Cavia's collapse

Curiously sold by Square Enix whose communication campaign remained particularly silent until the international release, *NieR* encountered serious issues on the Western market, where it sold with difficulty. Even in Japan, where *NieR* rose to the top of the sales rankings on PlayStation 3 during the first week following its release, the initial score was only sixty thousand copies sold, less than the first *Drakengard*–in which far fewer hopes had been placed. Yoko had already thought of a sequel with Saitô, or rather a spin-off, for which the two men would have been given *carte blanche* in the event of a resounding success. But this poor performance temporarily compromised Cavia's partnership with Square Enix[46] ; and precipitated the studio's demise. A few months later, it was absorbed by its parent company, AQ Interactive. Nevertheless, the company suffered not only from its results, but also from the economic situation and the holding company's plans: Feelplus and Artoon, the other two second party studios, actually shared the same fate.

At that moment, AQ Interactive's strategy seemed to respond to a threefold problem. Firstly, its subsidiaries were no longer profitable. *NieR* was a failure and Feelplus's *Mindjack*, a shooter also published by Square Enix, quickly sank into the abyss of the PlayStation Store. Secondly, its publishing activities on consoles had not been a huge success. And most importantly, the company had become involved in the rapidly expanding browser game sector and was seeking to consolidate its position. The absorption of Artoon, Feelplus and Cavia occurred at a time when the Web and mobile sectors were becoming the most profitable ones in Japan. Like its counterparts (Bandai Namco, SEGA Sammy), AQ Interactive sought, therefore, to centralize its talents in order to redeploy itself. And like its counterparts, it went on to merge, or rather allow itself to be absorbed by Marvelous Entertainment, which owned the *Harvest Moon* franchise. The stated goal of the new Marvelous AQL entity, similar to that of Square Enix and its "polymorphic content" concept, was to have a large enough production unit in order to control the entire value chain, as part of a multimedia activity taking various forms. By combining the office dedicated to browser-

---

46. *Catacombs*, a shooter secretly designed by Cavia for Square Enix, was canceled by the publisher during this period, for reasons that probably have as much to do with the absorption of Cavia by AQ Interactive as with the publisher's financial situation.

based programming with the console division, the company hoped to streamline the use of resources and create synergies. In short, the company founded by the former CEO of SEGA more or less replicated the consolidation and pool strategy imposed by Sammy after its takeover of the former manufacturer.

Unemployment and small jobs

After ten years, there was nothing left of the original Cavia launched in 2000—then renamed, absorbed and merged—to host the development of *Drakengard*, not even its two main figures. Taro Yoko left AQ Interactive some time before the merger to set up a freelance business, while Takuya Iwasaki founded and became the head of two companies: ILCA (I Love Computer Anime) specialized in graphic production and Orca, entirely dedicated to the production of video games. Naturally, the two friends met again after some time. And neither had stopped thinking about *NieR*. Together, they solicited Yôsuke Saitô and laid the foundations for a new project: the porting of *NieR* to the PS Vita. Saitô's aim was to bring the game to a wider audience, and to take this opportunity to add a little extra. Iwasaki should have hosted the production within Orca. But during the same period, in March 2011, the studio was chosen by Square Enix to support the *Dragon Quest X* teams. An offer that Iwasaki accepted. The porting of *NieR* was therefore canceled even before the pre-production phase due to labor shortage. As for Saitô, he dedicated himself entirely to his role as a producer on the tenth episode of the Slime series. Yoko, for his part, officially became unemployed—or almost. Having just turned forty, and while all his comrades-in-arms were scattered throughout the industry, Yoko was trying to make ends meet, in the hope that better days would come. His first contract led him to work once again for Square Enix, on the browser game *Monster X Dragon*. Management sought to permeate its title with a gloomy atmosphere, and therefore called on *Drakengard*'s director to supervise the script. Shortly afterwards, Yoko assumed the development of the rhythm game *Demon's Score*, released on iOS and Android—yet again for Square Enix. Designed by iNiS and endowed with a similar *gameplay* to one of the studio's most famous titles, *Elite Beat Agents*, this grade-Z rhythm shooter (inspired by *The House of The Dead*) primarily offered a good excuse to gather together the best Japanese video game composers: Keiichi Okabe, *NieR*[47]'s main composer, but also Naoshi Mizuta *(Final Fantasy XI)*, Yoko Shimomura (*Kingdom Hearts*, *Parasite Eve*), Kenji Itô (*Mana* and *SaGa* series), etc. Once more finding himself unemployed after this digital escapade, Yoko set out to find his old friend Takamasa Shiba. The break was over.

47. Cf. the chapter dedicated to the music of Taro Yoko's games.

DRAKENGARD 3
Takamasa Shiba's obsession

Takamasa Shiba is a stubborn man. And his obsession was called *Drakengard 3*. Ever since the second episode was released and the series he helped create was put on hold, the producer never stopped trying to revive it. He first asked his friend Taro Yoko, during Cavia's era, if he wished to take up the gauntlet. But the director had declined: he did not feel up to the task. After the studio was dissolved, Shiba wanted to give it another try and, therefore, turned to AQ Interactive. But to no avail. The publisher, too busy with its browser games and its merger with the "suitable for all audiences" specialist Marvelous, did not believe that the market would be receptive to such a violent game. And it was not necessarily wrong. Console game revenues in Japan had been plummeting for several years, the previously fanatical audience was diminishing and the Japanese role-playing industry was the first victim—*NieR* had just suffered a bitter failure, after all. So where did this persistent desire to revive a mid-range license, probably doomed to gather dust on the unsold stock shelf, come from two weeks after its release? As he was substantially determining what *Drakengard 3* would become, Shiba's reasoning is worth exploring. For the producer, identifiable thanks to his colorful caps and messy hair, the market for violent games like *Drakengard* had not vanished with the rise of smartphones. On the contrary, the transfer of activities by major companies towards the production of phone games (known as "casual[48]") left, according to him, a void to fill. Indeed, during this abandonment, the console audience would have been partly reduced to its durable core of regular players, who would ask them, again according to Shiba, to quickly deliver sensations reminiscent of the "old school" experience. In other words: old-school role-playing games with blood stains and colliding blades. At that point, Square Enix's executive believed that his company, by responding to the mobile siren calls, had turned away from the high fantasy[49] DNA responsible for its fame. His insistence on launching the production of *Drakengard 3* therefore stemmed from his desire if not to redirect, then at least to put a stop to this trend at the publisher level, which only fueled the global transfer of resources phenomenon and left, according to him, many historical fans by the wayside. Having spent his time gathering players' opinions in gaming

---

48. Used for games targeting an audience of casual gamers. By extension, designates said gamers. Popular a few years ago, this term is now somewhat overused. We reuse it here because this concept was explicitly part of Shiba's speech to the press in 2013.

49. A fantasy sub-genre that, most of the time, features a group of young heroes facing a serious threat to the world, during an epic journey.

arcades[50] , from his perspective it appeared to be compelling evidence: "Our core users–mature JRPG players–want something authentic," he hammered home over and over to the press. Yet nothing was more unauthentic and formatted than this inflated speech, oozing nostalgia and aimed at reviving past glories. Unfortunately, *Drakengard 3* would pay the price.

A highly outlined production

Through perseverance, and probably because Taro Yoko, unemployed, had not received a better offer, Shiba managed to secure the director's participation, and could therefore finally get to the heart of the matter. The producer had to deliver following his gamble, which meant proving that otaku games deserved to be given a place on consoles. And like every gambler in the world, he made sure to exercise caution. Through Square Enix, Shiba distributed questionnaires addressed to players, the results of which would reassure him on what fans preferred in *Drakengard*: the tormented universe. Subsequently, and thanks in part to the Internet, pre-production reflection phase was completed and the specifications were drawn up. First and last element written on the document: reproduce *Drakengard*–a better version if possible. Some kind of joke? Not really. *Drakengard 3*'s creation was set in an asphyxiating commercial breeding-ground, entirely subject to Shiba's mercantile certainties. However, surprisingly, his self-confidence contrasted with the attitude of his employer, Square Enix. Several elements did indeed suggest that the publisher had intended, from the outset, to provide minimum assistance for this game and did not fully share the enthusiasm of its producer. Poor promotion (except in Japan), a rather short development period (about two years, compared to three for *NieR* and *Drakengard*), complete absence of a physical version in Europe and the United States[51] ; if Square Enix was not completely out of the picture, the little effort made for the promotion campaign did not ruin it[52]. Shiba's replicative nostalgia combined with his publisher's nonchalance resulted in an easy and dull sequel, formatted on the model of its predecessor. In an interview, during one of his candid moments

50. Shiba is the producer of the arcade machine card game series *Lord of Vermillion*.

51. The collector's editions did not contain the game disc, but a code to download the game on the PlayStation Store, the only place it was available.

52. In its defense, the firm had just experienced the worst losses in its history during the 2012-2013 fiscal year, an event that would bring about the resignation of its president Yôichi Wada, replaced by Yôsuke Matsuda. According to the press release at the time, many of the projects supervised by the publisher were either canceled, or had their funds and scope reduced. It is unclear whether *Drakengard 3* had been affected, but it is interesting to note that its Japanese release, fixed for December 19, 2013, after an initial extension, occurred just before the holiday season and three months before the end of the 2013-2014 fiscal year.

which the video game industry rarely experiences, Yoko simply answered that *Drakengard 3*'s sales pitch was "the business of sequels." The comment was clearly not bitter, since the director regularly expressed his gratefulness for being allowed to work, but it was far from being innocent: in this regard, Yoko had much less room for maneuver than he had previously enjoyed.

In reality, by the time the director was approached by Takamasa Shiba, the main creative decisions had already been taken, and Yoko could no longer modify much when it came to the architecture and game systems, in many respects similar to the game mechanics of the first *Drakengard* (flight phases combined with the beat'em up genre, although the progression here took place in more restricted areas). The same applied to the script: his first drafts, considered too eccentric, were rejected. In one of them, the game was directly named *Drakengard 4*[53] and invited the player to look for the missing episode of the series. In another, the player was following the adventures of a Japanese high school girl who was able to summon her dragon using her phone. But this was not the strange and offbeat fragrance that Square Enix and Shiba were looking for. They wanted to get a whiff of past recipes, well-loved favorites, and thus forced Yoko to keep within the thematic framework of the first *Drakengard*. Logically, a similar creative process was used, inspired by otaku references from Japanese animation. The visuals of the Intoner sisters, for example, were based on *Puella Magi Madoka Magica*, a very popular animation series that reinvented the magical girls[54] genre. Even though Yoko found himself trapped in his old patterns, he did not give up on adding a hint of originality to distinguish *Drakengard 3* from its predecessor.

A different tone

Thus, the casting, mostly female, contrasted sharply with the violent action game models calibrated on the murderous imaginings of rough men (Dante in *Devil May Cry*, Kratos in *God of War*, Raiden in *Metal Gear Rising: Revengeance*, to name a few). Almost exclusively administered or exercised by the heroine Zero and her sisters during the adventure, the brutality was transposed to the other gender[55], both for the person who inflicted it and the person who received it, as illustrated by the death scene of Five, one of the antagonists. Willingly

---

53. Taro Yoko considered *NieR* as the true *Drakengard 3*.
54. Typical sub-genre of Japanese fantasy popularized by *Sailor Moon*, whose characteristic feature is the presence of young girls with magical powers.
55. Originally, the main protagonist was supposed to be a man. Yoko had to fight to get Shiba to agree to the change in gender.

burlesque, this scene[56] also highlights a significant change in tone compared to the first episode. More saucy and relaxed, yet also more sensitive and in touch with its characters, *Drakengard 3* extricated itself from the monomaniac examination of madness to deploy a richer emotional spectrum, nurtured by the sum of its protagonists' deviances. This was undoubtedly the lesson Yoko had learned from *NieR*: to superimpose points of view in order to diversify his narrative. Most likely driven by this idea, the director reused framing to disrupt the player's expectations, as he had done for *NieR*. Only here, the revelation logic was reversed. In *NieR*, the player initially believed that he was convinced of the legitimacy of his action and would only understand the detrimental effects linked to the fate of humanity much later. All that is known is that the hero is fighting for a noble cause, his daughter's survival, and that is enough to justify the act of killing. In *Drakengard 3*, however, it was quite the opposite. It was unclear at first why Zero became obsessed with her sororicidal quest or why such charming young girls like her sisters deserved to die. So much so, that the game appeared to rely solely on the many excesses of gratuitous brutality it inherited from the previous episode. With an introduction filled with murders and deranged laughter, but that was weak in reasonable discourse, Yoko indeed quickly summoned *Drakengard*'s ghost, and seemed to repeat its message: there is no other justification for murder than the madness of humans who wage war against each other. By failing to place a moral anchor to base this on, Yoko purposely placed the player in the judge's situation and let his own ethical code color the narrative. And unless you were a serial killer or a sadist, Zero's bloody killing spree could only seem unfair and illegitimate. That was the trick, since this prejudice would later be reversed, when the Intoners would reveal themselves to be emanations of the Flower's power whose existence threatened the world. Thus, if shifting points of view gradually made *NieR*'s main character evolve from the role of heroic father to that of mankind's gravedigger, conversely, in *Drakengard 3* it elevated a murderous prostitute to the rank of world protectress and demigoddess—the unsuspected Esmeralda. By thus articulating *Drakengard*'s harsh and coarse cruelty as well as *NieR*'s angle permutations, *Drakengard 3* produced a synthesis that allowed it to partly avoid repetition, at least in terms of themes. As for the rest, it was a case of "sticking to what you know best" or almost.

---

56. During which Zero confronts the corpse of her enemy while Five's disciple, Dito, protests about his role as a sex slave.

Access Games to the rescue

Shiba was aware of this: you can't make the same recipe without using the same ingredients. For this third production, *Drakengard*'s original team was back–Kimihiko Fujisaka for artistic creation, Sawako Natori for the script and so forth–with two notable exceptions: the absence of producer Yôsuke Saitô (busy on *Dragon Quest X*) and the replacement of Nobuyoshi Sano for composition by his friend and former partner at Namco, Keiichi Okabe, already mentioned for *NieR*. With Cavia floating in limbo, Square Enix entrusted the production to the Access Games studio, typically specialized in the development for handheld consoles. Selected by Shiba for its action game expertise–notably a few episodes of the *Sengoku Basara* series, clones of *Dynasty Warriors*–this small structure only really made its breakthrough in 2010 with the success and reputation of *Deadly Premonition* and the great performance of the *Monster Hunter*-like *Lord of Arcana*. Ironically, it had been in charge of several handheld episodes of the *Ace Combat* series–which never reached the refinement of *Electrosphere*[57]. In any event, *Drakengard 3* was at the time its first large-scale project after *Deadly Premonition*, and the biggest action-RPG in its catalog. It was therefore a matter of living up to expectations. The goal was simple: successfully remove the image reflected by *Drakengard* as a stumbling series, which was technically running out of steam and mechanically outdated. In order to preserve the technological structure, part of Square Enix's technical team was sent in to backup Gen Ishiyama, a programmer on *Deadly Premonition* promoted to head programmer on *Drakengard 3*. The difference was immediately felt: battles were much more intense, dense and varied than in the previous installments–without being radically different from the competition. For graphics and animation, Takuya Iwasaki's production company, ILCA, was called for support to help ensure that, unlike its predecessors, *Drakengard 3* would be worthy of its generation. However, the visual redesign was not quite convincing: the textures were poor, the environments were still equally empty and the colors hardly less dull than before. As if the mediocre graphics remained inextricably linked to the *Drakengard* style. However, this was to be expected. The Access Games studio, despite its ability to properly tie its game systems together, had seldom distinguished itself with its high mastery of graphic technology. *Deadly Premonition* had faced an onslaught of criticism for its display problems, its slowdowns and its numerous bugs. As it had benefited from Square Enix's very rigorous quality control, *Drakengard 3* was still more meticulous and could therefore at least pride itself on being clean, if not sparkling. The minimum, so to speak, for a game whose production required the intervention of more than twenty external service providers.

57. *Ace Combat 3*'s subtitle.

Drakengard 3, symbol of the sector's sedimentation

The use of subcontracting proved to be one of the most interesting pieces of data to analyze, since it clearly reflected the context in which the development of this third installment took place. While *NieR* had required the support of a dozen different enterprises, *Drakengard 3* involved more than twenty companies. However, only three years had elapsed between the two titles. Far from being insignificant, this leap actually revealed a basic shift in the video game sector: the explosion of outsourcing. In Japan, this phenomenon took on a particular form. Increasingly focused on the major players that emerged during the 2000s (SEGA Sammy, Square Enix, Bandai Namco), absorbed by the mobile revolution, and major loser of the duel that opposed it to the West on the seventh generation machines, the Japanese console game industry was disappearing. At the beginning of 2010, medium-sized studios in need of funds were unable to survive without sponging off major groups. The phenomenon also existed in the West, but the independent system allowed many creators to regroup and redeploy themselves, notably on the PC. On the Japanese archipelago, however, the independent ecosystem barely existed, and PC gaming was not very common. Many creators had no other choice but to turn—partly or entirely—to the profitable mobile sector like Media Vision (*Chaos Rings*), tri-Ace (*Chronos Ring*) or Mistwalker (*Terra Battle*). Others, or even the same, attracted by the conglomerates' center of gravity, sought to secure the latter's funds by focusing on subcontracting. But not just any. For risk or complexity reasons, these studios rarely hosted the entire development of a game, but rather specialized in certain areas of expertise: 3D modeling, animation, level design, porting and remastering, etc. By way of example, we have already mentioned ILCA, Takuya Iwasaki's company entirely dedicated to computer graphics, but we could also refer to HexaDrive[58] founded by Masakazu Matsushita, former developer of Capcom, valued by Square Enix and Nintendo for its programming skills, or even Mozoo, whose preferred field is motion capture[59]. These subcontractors were regarded by major publishers as a means of reducing costs by limiting the recruitment burden and, thus, better dealing with the international competitive pressure and Western expertise. They also allowed them to take over in the event of an internal labor shortage

---

58. Involved in the development of *Final Fantasy XV* and the porting of *The Legend of Zelda: Wind Waker* on the Wii U.

59. Motion capture technology which involves transposing the movements of actors performed in a studio into a video game (or a film in computer graphics).

or simply to free up part of the team[60]. Naturally, these contractors had always existed. Tose Software, both the most confidential and the most famous of them all, with over a thousand games to its credit, had been in business since 1979. A difference in scale, or at least the magnification of a trend, is particularly noticeable here. Little by little, instead of an independent developers' market with free competition, a strong service economy had developed around the major companies holding the capital–increasingly solicited as programming costs increased. Several of these subcontractors could be found in areas with relatively low labor costs; in Shanghai, for example, where Game Chain is located and whose members were involved in *Drakengard 3*'s 3D modeling. A typical feature of business strategies aimed at achieving economies of scale within an oligopoly, the use of subcontracting would reach new heights at Square Enix with *Final Fantasy XV*. In addition to the internal teams of Business Division 2, no fewer than sixty third-party companies were involved in the creation of this blockbuster, from Japan or abroad.

While the funds provided by Square Enix and the other leading publishers certainly helped the Japanese SMEs specializing in console gaming, the existence of the console gaming sector was, nevertheless, mostly thanks to the survival of the service provider network that came rushing to its bedside. The strong subordinate relationship between publishers and subcontractors, that emerged from this anticompetitive supremacy relationship, paradoxically explained the obvious lack of innovation from which Japanese mid-range titles had suffered in recent years, and which had caused their decline (before their more recent recovery). In a nutshell, the relatively generalized state of subjugation of SMEs in the sector–main suppliers in this market segment–by major groups had condemned these studios to take as few risks as possible, as they were systematically subordinated to the immediate profitability needs of publishers concerned about their business loss[61]. And one of the proven methods of ensuring profitability at low cost was to attract consumer niches, as Square Enix had done since the merger with the constant reissue of its greatest hits, *Dragon Quest* and *Final Fantasy*, or with the establishment of a studio dedicated to the creation

---

60. Without HexaDrive's help, the high-definition porting of Square Enix's *Final Fantasy Type-0* would probably not have been possible, as director Hajime Tabata had repeatedly referred to the resource allocation issue as playing a central role in this type of decision.

61. Investment in research and programming is the main victim of this process. Forced to produce "small" ordered games, many studios overlook this crucial variable, imperative even in video games if the company hopes to expand. Already at low levels compared to the West, R&D investment in Japan is therefore almost exclusively found in major groups such as Square Enix or Nintendo. This imbalance indirectly allows these groups to strengthen their oligopoly. Indeed, as long as the small and medium-sized studios are retained in the role of subcontractors with low technical capital, through the strategy of fund allocation and projects, they will never be able to extricate themselves from the major groups' grip in the hope of one day competing against them.

of old-school role-playing games, Tokyo RPG Factory. Most of the time, these niche-targeting titles were not managed internally, because they were highly defined and not very risky: a service provider is quite capable of recycling tasks and applying proven formulas. Service providers, extremely dependent on the international stature of publishers (and their capital), had to accept this task if they hoped to exist elsewhere than on the stunted Japanese console market. The design framework of *Drakengard 3* did not derogate from this context, which thrived, among other things, thanks to the effervescent retro trend (see for example the resurrection of the *Deus Ex* games) in video games and even in pop culture in general. Shiba had clearly understood this, since *Drakengard 3* ticked all the boxes: licensed game, formula replication, little innovation, minimal risk, largely developed by providers, short production time...

During its first week on the Japanese market, *Drakengard 3* sold one hundred and fourteen thousand and twenty-four copies, virtually the same score (one hundred and twenty-two thousand boxes sold) as the first episode over the same period. Early fans had obviously answered the call. However, it is difficult to draw a definitive conclusion concerning the producer's strategy on the basis of this result alone. After all, he had only partially fulfilled his challenge: he had failed to expand the player base, and the–digital–choice of distribution in the West suggested that the game did not sell very well in that market–probably not as well as *Drakengard*[62]. In any case, *Drakengard 3* hardly appeared in Square Enix's financial reports: briefly mentioned before its launch, it completely disappeared from the presentations on the group's strategy and results after its release, despite the subsequent release of the DLCs on the sisters' story. For such a costly product as video games, this is seldom the sign of a resounding success. Result: for the second time in three years, Yoko had failed to conquer a large audience. Nevertheless, the eccentric creator had already moved on behind the scenes.

The mysterious YoRHa

After having supervised the creation of two mangas connected to the *Drakengard* universe and written by Emi Nagashima[63], then finishing up his work on *Drakengard 3*'s DLCs, Taro Yoko announced to the world (i.e. on Twitter) that he was once again unemployed. But the break did not last long. A few fans noticed something in the Blu-ray data of *Drakengard 3*, which set them on the trail to discover the director's next activities. A song hidden close to

---

62. Since Square Enix and the main analysis institutes do not share their sales figures for dematerialized products, it is impossible to confirm this information, which nevertheless seems quite plausible.
63. Emi Nagashima, known through her pseudonym Eishima Jun, has been working with Taro Yoko since *Drakengard* and is in charge of transposing his universes into novels or mangas.

the data of the android Accord, which was impossible to listen to during the game. Its title: *Normandy*. This intriguing song was performed by the mysterious band YoRHa, also credited for the boss tracks. One thing leading to another, it was easy to understand that YoRHa was the name of a group of Japanese *idols*[64] who performed the songs of Monaca, the group of composers founded by Keiichi Okabe. The collective as a whole had been placed under the creative leadership of Taro Yoko since 2012. This would serve as a furtive means to distill the first elements of *NieR: Automata*'s plot, long before it was revealed at the E3 2015 expo. In the song *Normandy*, secretly placed in *Drakengard 3* as well as in the booklet included in the band's first album released in early 2014, the beginnings of the storyline already appeared: a dark story of war between androids and mechanical life forms and elite models sent onto the firing line to defend mankind, which had been banished to the Moon... However, the story will only be formally presented to the public a few months later, when the all-rounder Yoko adapted his script for the stage, at the Kassai Theater located in the Tokyo district of Ikebukuro. Soberly entitled *YoRHa*, the play produced by the DearStage agency (that held the rights to the *idols* group) told the adventures of an android contingent sent on a suicide mission to ravish the strategic Mount Ka'ala from the machines' grip. It was in this drama that Yoko really introduced for the first time, in October 2014, the universe of *NieR: Automata* and three of its central protagonists: the red girls, Anemone and Number 2, better known as A2. But obviously, nobody in the audience yet knew that, through this play, the producer was offering a taste of what was to come in the game he had been secretly directing for several months.

NIER: AUTOMATA

After *NieR*

While *Drakengard 3* would not have been possible without Takamasa Shiba's insistence, *NieR: Automata*, on the other hand, owes its existence to the perseverance of the license producer, Yôsuke Saitô. Even after *NieR*'s underperformance, the 40-year-old still hoped to build something with this universe as demonstrated by his first intention to port the game over to the PlayStation Vita. But naturally, Square Enix was not quite ready to give it another try immediately after such a

---

64. In Japan, the word "*idol*," unlike the English term, describes an activity rather than a status. *Idols* are teenage or young adult artists chosen by production companies for their image and are taught to sing, dance and perform on stage. Many *idols* do not become famous.

failure. Yet, something was happening; and Saitô felt it. Despite its poor sales, *NieR* struck an extremely unusual chord among players. Gradually, the symptoms of a lasting craze for the game began to appear. Across the Web, a passionate fan community was taking root. Needless to say, on Japanese boards[65], as well as in the West, *NieR*'s aficionados did not run short of fan-arts dedicated to Kainé and Emil, their favorite characters. Everywhere on the video game forums and in *YouTube* comments, Taro Yoko's praises were being sung and the smallest details related to his universe were devoured like delicious nectar. Definitely not millions, probably not even tens of thousands, but these fans were driven by a passion that made them extremely active and audible. As a group, they coordinated together to translate virtually the entire *Grimoire NieR*, exclusive to Japan, and then embarked on the transcription of Yoko's mangas or the short stories written by Eishima Jun. Nothing escaped their radar. Astonished by their enthusiasm, Yoko affectionately called them *ikkitōsen*, literally "a person worth a thousand." Powerful within the Internet community, the fans' zeal was also conveyed commercially: on the archipelago, the game's exquisite soundtrack, even several years after its release, continues to sell well. In the press, *Famitsu* polls regularly cite *NieR* as one of PlayStation 3's most prominent titles. More than perceptible, the craze was palpable. To such an extent that within the small video game community, the title gradually acquired status as an iconic work, alongside other great works such as *Okami* or *Shadow of the Colossus*. The game's value, difficult to pin down due to its limited distribution, skyrocketed and sometimes flirted with the symbolic threshold of a hundred euros on resale sites. Saitô's twenty years in the business helped convince him that this enthusiasm represented an opportunity, a niche market to be tapped into. The rest—as we don't know how else to explain it—seemed to be the result of celestial alignment.

Alignment of the stars

It just so happened that a member of Square Enix's management was not fundamentally opposed to *NieR* having a sequel. In an e-mail addressed to Saitô, Square Enix's finance and administration manager did not rule out the license's return, but set conditions by specifying the improvements that would have to be implemented in the new version. A good sign, which would soon turn into a blessing. The patron was indeed none other than Yôsuke Matsuda, promoted shortly after, in April 2013, to the CEO position of the company in replacement of Yôichi Wada, who had been held responsible for historical losses of more

---

65. Online meeting points where Internet users can discuss various topics, such as *4chan* in the United States or *2chan* in Japan.

than 130 million dollars over the past fiscal year. Having won the support of the hierarchy's highest level, Saitô found himself in a position of strength. Soon the situation would be confirmed by an extensive internal reorganization. Indeed, once settled in his new position, Matsuda unpacked from his boxes an investment and restructuring plan of a hundred million dollars for the firm. One of the aims of this reorganization was to replace an extremely centralized approach to project management with a clearer, more autonomous and better segmented structure for the production system. Thus, the famous Production Departments born after the merger of Square and Enix in 2003, doomed to agony[66], were redivided into twelve Business Divisions, in other words, twelve production offices. Through this review, Matsuda sought to streamline the approval process for new creations, which previously required the systematic consent of the Board of Directors. Following this restructuring, the producers in each work group were given greater freedom and responsibility in selecting their projects, which henceforth only required the approval of their own division. For Yôsuke Saitô, this loosening was the perfect opportunity. As a member of the Business Division 6 responsible for *Dragon Quest*, Saitô knew that he enjoyed a certain respectability within the company for his hard work on the series, in which he had been involved since his debut at Enix in the 1990s. Driven by his experienced producer aura, supported by management and in addition to being a smooth talker, Saitô managed to convince his employer to invest once again in *NieR*. It was not quite the time of *NieR: Automata*'s genesis, but it was already an incredible achievement, as the video game industry did not like to place bets on a horse that had previously lost the race. It took no less than this man's pugnacity and expertise to bring such an unprofitable license out of the closet. And this would not be his only feat.

Together with Taro Yoko, Saitô conducted the first brainstorming sessions. A few ideas emerged, a PlayStation Vita game, or better yet a mobile game. For a moment, the two friends contemplated the idea of creating the equivalent of a *NieR Farmville*. Meanwhile, Square Enix entered into negotiations with the PlatinumGames studio to discuss a possible collaboration, with no particular project in mind. With the help of providence, one of the Osaka-based company's employees was at that precise moment working on a game proposal. An avid fan of *NieR*, the young Takahisa Taura, unaware of Saitô's plans, had started to draw up a draft which, broadly speaking, reflected what the sequel to his favorite game could have been. Struck by the coincidence, Saitô decided to merge the

---

66. The simultaneous development of the *Fabula nova Crytallis* compilation (*Final Fantasy Versus XIII*, *Final Fantasy Type-0* and *Final Fantasy XIII*) seriously disrupted Square Enix's internal production system, in particular because of the teams' massive mobilization, tossed from one project to the next, and the technical gap accumulated on Square Enix's game engine, Crystal Tools.

two projects: by no means would there be the new *NieR* on one side, and the partnership between PlatinumGames and Square Enix on the other, but rather a *NieR* designed by PlatinumGames, on the PlayStation 4 and PC[67].

Far from being simply opportunistic, this collaboration could not have corresponded better to both the producer's and the publisher's *desiderata*. Renowned for the quality of their games and praised for their ability to build incredible combat systems, the Osaka creators were a much better solution than Access Games, both to improve the quality of the action and to ensure the technical and visual structure—so many elements that were cruelly lacking in the first episode. Still in search of an adult equivalent of its action-RPG *Kingdom Hearts*, Square Enix finally agreed to secure the services of a studio worthy of its ambitions. Most importantly, PlatinumGames's involvement ensured the support of a larger fan base for the project. Built on the ashes of Clover Studio and Capcom's former satellite studio, PlatinumGames benefited from the aura of its prestigious founders, including Hideki Kamiya, Shinji Mikami and Atsushi Inaba. All three were involved to varying degrees in the creation of some of the masterpieces of Japanese video gaming: *Okami*, *Resident Evil*, *Devil May Cry* and so on. By drawing on this heritage, Square Enix would at the very least arouse the curiosity of action game enthusiasts, and thus significantly increase the media sounding board for its future title. A winning strategy as demonstrated by the reaction of the players during the E3 2015 expo and the strong sales of *NieR: Automata*. In addition, the windfall was shared. Having lost momentum due to the disappointing results of its first games published by SEGA (*Bayonetta*, *Anarchy Reigns*, *Mad World*), Platinum had been forced, since 2013, to review its corporate strategy aimed at solely creating new franchises in order to adopt a more traditional subcontracting studio model, by borrowing licenses from leading publishers or major groups. To this day, its greatest commercial success remains *Metal Gear Rising: Revengeance*, published by Konami. The meeting between Square Enix and PlatinumGames was, nevertheless, unique in that it brought together the world's greatest role-playing game publisher, in an unprecedented way, with the best action game developer. While not unnatural, the partnership might nonetheless be considered curious and unusual in a market where, as has already been seen, each party was usually reluctant to think outside the box and preferred to remain within its territory. This eccentricity, as Yoko repeatedly suggested in the media, could undoubtedly have been the result of a new phase

---

67. Undertaken by developers such as Falcom (*Ys*, *The Legend of Heroes*) or SEGA (*Valkyria Chronicles*), the porting of Japanese console RPGs to the PC, more specifically to the Steam distribution platform, is one of the solutions developed by publishers in order to expand their audience at low cost and thus close the audience gap within the local market. So far, Square Enix, SEGA or Bandai Namco all claimed that PC sales of their games accounted for a significant part of their turnover.

that had just appeared in the Japanese console gaming sector. Its inability to copy European and American blockbusters (*NieR* wanted to copy *God of War*)[68] made the local market doubtful and unclear about where it stood or what it was supposed to produce. With no model to draw on, the designers proved more capable of experimenting with strange and innovative ideas, as illustrated by the freshness of *Gravity Rush 2*'s anti-gravitational gameplay, the first-person use in *Resident Evil 7*, or even the return to grace of the Team Ninja studio (*Ninja Gaiden*, *Dead or Alive*) with *Nioh*, whose universe radically reconnected with local folklore.

Dorīmuchīmu

Before being fully formalized, however, the decision concerning Platinum Games and Square Enix's partnership had to be examined: would the eccentric and demanding Taro Yoko be able to get along with this brand new team, and vice versa? There were reservations on both sides.

Yoko, who lived in Tokyo with his family and would have to spend a significant amount of time in Osaka (located over five hundred kilometers away) during the next three years to direct the game as a freelance, wanted to make sure that the project was viable. In his late forties, the creator was particularly apprehensive of having to work with young collaborators, who represented the majority of PlatinumGames's workforce. Not unrelated to the studio's demography, his biggest concern involved the changes that would be made to *NieR*: will they not want to transform it into a pure action game, adapt it to their own expertise and erase its original identity?

As for PlatinumGames's management, Atsushi Inaba was concerned about the iconoclastic methods of the director, to whom he would have to give a large part of his studio's resources. To test the viability of the partnership and lay the foundations for programming, Yoko and PlatinumGames collaborated on the development of a first game prototype, which was completed as early as July 2014, exactly three months before the first performance of *YoRHa*. This first collaboration was a real success.

On the one hand, Yoko noticed in his young team—and especially in Takahisa Taura, whom he took under his wing—an enormous respect for the original *NieR* as an RPG, and an extraordinary talent which reassured him regarding the direction of the project and made him hope for the best for the future. On the

68. We can also mention *Dragon's Dogma*, which attempted to emulate the Western-style RPGs; *Resident Evil 6*, which did not really convince with its American shooter gameplay, despite its strong sales; *Metal Gear Solid V*, which lost itself in a torrent of Ubisoft-like add-ons; *Mindjack*, a pale copy of *Gears of War*, etc.

other hand, Atsushi Inaba met a sincere and straightforward man with whom he felt confident enough to entrust with the position of director. "He understands that he is not orthodox in a number of ways, and because of that, people can trust him. He trusts the people on his staff, and they trust him, because he's honest," explained the head of the Osaka studio in the *Edge*[69] *magazine*. An idyll was born from this impromptu alliance.

Boosted by this emerging synergy, development got off to a flying start. Each more motivated than the next, the employees (chosen partly on the basis of their affinity for *NieR*) bombarded Yoko with new ideas. The director gladly compiled them. For once, he had the means to innovate, and intended to take advantage of the support of a studio at the forefront of development to refine his gameplay ideas. However, deviating from a certain spiritual lineage and betraying the essence of the original game were out of the question—early fans would not forgive him. In a nutshell, Yoko's guideline for this project was a respectful evolution. Temporary code name: *"NieR: Androids."* The aim of distributing key positions between longstanding partners and newcomers was to mirror this balance. Keiichi Okabe and his group, Monaca, invaluable architects of *NieR*'s melancholic and devastated atmosphere, were naturally reenlisted to work on the soundtrack, alongside Hana Kikuchi, who once again contributed to the script. In this respect, the unprecedented absence of scriptwriter Sawako Natori can be noted, whose sense of morbidity and troubling ability to infuse a shattering realism with the vilest emotions usually tainted the universes created by Yoko. DK Gashu, *NieR*'s character designer, would also have made a comeback if he had not injured his elbow. To replace him, Saito and Yoko asked for the moon: Akihiko Yoshida. A famous illustrator in Japan[70], with such prestigious titles as *Vagrant Story*, *Final Fantasy XII*, *Final Fantasy XIV* and the *Bravely Default* series on his résumé, this man seemed unapproachable—and more importantly very busy. But luckily, Kôichi Watanabe, manager of the Cygames studio which employed Yoshida, turned out to be a big fan of *NieR*. He therefore agreed to lend them his renowned artist, without the latter really having any say in the matter. Once again, a true master stroke. On the one hand, Yoshida's notoriety would help arouse the interest of RPG players in reaction to his name. Though on the other hand, the finer, looser, more sophisticated and less extravagant style of the designer compared to that of DK Gashu, more representative of Japanese art, led Saitô to think that the design would be equally well received in both Japan and the West, thus sweeping away, even before it emerged, the question

69. "Machine Learning" in *Edge* number 301, pp. 56-67.

70. In Japan, character designers, both in video games and animation, are much more popular than their Western counterparts. To such an extent that it is not uncommon to see their first and last names alongside the conventional proprietary rights notices referring to the names of the game publisher and developer.

of localization which had seriously handicapped the production of the first *NieR*. One crucial position remained vacant–the position of senior game designer. Given that he was in part at the root of the project, Takahisa Taura of PlatinumGames volunteered. Still young in appearance, the developer had in fact already honed his skills at PlatinumGames by being involved in the design of some of its major titles, including *MadWorld* and *The Wonderful 101*. Most importantly, he was one of the six craftsmen on the game design team behind the combat system of *Metal Gear Rising: Revengeance*, a great gem that, by comparison, turned most contemporary action games into mere trinkets. Yôsuke Saitô, Taro Yoko, Keiichi Okabe, Akihiko Yoshida, Takahisa Taura... The Japanese press quickly referred to this talented company as the "*dorīmuchīmu*"–dream team–, for good reason. Indeed, the team members' combined expertise took root in the finest Japanese video games on the market. For the first time in his career, Yoko saw the stars aligning in his favor–Saitô, for his part, easily declared that most of his work simply involved bringing all these artists together. But this was only the beginning, and many challenges awaited this dream team; most notably the design of a quality RPG in an open world by a studio that had devoted the past fifteen years to solely producing linear action games.

The open world challenge

With only one exception, the tactical RPG *Infinite Space* released on DS, PlatinumGames never strayed from its miracle recipe. Crisp action high on amphetamine and as straight as a die, strong scenes covered with colorful visual effects, grandiloquent characters from B movies: such were the ingredients of its success. In a certain sense, the studio kept making the same game. Building on his *Devil May Cry*, Hideki Kamiya had instilled in his employees and partners a sense of style and "feel-good gameplay," similar to that in "feel-good movies[71]." For PlatinumGames, the game was a choreography, almost a ritual, whose energy, stimulated by a surge of adrenaline, was dedicated to making the player reach a state of blissful satisfaction. This alchemy was complex and required rigorous discipline. Its game designers used it to balance visual feedback and the fluidity of the controller-to-screen transmission, like a chemist carefully dosing an active principle. Each push of a button had to be satisfying, each animation had to smoothly catch the eye and each victory had to be earned. In short, PlatinumGames employees were calibrators, who had become masters in the control and configuration of game mechanics, in predicting and scheduling the entertaining and emotional narrative. The characteristic "freedom of action"

71. A type of movie seeking to generate cheerfulness and happiness.

elements found in role-playing, such as contemplation, the management of extended time periods and large spaces, were consequently not covered by their area of expertise. With its open world, *NieR: Automata* therefore forced the studio to seriously alter its vision.

Enemy display was an initial issue. When PlatinumGames developed its action games, the designers' goal was to maintain a certain visual and mechanical intensity so as to hook the player. For example, if we use a musical analogy, they sought to increase the game's tempo so, much like a techno fan whose mesmerizing dance is synchronized to the music's beat, the player would feel constantly involved. This result could be achieved by channeling the action into a smaller area in order to obtain a sense of urgency. A narrow or linear environment also helps to condense the battle scenography, and thus to better adjust it (less space means more control over this space) while remaining in control of the rhythm. At the core of this equation lies the enemies' presence: the more targets there are, the more possibilities the player has to act and the more the intensity of the action increases. Generally, PlatinumGames preferred to set the action of its games in relatively confined environments and bombard the player with waves of enemies in order to increase the pressure. In an open world, however, and more importantly in an RPG such as *NieR*, this was a real game-changer. The goal was no longer to fight opponents in a furious deluge, but rather to enjoy the background and atmosphere that gave life to the universe. In order to free up space to allow the player to catch his breath, PlatinumGames had to reconsider the enemies' density and flow, much looser than in its previous titles—a clear sign that video games are largely a matter of rhythm, both in terms of space and narrative.

Space opening was also a challenge for sound designers. In most 3D games, each type of area, depending on its shape and its components, was assigned a variable informing the level of sound reverberation. Typically, the teams at PlatinumGames would set the required echo for each area of the game. Easy to apply in action games, strictly divided into several areas, the method proved too complex and time-consuming to use in massive and connected environments with no transition. So instead of manually adjusting the echo, sound director Masato Shindo had developed a technique to manage reverberation on the fly. The program scanned the character's immediate environment, analyzed the distance and the materials, and provided, on this basis, the necessary information to calibrate the echo in real time.

This small overview of sound problem-solving in video games, shared online by Shindo himself, also illustrates the diversification and enrichment dynamics that drove the studio, attributable to the development of *NieR: Automata*. By leaving its comfort zone to immerse itself in role-playing games, PlatinumGames actually calculated that its investment outside of the clearly marked territory of action games would allow it to extend the scope of its expertise–and consequently enable it to process more orders[72]. Demonstrating its seriousness and commitment, the studio created a position entirely dedicated to the implementation of *NieR: Automata*'s RPG elements, and appointed one of its main executives, Isao Negishi. Responsible for the game design on *The Legend of Korra* and director of *Bayonetta*'s Wii U port, the designer ended up at the head of an entire production section, starting with the supervision of numerous quests. Strategically positioned in the organization chart, just below Takahisa Taura, Negishi embodied PlatinumGames's desire to open up to other genres, and therefore to a new audience. Within the team, this mainstream ambition was conveyed by a key word which will become one of programming's leitmotifs: accessibility.

Reaching out to the general public

Yôsuke Saitô had still not completely come to terms with certain memories connected to the original *NieR*. He could handle the poor sales and the technical poverty criticisms, however the producer really felt bad when he discovered that some players could not reach the end of the story, because the game was too hard. With *NieR: Automata*, he would not repeat the same mistake: the priority was accessibility. The combat system was naturally at the heart of debates on the subject. As can be expected from PlatinumGames, the fundamentals were already in place only a few months after the beginning of development: weapon pairs, shuriken-like sword throw, movement range, etc. This aspect was handled entirely by Takahisa Taura, while Yoko, on the other hand, remained on the sidelines and was perfectly satisfied with delegating it to his right-hand man. Nonetheless, given PlatinumGames's demanding gameography, the concern was that the level of skill required to reach the last ending would be too high for neophytes trying out the game. Therefore, right up until quite late in the development process, Taura continued to plug away to ensure the action would be as smooth and accessible as possible. Exceptionally elegant and refined, the combat system he delivered easily ranks among the classics of Japanese action-RPGs. However, Saitô was not entirely reassured–or rather, the producer preferred not to take any risks. Together with the team, he decided to include

72. In September 2016, PlatinumGames announced its partnership with Cygames for the creation of the *Granblue Fantasy Project Re: Link* RPGs on the PlayStation 4 and *Lost Order* on smartphones, the latter being directed by Yasumi Matsuno, a big name in JRPG and responsible for *Final Fantasy Tactics* or *Final Fantasy XII*.

an extremely permissive easy mode in which all the player would have to do was move around, while the computer would fight on his behalf. Without doubt, with its "auto" mode (inspired by the one used in *Bayonetta*), *NieR: Automata* became accessible to the widest possible audience. In the process, he also overlooked one of the series' traditions: for the first time since *Drakengard*, the player could reach the last ending without having to collect all the weapons–the task would have been considered too complex and tedious by the audience otherwise.

A rougher game

Officially tailored to meet the requirements of a fairly wide audience, designed by some of the best creators on the circuit and unquestionably supported with greater enthusiasm by Square Enix than the previous installment: on paper, *NieR: Automata* could not fail. However, this favorable climate still had Yoko, the broken games expert, worried. "We feel we have these great ingredients now. Is it going to be too perfect? Is it going to be missing that thing that made it so endearing to our fans[73] ? ," the director wondered just after he unveiled *NieR: Automata* during E3. And what if *NieR* could not be *NieR* without all its clumsiness and awkwardness? What if *NieR*, like a forsaken dog, owed all its appeal to its pathetic appearance? Yoko, even if he enjoyed making people believe the opposite, was well aware that he owed the respect for his games to his unconventional style. And he knew, above all, that managing to replicate the formula at the root of such a craze would not be an easy task. So, why bother trying?

This was Yoko's hollow mindset during the writing process. Of course, the director intended to respect the legacy of the original episode, but not to the extent of venturing into the creation of a double theme or releasing an easy sequel whose sole purpose would be to reproduce the skeleton of the first installment, in the hope that the budget increase would be sufficient to guarantee its success. After all, *NieR* distinguished itself first and foremost by its contempt for conventions and its penchant for subversion. The best way to pay tribute to it would likely involve not copying its core and ideas, but rather decomposing them. From that point on, the creator attempted to take the opposite view of his previous work. While in the case of *NieR*, Yoko, according to his expression, had opted for a "wet" story with strong emotions, in *NieR: Automata* he wanted to turn the narrative climate around to create a more "dry" feeling. Undoubtedly rougher and less

---

73. https://www.gamespot.com/articles/new-NieR-will-stay-weird-but-this-time-with-platin/1100-6 428 262/

melodramatic, the curt naturalistic tone of this sequel was better suited to the approach chosen by the scriptwriter to explore his usual obsessions. Certainties and their consequences remained on the agenda, but while the player became the barbaric vehicle of a belief through his action in *NieR*, *NieR: Automata* shifted the point of view to the opposite side, where injustice inflicted by prejudice and dogmas gave rise to the oppressed. Yoko thus described a struggle, rather than a fight, a quest or an act of revenge; the characters' desperate struggle with their own condition and against the realities that were forced upon them. *Agaku* is the theme of the game, which in Japanese means struggling to overcome a predicament. But the same term could easily be applied to Yoko's trials and tribulations—of course prior to his arrival at PlatinumGames. Since its release, with its one and a half million sales achieved in just a few weeks [74] and its 88 out of 100 score on the *Metacritic* aggregator, *NieR: Automata* finally awarded him the public recognition he deserved. Naturally, he owed part of his success to his collaborators, and first and foremost to the composers.

---

74. And all this despite the extremely close releases of two heavyweights: *The Legend of Zelda: Breath of the Wild* on the Nintendo Switch and *Horizon: Zero Dawn* on the PlayStation 4.

THE STRANGE WORKS OF
TARO YOKO
From Drakengard to NieR:Automata

CHAPTER II — MUSIC: MONACA'S ANGELS

J ust imagine. You open your favorite newspaper on the page dedicated to music news. With one glance, you catch the results of the latest charts. In second place in the top 10 best-selling albums, you see... a video game soundtrack? From an RPG nonetheless? Out of nowhere, Taylor Swift and Ed Sheeran have been supplanted by the music from the latest blockbuster released on console. Surprised? Not if you lived in Japan shortly after the release of *NieR: Automata*. The album, featuring over three hours of music from the game, sold over 30,000 copies in one week. An impressive result, which placed the main composer Keiichi Okabe in competition with the country's most famous pop-rock artists like Amazarashi[75]. However, this success was by no means abnormal or unusual, since it was part of a larger phenomenon, related to the position of the soundtrack—and by extension of the composer—in Japanese RPGs. A phenomenon that we deemed necessary to briefly highlight as it underpins the popularity and creation process of the music of *NieR*, its sequel and *Drakengard 3*.

PRELUDE: THE IMPORTANCE OF THE SOUNDTRACK IN JAPANESE RPGS

From the early stages of mainstream Japanese RPGs during the NES era, the composer's role was crucial. And for one simple reason. Limited by the modest display capabilities of the first 8-bit consoles, developers could not rely solely on the graphics to create the illusion of epic and spectacular adventures, which were at the very heart of the genre[76]. Far from being a mere background element, the music thus played a key role by stimulating the player's imagination and amplifying the emotional intensity of the animated pixel blur. From *Final Fantasy* to *Dragon Quest*, including *Chrono Cross* or *Secret of Mana*, a myriad of iconic

---

75. Duo from Aomori with a distinctive modern J-Pop style, who would later also collaborate on *NieR: Automata*'s DLC.

76. A tradition inherited from the Western inspirations of the first *Dragon Quest* and *Final Fantasy*, including the RPGs *Ultima* and *Wizardry*, themselves adapted from the *Dungeons & Dragons* role-playing games and American fantasy literature.

soundtracks would go on to definitively establish music as one of the main pillars of the genre. So much so that Japanese RPG melodies are generally recognized as the most prestigious in video games. This is illustrated by the fact that the greatest Japanese video game composers, those whose scores have been awarded live performances in Japan and abroad, mostly come from the role-playing club: Yasunori Mitsuda (*Chrono* and *Xeno*), Koichi Sugiyama (*Dragon Quest*), Nobuo Uematsu (*Final Fantasy, Lost Odyssey*), Hitoshi Sakimoto (*Final Fantasy, Tactics Ogre* and *Valkyria Chronicles*), Yoko Shimomura (*Parasite Eve, Kingdom Hearts, Mario & Luigi RPG*), Yûzô Koshiro (*Ys* and *ActRaiser*) the list goes on. As in cinema, duos are spontaneously created between directors and composers[77], and last for years; another sign of the crucial role played by the soundtrack in the artistic identity of the Japanese RPG. Most importantly, the melodies leave their mark on the audience. Role-playing games generally last a long time. They can play out for ten or twenty times longer than a movie, whereas the soundtrack may contain half as many tracks as a feature film. Immersed for tens of hours in the same musical atmosphere, the players are given plenty of time to integrate the leitmotifs, to assimilate the melodies, and even to hum the battle theme with each new looming skirmish. More than just music, some compositions have acquired the status of anthems in the video game community, such as the *Prelude* or the *Fanfare* of *Final Fantasy*, or the theme of the character Frog from *Chrono Trigger*. Already eager consumers of *anime* soundtracks, the Japanese therefore gladly purchase albums from their favorite games, directly available from stores throughout the island nation. As a result, every year, the original soundtracks of the biggest Japanese RPGs become chart-toppers in the *Oricon*[78] weekly rankings.

To sum up, our point is the following: among the elements that determine the substance and texture of a Japanese RPG, the soundtrack is by convention one of the most scrutinized and analyzed, one of the most important components of its alchemy. It can refine the original material as well as corrupt it. The compositions of Keiichi Okabe and his colleagues from Monaca, however, did not follow either of these two eventualities—they transcended them.

---

77. Yoko Shimomura and Tetsuya Nomura (*Kingdom Hearts*), Nobuo Uematsu and Hironobu Sakaguchi (*Final Fantasy*), Hitoshi Sakimoto and Yasumi Matsuno (*Vagrant Story*), Yûzô Koshiro and Masaya Hashimoto (*ActRaiser*)...
78. The equivalent of music charts in Japan.

KEIICHI OKABE, FROM *TEKKEN* TO *NIER*

Keiichi Okabe was born on May 26, 1969 in Kobe, on the island of Honshû in Japan. From an early age, his parents enrolled him in electronic organ classes. He was trained in a repertoire which included classical music, but also Western pop songs and movie soundtracks from the 1960s and 1970s. At the age of sixteen, he started his own music band and learned to play the synthesizer, the drums and the guitar. Nevertheless, at the end of high school, he turned to design studies at the University of Kobe, fearing that music would not allow him to earn a living. It was here that he met Taro Yoko. They became friends and joined the ranks of Namco almost simultaneously at the end of their studies in the 1990s. Despite his CG design training, Okabe assumed the sound designer position. He earned his first stripes on the *Tekken* fighting game series (to which his name is still associated today), collaborating with Nobuyoshi Sano, future composer for *Drakengard*. A few years later, he left Namco to go freelance. He then founded Monaca, his own music production group, for which he recruited several former fellow composers from the Namco Sound Team (Ryuichi Takada, Satoru Kôsaki). Okabe's compositions, and in following those of Monaca, mainly distinguished themselves by their rock, pop and jazz rhythms whose main role consisted in setting the atmosphere for the levels or areas of Namco's arcade games. When Taro Yoko called on his old college friend to replace Nobuyoshi Sano on *NieR*, Okabe had yet to experiment with role-playing games.

NIER: SHADES OF SADNESS

A wide gap separated the worlds of *Tekken* and *NieR*... On one side, an intense and nervous fighting game, on the other, a role-playing game full of cutscenes and dialogs. In the case of *Tekken*, the player, tested by the intensity of the duel, generally ignored the peripheral gameplay components. Thus, the composer's goal was to merge the music into an atmosphere that resonated with the subconscious, rather than trying to capture the player's attention at all costs. This is why Okabe usually highlighted the rhythms of his compositions to match the action. "I would write tracks that would evoke a sense of competitive spirit," concluded the Japanese composer during an interview about his work on the Namco series[79]. In the case of *NieR*, Okabe adopted the opposite approach and placed all the emphasis on melodies. "It's not all about the player being driven to concentrate on his or her own gameplay especially in an RPG like

79. https://www.gamespot.com/articles/sound-byte-meet-the-composer-NieR/1100-6 393 188/

NieR. In some instances, there are scenes in which the player's mind can shift to the story, graphics, and the music," he continued. Okabe described a fairly classical approach to composition in Japanese RPG. Kôichi Sugiyama, composer for the *Dragon Quest* games and symbol of RPG music, laid the foundations of his discipline with the eight melodies of the first episode of the series[80]. His baroque and classical style, sometimes influenced by the movie soundtracks of the 1950s and 1960s, remains palpable in many role-playing games that replicate this pattern. How many "imperial capitals" are accompanied by baroque music? How many ethereal and flowing compositions are used to illustrate plains or world maps? Ever since Sugiyama, Japanese RPGs have been a matter of melodies, anthems and tunes, musical narration and tonalities rather than percussions. For *NieR*, Okabe and Monaca (Keigo Hoashi, Kakeru Ishihama) adopted this basic principle, but broke Sugiyama's nomenclature. The soundtrack was not imagined, as was usually the case, to illustrate a scene, a movement or a place. Okabe did not seek to bring out the essence of these elements, nor to make his music a simple addition to the game's content. Instead, Taro Yoko set him a theme—sadness, moroseness—which he then diversified into different shades to compose the melodies. Ranging "from a quiescent sadness to intense sadness," Okabe explained, his music was designed to create the atmosphere, to permeate the game and its world, rather than to simply accompany it. Hence, there were no battle, victory, dungeon or village themes here. Sudden shifts in tone, typical of transitions between different areas in the Sugiyama structure, were carefully avoided. Only the entire spectrum of melancholy could be experienced here, declined in countless poignant melodies that confer to the game its consistency, and its unique end-of-the-world atmosphere. It is worth noting that in order to make it seem like the music was intermingled with the game, Okabe and his team used different instrumental layers. These shifts are noticeable during transitions between combat and exploration phases, but also at more precise moments, such as when Devola's voice appears in the *Song of the Ancients as* Nier approaches her in the village. Or when the Shadowlord is on the verge of being killed, then the *Shadowlord* track is reduced to the simple melody of a music box.

The process, by coloring the narrative and offering an interpretation of the world through music, was not dissimilar to the extremely graphic scores of Ennio Morricone—one of Okabe's main influences—in the way they enhanced the narrative by taking it over. And following the example of his Italian counterpart, Okabe distinguished himself by his abundant use of voices.

---

80. Opening, Castle, Town, Field, Dungeon, Battle, Final Battle, and Ending.

Nevertheless, this request came from Taro Yoko. During *NieR*'s development, the director pressured Okabe into recording lyrics on his music. But not just any lyrics. Yoko stipulated that the language must not be recognizable, and could even give the player the impression that it was another world's dialect, in order to match the dystopic plot of the game. Logically, the request involved inventing a new lingo. Fortunately, the composer had recently met an Anglo-Japanese singer who was fascinated by languages and whose voice could match *NieR*'s melancholic tone.

Emi Evans (born Emiko) emigrated from the UK to Japan in the early 2000s to pursue a singing career. Together with a friend she met there, she founded the trip hop band "freescape" and became its lead singer. A few albums and performances later, she made her first steps into the video game industry by singing on an arrangement CD of the *Etrian Odyssey* RPG series. Then, thanks to her network, Evans contacted Monaca and Keiichi Okabe, who were looking for an English singer to record a *Dance Dance Revolution* album. The composer did not select her for this project, but later contacted her to make her the voice of *NieR*'s soundtrack. Her only condition was that she would be in charge of writing the imaginary lyrics that would accompany Monaca's melodies. Born to a Japanese mother and a British father, Evans speaks both languages and learned the basics of French at university. Her passion for linguistics led her to accept the project. The first song she wrote was *Song of the Ancients* performed in the game by Devola and Popola. She recounted the prophecy according to which a white book, the Grimoire Weiss, would restore peace in the world after defeating the black book, Grimoire Noir. For the lyrics, Evans combined English, Japanese, Italian, Spanish, Portuguese and French elements. *Song of the Ancients* was nonetheless the only track whose language was completely invented.

For the rest of the soundtrack, Okabe and Yoko refined their vision and asked Evans to write the next songs in futuristic versions of existing languages. With only the first drafts of the melodies composed by Monaca as a basis to work on, the lyricist decomposed and rearranged several languages in order to simulate their erosion over millennia. Thus, she wrote *Kainé*'s track in futuristic Gaelic, used a science fiction French for *Grandma*, and *The Wretched Automatons* envisioned what English would sound like in more than a thousand years. The only track written in an understandable language, English, was the final song: *Ashes of Dreams*. "With Yoko, we wanted players to first imagine what the songs were about, so that when they would reach the end and hear the English lyrics, they would have a sort of revelation," explained Okabe in an interview with *Famitsu* magazine.

But Emi Evans believes that the power of her songs lies precisely in the emotional release of abstraction, rather than in the intrigue it provoked: "When everyday language is used, the duality of sound and meaning, the tone of the voice, help to convey feelings. But when the meaning is completely set aside, the voice has to transmit many more emotions, by making the best use of sounds and tones. Since emotions are no longer conveyed by thoughts, the form of expression becomes purer and more direct. As a result, and especially with respect to singing, it is possible to transmit emotions to anyone, regardless of their own language. When you speak a real language, communication takes place on an intellectual level, you have to think and reflect. When different tones and sounds are used, thinking is no longer necessary and communicating on a deeper emotional level becomes possible, as we simply gain the freedom of perception[81]. "

Ironically, it was on the *Ashes of Dreams* text, written in her native language, that Evans struggled the most. Yoko had requested the lyrics to be heartbreaking with sadness to conclude the game on a note of despair[82]. Evans, at the time employed by Club Med on the beautiful island of Ishigaki in the heart of the Yaeyama archipelago in the south of Japan, was unable to muster the resolve to set down such dark feelings on paper. However, it was only after facing the depressing British rains again during a trip home to her native country that she found the strength to write the lyrics to this crucial song. She explained that the melancholy that struck her then, which manifested itself in her voice, celestial and haunted, as it did in the overwhelming lyrics of *Ashes of Dreams*, "must just come from growing up as an only child in rainy England[83]".

But although the sullen echo of the British Isles had undoubtedly seduced *NieR*'s fans, part of the credit for the exquisite soundtrack must also go to the woman in the shadows, Nami Nakagawa. Assigned to the chorus on a significant part of the soundtrack (*Dark Colossus Destroys All*, *Wretched Automatons*, *Shadowlord*...), the singer delivered an impressive vocal performance, capable of reaching the highest notes, as high as the firmament before dropping down in a flash into the most hollow depths. When Emi Evans's voice, wavering and sincere, sometimes lacked power or variety, Nakagawa would take over to strengthen the score. The complementarity was perfect. As a matter of fact, the music team, as a whole, worked wonders, as demonstrated by the commercial success of the soundtrack and subsequent arrangement albums[84]. For this very

81. http://www.dixiemeart.com/2010/06/08/emi-evans-la-voix-de-NieR/
82. The song ends with the following verses, echoing the counterproductive efforts of the group of heroes and the impending end of the Replicants after the Shadowlord's death: "Stories of danger, fearless attack,/Specters of plague and pain./All of these ghosts of our own delusions are back;/Have we been fighting in vain? Fighting in vain?"
83. http://www.originalsoundversion.com/deep-into-NieR-interview-with-vocalist-and-lyricist-emi-evans/
84. *NieR*'s soundtrack and the first two arrangement albums that followed managed to make their way

reason, the composition would not change much on *Drakengard 3* and *NieR: Automata*.

DRAKENGARD 3: A MATTER OF CONTRAST

For *Drakengard 3*, Taro Yoko wanted to allude to the concept of contrast through the compositions. For two reasons. The first involved his desire to mark the transition between stillness and motion. In the game, these notions were central to the dialectic between the casual dialog phases around the campfire, the exploration periods and the bloody rage unleashed on the battlefields. The "motionless" tracks, such as the main menu *Descendeus*, were mainly composed by Keigo Hoashi from Monaca. In substance, they were very close to the melodies of *NieR*—Emi Evans occasionally added her voice and imaginary lyrics to evoke an atmosphere both sad and peaceful. As for the music evoking motion and movement, it corresponded to the many boss themes. Their rock and aggressive melodies filled with distorted riffs contrasted violently with the orchestral compositions of exploration music. Okabe, in charge of conducting these tracks, endeavored to cast a different atmosphere than the ones in *NieR* and *Drakengard*. "I think *Drakengard*'s fans have a lot more of a love, or a pre-made image at least, of the series. That makes it hard to figure out what to create to keep them satisfied. I thought at first that there'd be no purpose to rehashing Sano's work, but there were times when I thought that was what I should do instead, even though I knew it'd just be an inferior copy[85]." Okabe finally chose to rule out this possibility, but still invited Nobuyoshi Sano, *Drakengard*'s original composer, to revisit one of the emblematic themes of the first episode: *Exhausted*. This song reflected Furiae's point of view, who confessed her incestuous feelings to her brother Caim. In *Drakengard 3*, the new lyrics written by scriptwriter Hana Kikuchi were recited by Zero, who lamented about the curse that dwelled within her. Sano's arrangement concluded the C branch of the game, and it was Maaya Uchida herself, Zero's voice actress, who sang the lyrics.

The second reason that led Yoko to highlight contrast in the soundtrack lay in the characters' representativeness. *Drakengard 3* features six sisters with personalities at opposite ends of the spectrum. Moreover, all are endowed with the power of song, which made singing a key feature of their way of expressing themselves, and therefore also of their dissimilarities. Okabe adopted a two-step

---

into the *Oricon* rankings the week they were released.
85. https://www.polygon.com/2013/7/17/4530966/abot-Drakengard-3-and-making-the-music-for-a-very-strange-game

approach to reflect these abundant disparities. First, he encouraged several composers to color the melodies with their own sensitivity. Nobuyoshi Sano and Keigo Hoashi have already been mentioned, but Kakeru Ishihama and Kuniyiki Takahashi from Monaca should also be credited for their contributions to the exploration and combat themes. Akitaka Tohyama, former music director of the *Tekken* franchise, was responsible for the themes of Three. To reflect the differences and diversity within the songs, Okabe next called on a handful of female singers each with different vocal characteristics. Thus, their voices impregnated each style of composition with a particular emotion or personality. As mentioned, Emi Evans depicted *NieR*'s atmosphere with her tender and melancholic songs. Nevertheless, she did not intervene much, and mostly stood out for her performance of *The Final Song*, the final boss song of the D branch, shifting between hope and despair. In a similar style, though more romantic, artist Eir Aoi (known for the theme music of the Japanese anime *Kill La Kill*) sang *Kuroiuta*, one of the two main themes of the game and the song for ending B[86]. As for Nami Nakagawa, she resumed her role in the chorus, and sometimes took part in the leading vocals. Her powerful voice mainly benefited the many orchestral tracks of the battlefields. Like a distorting mirror effect, the glitchy electronic voices of the trio of YoRHa singers added to the riffs of the boss fights generated a crystal clear contrast between the different phases of the game. Finally, there was independent artist Chihiro Onitsuka's mesmerizing performance of the second theme of the game concluding the D branch: *This Silence is Mine*. Her raw and rasping voice concluded Zero's sororicidal quest in a long, dark and nerve-racking lament, a plea for a return to silence and tranquility after hours of brutality.

In short, Okabe's method allowed *Drakengard 3*'s soundtrack to produce interesting tone variations. However, the heterogeneity of the tracks and the numerous collaborations undoubtedly ended up subverting the overall coherence, which is more disjointed than the *NieR* soundtrack. By adopting a more classical division between rest, exploration and combat phases, the music director had, in a sense, moved closer to Sugiyama's formula. More run-of-the-mill than those of *NieR*, the compositions thus struggle to cause surprise, and especially to show any clear direction. Evans's melancholy competes with the frenzy of the boss tracks, which in turn compete with the grandiloquence of the orchestral music. However, the fact remains that, taken separately, the melodies of Okabe and his team still compare rather favorably against those of the competition. The composer remains one of the safest bets in video gaming, and he would go on to prove this once again with *NieR: Automata*.

86. For legal reasons, this version was not included in the Western port. Outside Japan, the international version of *Kuroiuta*, renamed *Black Song*, is sung by Emi Evans.

NIER: AUTOMATA: RETRO-MELANCHOLY

For *NieR: Automata*, Keiichi Okabe had no other ambition than to revive the style of the previous episode. So he virtually surrounded himself with the same team. Keigo Hoashi, his right arm in Monaca, assisted him with the composition, accompanied by Kuniyuki Takahashi who started out with *Drakengard 3*. The singing was performed by Emi Evans and her unique language, enriched here by the influence of dialects inspired by lost or forgotten languages. Nami Nakagawa was also involved, with a role that was considerably more central than last time. In addition to her chorus work, she become the iconic voice of some of the most poignant tracks in the game, such as *Possessed by Disease*. Her enchanting polymorphous performance with tribal accents placed her on an equal footing with Emi Evans. The main addition to the vocal cast was J'Nique Nicole, an American R&B singer who had recently immigrated to Japan. Her voice was smoother than the voices of her colleagues and warmed up the ethereal theme of the desert in *Memories of Dust*–among other performances. However, she mostly sang the main theme (and first ending theme) of *NieR: Automata*, *The Weight of the World*, a pop track, almost reminiscent of Disney songs, projected into the atmosphere by the singer's powerful voice.

Monaca did not skimp on the covers and references in order to revive *NieR*'s sensations. The most emblematic tracks of the title, like *Grandma*, *Song of the Ancients* or even *Dark Colossus Destroys All*, were rearranged in new versions respectively subtitled *Destruction*, *Atonement* and *Kaiju*[87]. The soothing melody of *Dispossession* was incorporated into *Faltering Prayer*, used after the completion of certain side quests. Okabe even went so far as to create several versions (one for each ending) of the final song *The Weight of the World*, as he had done with *Ashes of Dreams*. Nevertheless, it would be misleading to say that *Automata*'s soundtrack is just a 2.0 version. For the most part, the music contained more brutal and mechanical sounds (factory sounds, notably in *Wretched Weaponry*) in order to reflect the change of tone between the pastoral world of *NieR* and that of *NieR: Automata*, more heavily influenced by science fiction and cyberpunk. In addition, the change in scale and budget compared to *NieR* allowed Okabe

---

87. It is worth noting that, with the exception of *Grandma*, these covers follow a certain thematic pattern. *Dark Colossus—Kaiju* punctuates the encounter with the giant boss Grün and echoes Nier's fight against the Shadow which attacked the village on the same musical theme. Devola and Popola's song in *NieR*, *Song of the Ancients*, is used as a fighting theme with *Atonement* when the other twin sisters protected 9S to redeem themselves from their sins. Likewise, Emil's theme is rearranged into fighting music with its *Despair* version, which illustrates the fight against the magician's clones, and can be heard in a side quest.

and his team to move one step further: firstly on the finish and variety of the instrumentation, but also on the originality of the implementation.

The main sound component of *NieR: Automata* did not lie in the compositions themselves, but rather in the way they were presented to the player. The more open nature of the environments in this episode meant that Okabe had to find a way to soften the transitions between the different atmospheres he had created, without causing an excessively abrupt tone break. His decision to use this method extended the music transformation process he had begun on *NieR*. At the beginning of a zone, the player was greeted by a raw version of the accompanying track. Then, as he progressed, engaged in combat or met a character, successive layers of instrumentation were added. The power build-up was achieved through a dynamic system that combined four levels of instrumentation (classified by intensity) and the possibility of adding voices on each of these levels. The malleability of this process allowed a smooth evolution of the melodies and thus favored painless transitions. The remarkable effect of fades sliding, intertwining and strengthening from one area to the next, never rushed the player. Even better, his curiosity and his thirst for exploration were organically rewarded. In this respect, the discreet arrival of J'Nique Nicole's powerful voice upon entering the desolate desert area is shockingly beautiful. Likewise, it was in this spirit of composition and assembly that the sound team had fun incorporating the machines' voices into *Possessed by Disease* (*"Become as Gods"*) and *Birth of a Wish* (*"This Cannot Continue"*), reinforcing the feeling that the sound and game dimensions coexisted in the same space and influenced each other–the concept behind *NieR*'s compositions.

Full credit was awarded to Masami Ueda, composer at PlatinumGames, for the music integration. A small legend in the industry, this former Capcom and Clover Studio artist had already made a name for himself on *Resident Evil*, *Okami* and *Bayonetta*. For *NieR: Automata*, he put aside his scores and focused exclusively on the implementation of the soundtrack. In addition to the transition system, he was also credited with the trick that enabled the automated transformation of gaming music into 8-bit. These versions can be heard during 9S's hacking sessions. When he breaks into a safe or steals from an enemy, the background music transforms into a computer synthesized melody which emulates the full version. But only a small part of the soundtrack was given an 8-bit arrangement by Shotaro Seo from Monaca. While the rest underwent an audio reduction process called tone filter. This roughly filtered the track signal and transformed it into a square wave typical of 8-bit sounds. However, since it was automated, the result was not as pure as an arrangement. To preserve the 8-bit style while properly highlighting the melody, Ueda combined the two in the output signal:

the filtered version was boosted to 80% of the signal, while the original music filled the remaining 20%[88]. Most of the time, the player therefore heard this hybrid version during the hacking phases.

Full of intoxicating compositions, refined by the stellar voices of its singers and cleverly implemented, *NieR: Automata*'s soundtrack was on the verge of perfection. Seemingly acknowledging Keiichi Okabe and his company for their merit, the Japanese industry awarded the game with the CEDEC Award[89] 2017 in the sound category, beating Yoko Shimomura's score for the imposing *Final Fantasy XV*. National recognition that was long in coming for the *NieR* dream team, seven years after having produced what represented, in the minds of many players, one of the most beautiful video game soundtracks. The aura and magnitude of Monaca's (and Nobuyoshi Sano's) scores stemmed from the fact that they served as a projection of the universe developed in Taro Yoko's games—a strange and tragic world engulfed in insecurity, shaped by man's conquering grip, infused with his violent and hateful instincts and condemned to eternally perish in an endless melancholic spiral. At the heart of this chaos, Yoko's antiheroes try to make their way through the walls of flesh that block their path.

88. https://www.platinumgames.com/official-blog/article/9581
89. The equivalent of the Oscars, but for video games, in Japan.

THE STRANGE WORKS OF
TARO YOKO
From Drakengard to NieR:Automata

CHAPTER III — UNIVERSE

T aro Yoko[90] has developed, in spite of himself, an extremely deep universe as the setting for his plots. This alternative and polymorphous world, a combination of heroic fantasy, science fiction and realism, started with the first *Drakengard*, released in 2003 on the PlayStation 2. At the beginning, as we will see, it was nothing more than a rather classical medieval fantasy universe mixed with gloomy and Gothic elements. Then, over the years, as the director followed up on his first work with *NieR* and *NieR: Automata*, and his addition of the prequel *Drakengard 3*, this space, this world, gradually became denser, until it encompassed more than ten thousand years of history. This has continued to such an extent that today the storylines of the games only constitute brief epiphenomena in the midst of this vast saga. For the past fifteen years, Yoko's universe, driven by a myriad of cultural products—mangas, *dramas*, news, guides—of which it is useless to list an exhaustive inventory here, has reached an intimidating scope, however it easily drifts. Indeed, we should not be misled: despite its scope, the backdrop set up by the developer does not share the consistency and tangible nature of great global works such as those created by J. R. R. Tolkien (*The Lord of the Rings*, 1954-1955), Frank Herbert (*Dune*, 1965), or even, to stay in video game territory, those by Bioware (*Mass Effect*) or Yasumi Matsuno[91]. In truth, fascinated by humans above all else, and undertaking to explore their contradictions, Taro Yoko had little concerns about what unfolded in the background, and simply used the generous background he had envisioned as a pretext, a simple framework into which he inserted his script and characters. This is why Taro Yoko was never committed to building a new structure from scratch for the stories he wanted to tell. He simply preferred to dip into what already existed. Thus, his world was perceived as the chaotic reproduction of a patchwork of influences, rather than as the result of a carefully devised design process. The history of humanity, the characteristic themes of medieval fantasy literature (spiritualism, mysticism, Church) and science

90. Supported by two lead scriptwriters, Sawako Natori and Hana Kikuchi.
91. Director of *Vagrant Story* and *Final Fantasy XII*, in charge of the creation of the world of Ivalice at Square Enix.

fiction literature (eugenics, robotization, genetics), notions of philosophy and psychology, a good dose of otaku culture, etc. were mixed pell-mell.

The storylines, one of Taro Yoko's signature game mechanics, were symptomatic of the director's contempt for his universe's consistency. Throughout all these works, several alternative paths would lead the player to successively explore significantly different endings (identified by the alphabet letter assigned to them). However, only one path was the "right one," in the sense that it historically linked the games together. In order, the ending E of *Drakengard 3*, not included in the game, but published as a novel, led to *Drakengard*, whose ending E in turn led to *NieR*. The latter's ending E, once again missing from the title, but published in the book *Grimoire NieR*, which followed the ending D, eventually led to the events of *NieR: Automata*.

We have thus attempted to outline here, as accurately as possible, the canonical structure of events in Taro Yoko's universe, insofar as it may be reproduced on the basis of our current knowledge. As has been mentioned, the creator never intended to outline a nice, long, straight storyline. As a result, some gray areas must still be cleared up, especially those between the games. Hence, we will have to extrapolate some information to connect all the elements, while always keeping the overall coherence of the story in mind. Besides, not everything will be covered exhaustively in these lines. For the sake of clarity, some obviously secondary or minor parts of the plot, despite their success, will be omitted, with hopefully no impact on the detailed and precise understanding of the main events[92][93].

THE CATACLYSM

In Eastern Europe, the Eastern Roman Empire prospered under the Amorian dynasty. In the West, the Carolingian Empire had just been divided between Charlemagne's three grandsons. In Asia, inspired by the Chinese administration, Japan had adopted the Code regime, while in the Middle East and in sub-Saharan Africa, the Arab civilization had conquered large territories and settled as far as the gates of Aquitaine. This was the year 856. All year round, devastating earthquakes ravaged Tunisia, Iran, Kyoto in Japan and Corinth in the Byzantine Empire. Hundreds of thousands perished. The Iberian Peninsula was also struck by a violent 7.0-magnitude earthquake of such immense intensity that it became

92. All the alternative endings that were not part of the canonical structure, namely the endings A to D of *Drakengard*, A to C of *NieR* and A to D of *Drakengard 3* will therefore not be covered in this chapter.
93. Some extracts are taken from partial translations of the short stories contained in *Grimoire NieR* and *Drakengard* art books.

known as the Cataclysm. Following this event, a huge city with a cathedral at its center emerged on the peninsula: Cathedral City.

In the space of a few years, hordes of dragons fleeing the city had burnt empires and nations to the ground: the Byzantine Empire and the three kingdoms of France fell one after the other, while riots broke out all over Europe. The continent was devastated, the borders destroyed. Hordes of refugees fled in the hope of finding a peaceful place to live. What remained of the region and the old empires was henceforth commonly called "Midgard."

While death engulfed the world, the rumor of Cathedral City's appearance became increasingly persistent and many considered it a last refuge for humanity. The former European elite, henceforth stateless, decided to transform the city into a sanctuary so that nobles and intellectuals could study the calamity that had struck the continent and unravel the secrets of the strange phenomena occurring all over the world. To this end, they founded the Pythagoras Institute, de facto reining institution of the city. The refugees tried in turn to enter the city walls of Cathedral City to take advantage of its wealth. Though they were systematically rejected by the Institute. In response to the migrants' arrival, the organization built an enormous gate–known as Chaldea Gate–to control incoming flows and manage resources, especially food. In reaction to what was perceived as injustice, the refugees rose up in revolt against the city's defense forces during a bloody week that became known as the "Ten Days of Tragedy."

The appearance of magic

While Cathedral City withdrew into complete isolationism, many Midgard residents began to master strange powers that were considered "miracles," such as the power of destruction or the ability to detect water veins in the ground. Upon researching the phenomenon, the Pythagoras Institute proclaimed the existence of magic. The "Users" of these miraculous powers quickly acquired a high social status which gradually enabled them to become leading figures within the city. They brought order and social harmony. As old faiths and religions deteriorated, the User's dominance was perceived as a new way of inspiring people and controlling the masses. A new faith devoted to them developed and spread swiftly: the Pythagoras Institute Church, more commonly known as the Church. For the first time in ten years, Cathedral City reopened the Chaldea Gate and undertook its first territory expansion. Meanwhile, the Church pursued its research into magic and experimented with techniques–known as Seal Magic–to try and contain it, should a User ever lose control of it. The situation got out of control during one of these experiments. The caster's foot unfortunately became gigantic and crushed two thousand people living in the slums with its massive weight. The two thirds of the city were destroyed. The Church concealed the event.

Despite this horrific outcome, the city continued to expand and sought to extend its influence to the surrounding regions. In this context, the Church created the Church Investigation Committee, an armed force with powerful magical equipment whose sole mission was to take control of the various self-governing regions surrounding Cathedral City. Once this goal was achieved, the Committee members who were scattered throughout Midgard, although still affiliated with the Church, independently ruled over their own respective dominions. As a result, a new political organization emerged on the continent—that of the "Lords of the Lands." On the British Isles lay the Land of Seas, while to the west, once under Charlemagne's rule, stood the Land of Mountains. At the center of Midgard, on the territory of the Austro-Hungarian Empire and part of Italy, a Lord ruled over the Land of Forests, while to the north, the sand-flooded Land of Sands skirted the North Sea. As was customary in Europe, territorial division heralded a period of conflict in which the Lords of each Land would compete over the sovereignty of vast regions. The Church, while in the background, nonetheless attempted to preserve its hegemony and its stranglehold on the region by establishing close relationships with the Lords, with certain senior religious officials willingly accepting bribes in exchange for services. More importantly, members of the Church took advantage of these new local footholds to pursue their research on magic. Thereby, the Church established Magic Academies dedicated to its study in every Land, collectively placed under the authority of the Central Magic Academy located in Cathedral City. Thanks to the fantastic progress achieved within these institutions, magic was no longer the privilege of an elite and quickly became a common technique. With these achievements, the Academies acquired stature and lastingly settled in the social, technical and political landscape of Midgard. In 960, over a century after the Cataclysm, the first Magic Academy President was elected by the Lords of the Lands. His unusual profile, totally ignorant of the mysteries of magic, caused a disagreement between the Lords and the Church, but more importantly, provoked anxiety and unease among magicians. After ten years of dissatisfaction about the Lords' stranglehold on the elections, young magicians decided to rebel and marched through Cathedral City, demanding the replacement of the Academy's president. They were all suppressed in a single night during the White Rebellion.

In 985, a widespread famine struck the entire continent. The food usually shipped to the city from the Lands was becoming scarcer. To survive, Church dignitaries and influential politicians abused their privilege. In exchange for money, goods and weapons, or even women and children, the Lords provided them with food, to the detriment of the people. Outraged by the level of corruption unveiled by the famine in the very heart of the Academy and disgusted by the abandonment of the poor classes, a few magicians formed a secret organization to spark a revolution: the Blue Corps. Four years later, when famine had weakened the Church's military capabilities, revolutionary magicians began to set things in motion. They received support from many of their young colleagues and from a few lords who were dissatisfied with the Church's actions. Finally, in 991, an uprising on an unprecedented scale broke out in Cathedral City–the Blue Rebellion–led by the Blue Corps. Its magicians occupied the Central Magic Academy in the hope of overthrowing the Church and the Institute's government. Their main demands included the freedom and independence of the Magic Academy and the abolition of the rule of the Lords of the Lands. Despite all its efforts, the Blue Corps was completely decimated overnight by Seal Magic that encompassed the entire city. More than three quarters of the citizens located within a radius of two districts around the center of the city were killed while serving as catalysts for the execution of the spell. Among the survivors, many appeared to have completely lost their minds. Deemed potentially dangerous, the Church buried them alive.

Following the Blue Rebellion, the Church, in an effort to avoid repeating such a disaster and to ease fears, granted independence to the Magic Academy. By cutting itself off from its magical military power, it increasingly became dependent on the strike force of the Lords of the Lands, thus raising the question of its future and its hegemony over Midgard. Despite its newly acquired independence, the Academy declined due to a shortage of magicians, to the point of totally losing the support of the Lords of the Lands, still affiliated with the Church. In order to regain its former power, the Academy lifted the ban on a multitude of extremely dangerous magical arts. In the aftermath of this violation of the balance of power in the region, Midgard sank into chaos. The climax of this instability occurred in 995, when a massive incident marked the end of Cathedral City such as it had existed since the Cataclysm. It is believed that a magician from the Central Magic Academy, in her attempt to summon the forbidden art of the song, had made a singing error which caused a terrible explosion. In an instant, the city had been reduced to ruins and all traces of life disappeared. The dust produced by the blast of the explosion had formed a gigantic flower in the night sky overlooking the Iberian Peninsula.

Two years later, in one of Midgard's jails, six young women were held prisoner. Five of them were severely tortured for having conspired against the Lord of the Land, regarded as a tyrant by the people. The sixth was a former teenage prostitute suffering from plague. Her name was Rose, like the color of her eyes. Her life was fraught with blood and death. She had been found guilty of theft and more than a hundred murders, starting with those of the entire staff in the brothel where she had been forced to work. The bodies of the rebels, wounded by the abuse of their torturers, lay before Rose's eyes: their eyes gouged out, their flesh burnt, their bones shattered, their nails ripped from their fingers. Lying there, in agony, were five brave souls driven by the will to face the established order, to rid the world of despots, but also of bloodthirsty assassins of her kind. At that moment, the contrast between the dignity of these resistance fighters and the pure malevolence she embodied could not be more prominent. Drenched by the rain that seeped into the cell, with blood trickling down her body, the murderess cursed the universe; for lashing out at decent people taking it upon themselves to protect the weak and defenseless, but also for transforming her into what she had become: an empty stomach whose only resort was to steal food from potbellied people along with their lives. "Fuck the world! Fuck you all! Fuck you, fuck you, fuck you! Fucking die!" she raged inwardly.

But the world was hardly offended. She watched her tormented comrades draw their final breath, one after the other, until she found herself alone and dying, her trachea clogged with the blood accumulating in her lungs. Her time was coming. Before drawing her last breath, her gaze fell upon a beautiful pale pink flower. She had never seen one so beautiful. Her field of vision became obstructed as the petals grew larger until the flower had taken full possession of her body. Rose was dead, Zero was born.

The Flower

Miraculously resurrected and thus cured, Zero awoke with new powers and a white flower with pink pistils in place of her right eye. She could henceforth use magic through the forbidden art of the song. In the ancient texts of Cathedral City, the beings who mastered this ability of immeasurable power were called Intoners. Zero had also acquired incomparable healing skills. However, she realized that her body no longer completely responded to her. Her brain, her heart, her muscles, nothing seemed to obey her will. Reduced to the role of an articulated puppet, or rather an undead given the circumstances, Zero concluded that it was the magic of the flower she had seen before dying that now controlled her actions, and that all traces of life within her had disappeared.

Freed from the depths of Cathedral City during the incident which had devastated the city, the Flower was a terrible evil creature. It parasitized Rose to turn her into a tool to destroy humanity. It fed on her body and her resilience, devouring her from the inside, in order to one day fully control its host. At which point, it would possess a tremendous magical power capable of destroying the world. Sensing the danger embodied by the Flower and determined to die for good, Zero attempted to take her own life. She stabbed herself in the heart—but did not die. At that moment, a gigantic budding flower ripped through her entire chest, and blossomed in a violent deluge of shrieks. A torrent of blood splattered the ground from the ovary of the pistil. Five little girls bathed in liquid emerged from the puddle that had formed. In response to its host's life-threatening suicidal urges, the Flower had shaped five children to whom it had granted a share of its power, inventing false memories to give them a human essence. Therefore, One, Two, Three, Four and Five were also Intoners. Alarmed by the danger they represented as receptacles of the Flower's destructive magic, Zero considered immediately killing her "sisters" while they were still frail and defenseless. As she approached Two to destroy her, another sister, One, intervened, then escaped with the other girls cursing her eldest sister, traitor to her own siblings. Weakened by her suicide attempt, Zero was unable to move and could only watch them leave. Feeling the burden of her new responsibility, the original Intoner set out to destroy the abominations she had given life to.

The Battle of Cathedral City

Led by One and her strong sense of justice, the five young sisters traveled the lands of Midgard acting as protectors of the poor and the abused. But their real purpose was to figure out a way to gain more power in order to kill Zero. Not a single one of them realized that the Flower was manipulating them. As they traveled through the Land of Sands, they fought and then killed the despotic Lord of the region, Bass. The latter's assistant, Partition, a magician with more than enigmatic intentions, showed them the way to the Iberian Peninsula and Cathedral City, the origin of all magic. In the bowels of the ruined city, behind Mercurius Gate, dwelled a power beyond all comprehension capable of defeating Zero. With Partition at their side, the Intoners boarded a ship and sailed to their destination.

Meanwhile, Zero had recovered her strength and thrown herself into researching the Flower's origin in order to find a way to annihilate it. According to her research, dragons appeared to be the Flower's natural enemies, the only ones capable of destroying it. After meeting the most powerful of them,

Michael, on a battlefield, Zero asked for the beast's help to wipe the Flower off the face of the earth. To achieve this, he would have to wipe out her sisters and eventually herself. Michael was hesitant: a dragon's pride normally prevented it from associating with humans. To prove her worth, Zero agreed to take up the challenges set by the legendary monster. And she successfully completed all of them. Forced to acknowledge the Intoner's worth, Michael agreed to lend her his support and became her friend. Shortly after this, a strange person named Accord paid Zero a visit. She introduced herself as an android from a different era in charge of overseeing the right course of history. Accord warned Zero that she represented a "singularity" in the space-time continuum, in other words, a specific presence that caused the future to diverge into several branches. She explained that Zero's existence, due to the Flower, threatened the world, and her actions would determine the future. The android's task involved finding the time branch in which the young woman successfully completed her quest with Michael's help. If the Intoner were to fail, she would be forced to seal the current branch and explore other time ramifications until she finally found the one where Zero triumphed. Determined to unfailingly fulfill their mission, rider and dragon headed together for Cathedral City, where the battle would take place.

But neither the sisters nor Zero were the first to reach the capital. The Lords of the Lands of Forests, Mountains and Seas were already there. They had also gotten wind of the power sealed behind Mercurius Gate and wanted to seize it. Nevertheless, they had not yet managed to access it. Notwithstanding the help of the enigmatic gatekeeper, Bartas, the Seal refused to disappear and kept them out. The Lords then proceeded to place their troops inside the city and patiently awaited the Intoners' arrival to ambush them.

During her voyage to the peninsula, One met the dragon Gabriella. After several battles with mixed outcomes, the young girl and the creature fell in love with each other and decided to join forces to accomplish One's quest: saving the world and killing Zero. Together, accompanied by the other four sisters, they landed in the heart of Cathedral City near Mercurius Gate, where the Lords reserved a bloody welcome for them. Shortly thereafter, Two, Three, Four and Five were killed, torn to shreds or beheaded by Caerula and her counterparts. Traumatized by this infuriating and unbearable vision, One flew into a terrible rage during which she sang her songs. Receptive to the magic song emanating from the Intoner, Mercurius Gate opened, releasing a putrid and slimy black matter similar to oil onto the ground. Contorted arms emanated on the liquid's surface, like tentacles desperately attempting to cling to living entities. The crawling limbs eventually scavenged parts of the young sisters' bodies, assembling them and wrapping them in their lumpy fluid which seemed to bring the dislocated bodies back to life. However, the four sisters thus resurrected were nothing more than puppets with no control over their actions. As if paralyzed by a magic trance of incredible intensity. In the surrounding area, the shapeless mass of matter increasingly grew and took the form of a large flower as black as ink and the size of a building. Four circles of light suddenly appeared, in contrast with the bright blue sky, and spewed out strange monsters of immeasurable power in the form of babies or titans: Daemons. In no time at all, the Lords of the Lands were obliterated by these terrible creatures.

Therein lay the real power bestowed by the Flower upon the Intoners: the power to lead the Daemons to earth, God's pawns[94] devoted to the destruction of humanity, which must be punished for its vanity and the devastation it has caused. The Flower that parasitized Zero and her sisters actually represented only a fragment of this greater divine power; the Black Flower which had just appeared was its origin. Without the Mercurius Gate to contain the full power of the original Flower, the latter was entirely free to use the bodies of the Intoners as catalysts of the apocalypse, with no need to undergo a time-consuming process involving the seizure of power.

When Zero got to the scene, riding Michael, she realized the seriousness of the situation. In order to neutralize the Black Flower's power, she enchanted four doves with her magic, then sent them to Two, Three, Four and Five. The birds absorbed the Intoners' energy, thereby depriving the Black Flower of its ability to summon the Daemons, which immediately disappeared. Then, Michael obliterated the Flower with a salvo of fireballs. A few steps away, the four sisters were knocked down, unconscious, but alive. However, Zero's goal remained unchanged: defeating her genetic monstrosities to annihilate once and for all the Flower still hidden within them. As she prepared to fight One, Bartas, the gatekeeper, blocked her path.

When Mercurius Gate was opened, Bartas realized that he had failed in his task. Deprived of his raison d'être, he turned to another one of his hobbies: fighting. He would only die after finding someone capable of defeating him, and intended to challenge both Intoners to achieve this. Zero was the first to bite the dust, followed closely by One. Bartas's strength seemed unrivaled. Even Michael's flames were no match for him. Gabriella, the dragon who had fallen in love with One, chose to use the hidden power of her species to defend her protégée: the "Beastification." In exchange for losing consciousness, dragons possessed the ability to transform themselves into dreadful monsters with a

---

94. In Taro Yoko's universe, the notion of "God" is never really defined in detail. All we know is that it appears to be a unique God, since the Japanese version of *Drakengard* never uses the plural form to define it (whereas Western translations do), and that it is more or less responsible for all the disasters that befall men, like the White Chlorination Syndrome (or WCS) in *NieR*.

tremendous offensive potential. Upon completion of the process, no trace of their memory or ability to think would remain; they would become mere killing machines. Halfway through her transformation, Gabriella disintegrated Bartas then, blinded by her devastating fury, turned against her friend One. In a desperate attempt to stop the Beastification and to bring Gabriella back to reason, the Intoner resorted to the most ancient piece of forbidden magic conferred by the Flower's power: the Pact. Its general principle, when used by a human being, was to save a life—its own or that of the partner entity, or both—in exchange for the removal of a feature or characteristic from the one invoking the Pact. The souls of those who are bound by a Pact would then be intensely connected and if one were to die, the other would immediately follow.

In the ruins of Cathedral City, coiled on a long scaly tail, One awoke to the voice of Gabriella. The Intoner, forever trapped in her teenage physical form, burst into tears of joy. The Pact was a success. Her sisters, who had recovered from their ordeals, joined her and shared this moment of happiness. In the air, Michael flew away holding Zero in his mouth, still unconscious after this grueling fight.

One was aware that her older sister would try to destroy her again. In anticipation of this eventuality, she created a brother in her image, also named One, out of one of her ribs. His only purpose would be to stop Zero if his sister should ever fail and die before delivering the fatal blow. Equipped with a dragon bone sword carved from one of Gabriella's teeth, the male One trained in absolute secrecy whilst waiting for the fateful day, occasionally satisfying his sister's sexual desires. Nevertheless, the threat posed by the dragon Michael remained. Gabriella, feeling unable to face him, allowed One to transform her into the Daemon Gabriel. This new form granted him powers that were greater than Michael's, but like the Beastification, it blocked his consciousness. Only an unfailing loyalty towards One remained, his Pact partner.

Two, Three, Four and Five, scattered across the continent, grow unusually fast—a side effect of the Flower's power. Henceforth young adults, they roam throughout Midgard. During their wanderings, they each met a "disciple" whom they took under their wing. These men would act as the protectors of their respective Intoners, but also as lovers expected to satisfy the uncommonly intense sexual urges of their mistresses. Nonetheless, the disciples were hardly ordinary. These guardians were, in reality, reincarnations of the doves used by Zero to calm her sisters' trance during the fight at Mercurius Gate. Since they had drawn their energy from the Intoners, they too were endowed with the abilities granted by the Flower, including the summoning of Daemons.

A few months after The Battle of Cathedral City, the five Intoners, celebrated as the glorious sworn enemies of tyrannical lords, reigned supreme over the Lands. They were worshiped as Goddesses bringing prosperity and peace throughout Midgard. A cruel irony as the entire world adulated these abominations that would cause its downfall.

DRAKENGARD 3

Long ago, in an age tarnished by endless conflict, five beautiful goddesses descended upon the land. The goddesses sang mystical songs that restored peace and harmony to our broken world. The people began to worship these holy songstresses, and came to refer to them as "Intoners." Thanks to the efforts of these Intoners, the chaos of war became a distant memory. And as a result, mankind enjoyed an age of sweet reverie, basking in the newfound light and beauty...

Zero's sword cut right through Partition and sank into the table. The blood of the Lord of the Land of Sand's former assistant ran abundantly on the illustrated parchment he was carefully reading. He would never be able to finish his story; in any case a myth devised to entice the people of Midgard under the new reign of the Intoners. Removed from the inert body, the blade bled onto the floor of the fortress library. Outside: the clanging of armor, the din of cannonballs, and the cries to kill the "traitor." The manhunt had begun. On March 3, 999, Zero returned to Cathedral City, where One, who had established the city as her headquarters, had repatriated her sisters from the surrounding Lands. The six Intoners were once again reunited. It was time to die.

Zero, supported by Michael's devastating flames, cleared a path through the city's streets full of soldiers, though not without shedding hectoliters of blood in her wake. At the cathedral's gates, Zero challenged One, Two, Three, Four and Five in a sororicidal battle. The stakes were enormous for One. The noblest Intoner dedicated her life to defending order and justice and in doing so had succeeded in bringing peace and stability to Midgard. Zero was not part of this plan. She represented a hindrance, more so the personification of madness and evil. In short, One's antithesis.

"Gabriel..." she whispered. The Daemon flew down from the sky and assailed Zero. Hit by one of his shots, she lost her left arm and collapsed. Michael attempted to contain the enemy fire, but found himself completely overwhelmed by Gabriel's power. Fatally wounded, he nevertheless managed to protect his friend who was able to flee Cathedral City, severely weakened. In his last breath, Michael wished to be reincarnated.

Zero minus five equals Dito

After one year of convalescence hidden somewhere in the Land of Seas, Five's territory, Zero had finally fully recovered. A mechanical prosthesis replaced the limb ripped off by Gabriel. By her side to support her on the umpteenth quest to overcome her sisters stood Mikhail, Michael's reincarnation. More naive and idealistic than his predecessor, and in particular much less ferocious, the young dragon loved Zero as if she were his mother, and she returned the sentiment by calling him every name under the sun whenever she had the chance. Not knowing all the facts about the Flower and its effects, Mikhail did not really understand why Zero wanted to murder her sisters. But driven by his boundless affection for his mistress, he nevertheless agreed to help her. This explosive duo, to say the least, started searching for Five, the first on the list of Intoners. Not because she lived nearby in the castle of the Land of seas, but because Zero though it easier to kill her stupidest sisters first.

After she had carved her way through the flesh of the soldiers who protected the Land, Zero quickly reached the sanctuary where Five was awaiting her. Assisted by her disciple, Dito, Five summoned the Daemon Phanuel and fought against her older sister. Victorious thanks to Mikhail, Zero nevertheless unleashed her rage and butchered Five's defenseless body with her sword. The Intoner, or what was left of her, managed however to rise one last time, before being cut in two. Dito was the one to give the fatal blow. The disciple was terribly frustrated with the way his Intoner used him as a sex slave all day long. Joined by the young man, Zero and Mikhail headed for the Land of Mountains, Four's refuge.

Grappling with her sister's army and the monsters who inhabited the region, Zero was in trouble. During a confrontation with a huge beast resembling a dog, she lost her right arm, but managed to use her regeneration skill to create a new body. Her left arm, however, severed by Gabriel, remained amputated. The Flower's power ended where the dragon's power began. As for Dito, he began to reveal his disturbed personality. Throughout the battles, the disciple relished the cries of agony of the men torn to pieces on the battlefield, and did not hesitate to offer his favors to Zero in order to protect her from the biting cold that reigned over the Land of Mountains' high altitudes. After having been turned down, Dito asked Zero about Four's nature. Laconic, she replied simply that her sister was a virgin, presumably thinking that this was her dominant trait. Albeit strange, her intuition was about to be confirmed, since following this interlude, the group met Decadus, Four's disciple, who had just been sent away by his mistress. The guardian revealed to Zero that the mental state of his Intoner was at its worst. Overwhelmed by the Flower's power and frustrated by her inability to satisfy her own sexual desires, Four sank into paranoia, to the point of believing that everyone on earth had become her enemy. She had already slit the throats of her entire staff and even appeared to be targeting her own subjects from the Land of Mountains. It seemed that nothing could appease her wrath. Thanks to Decadus's indications, the group set off to meet Four to put an end to her madness—and to the Flower's misdeeds.

Two bad, Two cries

Meanwhile in the Land of Sands, Two and her disciple, Cent, presented a perfect match. Both ruled their subjects with kindness and altruism, taking in orphans and tending to cripples. They even shared their power with the warriors protecting the Land. Indeed, Two had agreed to increase their strength with her songs so that they could repel monsters and invaders. Safe and cherished by their people, Two and Cent were overjoyed. But the couple's idyllic life was smashed to pieces during a picnic organized in Cathedral City for the two darlings of the Land. In the capital's streets, the two lovers unexpectedly found themselves facing off against their own soldiers turned into an army of undead by an unknown force. After entering the city's crypt where the children were sheltered, Two realized that the evil had been caused by the enchantment of the song. The Flower had corrupted the warriors. Two, an altruistic and loving woman, was devastated. This was all her fault. But she had no other choice, the crypt had been overrun by the undead, the children were in danger. She therefore plunged into the depths of Cathedral City, decimating her own army. At the very bottom, a horrifying scene awaited her: the orphans whom she loved as her own family and protected with all her being had mutated into a horrible monster. The Flower's curse had struck first. As Two rushed forward to kill the abomination and to put an end to this nightmare, the crystalline voices of the children resounded in the vault; they were saying their last goodbyes to their substitute mother, before she dealt the final blow.

Overwhelmed by the guilt of having taken the lives of so many innocents, and devastated when she realized the danger she represented for those she cherished, Two plunged into a near-catatonic state of shock. Her mind was shattered, her happiness had vanished. There was nothing more she could do. The Intoner was paralyzed by the fear that the Flower would someday completely take over her body and mind. Two therefore made Cent promise her to keep on living, and then committed suicide. The disciple then joined forces with Zero who was on her way to kill Four, with the shared goal of eliminating the Flower.

Four and three subtracted from zero

The group finally faced Four on the shores of the Land of Mountains. Under the Flower's influence and in a paranoiac state, the fourth sister no longer felt anything but hatred towards the world. She summoned the Daemon and ancient dragon Zophiel, God's protector. Riding Mikhail, Zero triumphed over the beast and then faced Four in single combat. The older sister prevailed with one blow of her rapier to the head. Mikhail, naturally predisposed to fight the Flower, devoured the remains of the Intoner. In a festival of magic lights, the dragon transformed himself: his horns grew, his scales thickened, his wings expanded and his claws became sharper. These new features gave Mikhail a more dangerous and ferocious appearance, comparable to Michael's, but his reedy voice, typical of young dragons, automatically dismissed him from the position of worthy successor. Worn out by the battle, Zero and her disciples Dito, Decadus and Cent, set up camp.

During another unexpected appearance, Accord explained to the group everything Zero already knew, namely that Intoners and dragons had been rivals since time immemorial. Which explained Mikhail's sudden appetite. Unable, however, to clarify the reasons for this antagonism, the android withdrew from the scene while warning Zero of the dangerousness of the time branch on which she had embarked. In the purlieus of the Land of Forests where Three resided, they ran into the latter's disciple, old Octa, who provided elements confirming Accord's theory. According to the old man, Three had become utterly obsessed with the creation of extremely dangerous magic "dolls." So much so that his mistress no longer deigned to sleep with him. This was a real reason for disappointment for this lecherous and eternally dissatisfied old man. But it was not the underlying reason for his departure from the Land. It so happened that

Octa—who was nonetheless endowed with a degree of ethics—was horrified to learn that Three's dolls were actually more than mere dolls. The Intoner had in fact tortured dozens of men and then transformed them into colossal and inhuman things; she had created patchworks of several species, men, monsters and animals, with one arm attached here, one leg sewn there, like jigsaw puzzles of flesh and bone. She was often unhappy with her creations. She would release her monstrosities into nature, which would then cause chaos in all the Lands. One, whose priority was to maintain order over Midgard, was also opposed to these necromantic experiments, which undermined the continent's stability. On several occasions, she ordered her little sister to destroy her creations. Upset that someone should come between her and her beloved dolls, Three unsuccessfully attempted to set a trap to kill One. She henceforth hid in her Land and watched over her puppets of ill omen. In the hope of finding Three's hiding place, Zero and her companions plunged further into the twists and turns of the inextricable forest which covered a large part of the Land.

Death fumes and chills of displeasure: the gloomy atmosphere in which these woods were immersed perfectly suited the fauna that had taken up residence there. Oozing and pestilent, plagued by madness, the zombified creatures from Three's toy chest roamed dangerously, driven by a dark force. The group progressed cautiously, accompanied by the echo of long and disturbing laughter. Dito, the great sadist, made it clear that he was in his element.

Once at the heart of the woods, it was not Three, but Five that Zero met. Resurrected by the Flower's power and its insatiable desire to live, the youngest of the Intoners was no more than a shadow of her former self. The lack of any trace of life in her eyes and her strange gait suggested that she was responsible for the evil that plagued the forest. Without delay, she summoned the Daemon Galgaliel, who was none other than an army of undead. Dito was on the verge of pleasure. Delighted by the morbid transformation of his former mistress, the disciple joined Five and expressed his wish to live forever in this place—rotten from the inside. In an effort to renew his allegiance to his Intoner, he summoned the Daemon Phanuel on his own to destroy Zero. Cent immediately responded by summoning Two's Daemon, Egregori. Two massive soldiers entirely made of water emerged from the ground to fight Phanuel, blocking the claws of this enormous crab. While Dito and Cent faced off against each other with Daemons, Zero was free to kill Five once and for all. A fierce battle ensued during which Five never seemed resolved to die, constantly feeding on the bodies of the Galgaliel to restore her life force. However, Zero took advantage of an opening created by Five's brief return to reason to deliver the fatal blow. Five passed away for the second and last time. Not far from there, the battle between Dito and Cent was coming to an end. Neither one had gained the upper hand over the other. Soon, they would both disappear. As both disciples had summoned their respective Daemons without the help of their Intoner, their destiny would be to revert to their primitive and original dove form. Surrounded by a halo of magic light predicting his imminent demise, Dito cursed his fate, he who had finally found what he was looking for in this forest of madness. Cent, on the other hand, had no regrets. After all, Two was his entire life, and she was no longer a part of this world. With a flap of their wings, Zero's former companions in misfortune, whom she had herself created, vanished into the sky of the Land of Forests. As she watched them leave, the Intoner contemplated the solitude that awaited her at the end of the path she had set for herself. Her next battle against Three would indeed bring her a little closer to her goal: the nothingness to which she had long been destined. But where was her sister hiding?

Nowhere to be found in the fief of the Land of Forests, the penultimate sister on the list could only be hiding in the two places that the company had not yet visited: the Land of Sands or Cathedral City. Around a campfire, Zero and her disciples planned a course of action. But just before that, the lady believed it necessary to report on Decadus's and Octa's poor sexual performances. Since the Intoners had an inexplicable and particularly high appetency for the pleasures of the flesh, it was important to ensure that the disciples were keeping pace. Zero advised Octa not to focus so much on the duration and size of his equipment, but rather to optimize performance, while Decadus was reprimanded for the systematic nature of his masochistic demands. Once the records had been set straight, they headed for the Land of Sands. Mikhail would keep watch over the skies while Zero and her guardians explored the underground ruins, Three being particularly fond of confined spaces and high altitudes. The young dragon finally managed to unearth the necromancer, suspended in the clouds with the help of three Wyverns. Zero joined her mount and engaged in combat. Galvanized by the resentment which had never stopped growing inside her as a result of One's reprimands, Three managed to summon the Daemon of death, Ezrael, a titanic ancient dragon. Usually, resorting to such a power, moreover without a disciple's help, should have forced the Intoner to succumb to the Flower as it had been the case for Four. Three, however, thanks to her sturdiness and natural insanity, managed to keep the situation under control—which made her all the more dangerous. Exceeding by far Mikhail's abilities both in speed of movement and in firepower, the mythical beast put Zero in great difficulty, preventing her from delivering even a single blow. As for the young dragon, he was terrified both by Ezrael's profile—massive and glistening with a disturbing purple light, his face resembling a killer clown—and by his ancient dragon appearance, a sacred and untouchable species, according to him. While searching for a solution, Zero strove to reassure him when suddenly, from even higher skies, Decadus landed on Mikhail's back. Propelled from the ground by Octa, he had come to lend a hand to his mistress. He intended to summon Four's second Daemon, Armaros, to get them out of this sticky situation. However, he knew that using his disciple magic would cost him his human form. During a rare moment of complicity, as if to say goodbye to her partner and dispel his anxiety, Zero slapped him tenderly. The disciple welcomed it and smiled. Back in his dove form, he flew away. Tearing the sky behind Three, Armaros, the flying fortress, came into play. Thanks to his attraction and paralysis spell, Ezrael's movements were drastically slowed down. Mikhail used this window to shoot his nightmarish opponent to death with his fireballs. Nevertheless, Three managed to escape. Zero, Octa and Mikhail tracked her into the Land of Forests where she had taken refuge. Cornered, Three cast a manipulation spell on Octa and ordered him to summon the Daemon Armisael, a legion of soldiers in the form of large babies. Before this army could cause any serious damage, Octa managed to pull himself together and turned these strange servants against their progenitor. Struck by the same curse as his peers, the final disciple escaped into the heavens, finally freed from the Flower's curse and the Intoners.

In her final moments, Three inwardly contemplated everything she had achieved with her dolls—her precious dolls. She would have loved so much to combine dragons and humans, just to see, just to know, just to have fun. But the whole world had rallied against her: One, Zero, Mikhail, even Ezrael, her Daemon, who had failed to protect her. This was the end. Famished, Mikhail devoured the remains of Three, causing a second metamorphosis. With this new form, Zero had no more doubts: Mikhail was indeed Michael's reincarnation, the friend she had lost. The same tail in the shape of a mallet, the same fierce mouth, the same presence induced by his appearance, and above all the same white coloring, the sign of nobility. The dragon was ready. The final battle was looming. One last time, Zero urged her winged partner to keep the promise he had made to kill her once everything was over, as she had previously asked Michael. The creature reluctantly agreed.

Only one left. The most powerful sister was waiting in Cathedral City, seated on her throne: One.

The Intoners' fall and the birth of the Cult

Cathedral City: its wrecked buildings, its hordes of deranged soldiers and its protector Gabriel. Pursued by One's Daemon as soon as they had reached the city, Zero and Mikhail were forced to split up. The dragon tried to contain the Daemon while Zero continued her progress on the ground. But One stood in her way. After the two sisters had exchanged a few blows, a horde of wyverns stormed Mikhail just as he was beginning to gain the upper hand over Gabriel. Wounded, the Daemon fell back with One into the cathedral at the center of the city. Zero and her white dragon chased them to the lair in which they were hiding. Face to face, the two Intoners knew that their path would end here. But first, they exchanged a few words. One wondered about the Intoners' true nature and the reasons behind their power. Zero answered that her quest for truth was pointless. One agreed: if she had discovered one thing during her research, it was that this world did not need the Intoners. She finally summoned the Daemon Abdiel.

Three golems rushed upon Mikhail, who tried his best to push them back. The narrow space of the cathedral's nave only offered him a small margin to dodge their attacks. One had foreseen that the dragon would have trouble fending them off. While Zero was murdering her sisters, the smartest and most gifted Intoner had had the time to come up with a plan to defeat the white dragon. Abdiel was only the first Daemon on the list. His purpose was merely to weaken Mikhail, who, as expected, had no trouble getting rid of him. One then summoned the Daemon Raphael, Two's protector—to Zero's great displeasure, who was both amazed and terrified by the extent of her little sister's powers. The toxins released by this colossal tarantula filled the cathedral's air and severely poisoned Mikhail, who nevertheless managed to overcome it. By this point Zero and her dragon were exhausted, and One wanted to end this. She once again summoned her lifelong friend, Gabriel. Subsequently, two parallel jousts took place. A wearied Mikhail battled with the Daemon, while Zero and One waged a hand-to-hand combat of rare violence. In the face of the impending extinction of the Intoners, One, on behalf of her little sisters, unleashed all her fury, despair and hatred towards the woman who had brought her into the world. She screamed against injustice: before being killed, Two, Three, Four and Five had lived, and Zero had no right to wipe them out. One could not be content with resigning herself to dying, to quietly fading away.

In that very moment, Zero finally understood why One, such an upright and fair being, could have originated from her rotten flesh and tormented spirit. It was her, on the scaffold, ready to die, two years ago. It was her, who had watched those rebels die and did not understand the injustices that plagued this world, seeking a purpose, an answer, a noble reason for her ineluctable death. She realized that the question was not to do what was right, but rather not to be satisfied with the anomalies of corruption, tyranny and oppression. One personified Zero's deep desire for a logical and orderly world, where all who were righteous would be rewarded and sinners would be punished. But it was too late for that. She had blood on her hands, the blood of her countless victims–and now One's blood, fatally wounded. Drawing her dying breath, Cathedral City's sovereign and the last member of the fake siblings instructed Zero to seek forgiveness for her actions. But she had no intention of doing so. With a decisive blow, Zero killed her flesh and blood. Through the virtues of the Pact that bound One's soul to that of her Daemon, Gabriel collapsed and died on the cathedral's ground. His opponent Mikhail, seriously wounded, lay lifeless. He had succumbed to the Daemon's attacks. Once again, Zero had lost her one and only friend in her struggle to defeat the Flower. Furious, she tried to tear it out from her eye before suddenly stopping herself. She had already experienced a similar situation. The consequences would be far too dramatic. Inconsolable, Zero finally called upon the power of her song to form a Pact and bring Mikhail back to life.

The white dragon awoke next to a rejuvenated Zero–the price of the pact–and both rejoiced over being alive for each other. But the reunion was short-lived. One's twin brother, created in her image, suddenly emerged and ran through the Intoner with his dragon tooth sword, fatally injuring Zero. Bound to the girl by the Pact, Mikhail was also wounded. Lurking in the cathedral's shadows and terrified by the fierceness of the battle, the murderer had waited for the right moment to fulfill his mission. His target's new and more innocuous appearance had offered him the perfect opportunity to strike. At death's door, Zero apologized to Mikhail who was about to die. And before closing her eyes forever, she engraved the image of her dragon in her memory. This was the end of the Intoners. But the Flower, as well as the Daemons' devastating power continued to live in the body of the male One, created in the image of his sister thanks to the parasite's magic.

After having completed the mission entrusted by his sister, the twin felt disoriented. With no more purpose, without the warmth and comfort of his alter ego, what should he do? He realized that he should have died in order for the Flower to be permanently annihilated. It was, after all, One's will. But she was gone for all eternity. He would have liked to see her again, to feel her once more. In her room, in front of her mirror, dressed in the clothes she was wearing, he seemed to see her. Beyond the cold facade he touched with his fingertips, his sister was there. His reflection, his sister, himself, everything was intertwined. She was alive again. Through him. The idea came to him to honor the memory of One and her sisters who had fought for peace. So that they could live forever. So that they could be worshiped. Impersonating his deceased sister, One undertook to build a new Church on the foundations of the old Pythagoras Institute Church. A new order would emerge from the ruins of Cathedral City. Its symbol would depict two three-eyed Siamese twins, One and One. Its name: The Cult of the Watchers.

In the following years, Midgard's world underwent radical changes and the Cult became a key figure in the region. Following the death of the Intoners, countless monsters and demons appeared all over the continent, spreading terror and misery in their wake. The Cult, whose main mission was to protect the world in accordance with the wishes of its leader One, tried to fight against them. In the meantime, the intellectuals gathered within the Cult became aware of the constant threat posed by the Watchers[95] and discovered the existence of the Seeds of Destruction, divine playthings capable of plunging the world into chaos. In order to counter their power and to prevent the Watchers from entering this dimension, the Cult developed the Seal system. The system featured four extremely powerful magic seals. Three were split up into the desert, the ocean and the forest, while the fourth was embodied by a person: the Goddess of the Seal. Chosen spontaneously by the mark that appeared on her body, the Goddess carried the weight of time, space and dimension on her shoulders. It was the ultimate seal, the last defense against the Watchers should the others fall. However, this protection came at a price. The chosen one, inevitably a woman, was condemned by the Cult to live as a recluse, without ever being able to marry or give birth. Worse still, the mark caused her daily physical suffering. The hardship was so violent that many Goddesses chose to commit suicide rather than continue to endure this eternal ordeal. About fifteen years after the Cult's foundation, the second Goddess of the Seal was vested with its powers. She was one of One's assistants. Due to the controversy over the selection of the chosen one, a series of ethical conflicts within the institution led to One's exile, who had forced into a difficult position by the bishops, the real authorities within the Cult. Shortly after this banishment, a disease began to spread among the faithful, with the main symptom being red eyes. All those infected by the epidemic lost consciousness and became extremely violent, as if possessed by the devil. Overwhelmed by this new affliction and the management

95. "Watchers" is another name for the Daemons. The name was translated differently in the English versions of *Drakengard 1* and *Drakengard 3*. However, in the Japanese versions the names remain the same in both versions, 天使 or "Angels".

of the monsters, the Cult could not fully establish its authority over the entire continent, undergoing a drastic territorial redefinition. Successive famines, neighboring wars and the subsequent refugee flows redefined the borders of the Lands, and even hastened their collapse. In this context, small independent states had emerged, such as Caerleon, located at the heart of Midgard. Nevertheless, the Cult had managed to strengthen its military power thanks to the regular flow of the faithful who joined its ranks, and forcefully established its yoke over a large region around the Iberian Peninsula. The Empire was born. In response, the independent provinces and nations formed an alliance of countries under the banner of a confederation of states: the Union. The balance of power between the two great powers was, however, largely unequal: on the one hand, the Union only counted ordinary men, while the entire infantry strength of the Empire was infected with the Red Eye disease. On the battlefield, the cruelty that drove those stricken by this affliction represented an important strategic asset.

No one knew exactly why or how this evil had appeared. However, it seemed that One, or more precisely the traces of the Flower that he hosted, was at its origin. During his exile, he had continued his and therefore the Flower's lineage by sleeping with a refugee from the former Land of Forests. Although the former leader had been dismissed from the Cult, his biological successors would become the heirs and leaders of the Church by acquiring the title of High Priest of the Order. In 1099, the Cult's mission completely changed when his great-great-granddaughter Manah became High Priestess.

Abandoned in the woods by her own mother, Manah was distraught. In this moment of intense weakness, definitively deprived of maternal love, a voice offered her an alternative. The Watchers' love. So many years after the Intoners' death, One's cursed blood still ran in the veins of his descendants, and the Watchers still had a gate to this dimension. A godsend for them. Desperate and suffering from her family's rejection, Manah succumbed and allowed herself to be possessed.

To continue living off the Watchers' love, the child used her powerful position to hasten the world's end. Thus, under Manah's yoke, instead of perpetuating the tradition and protecting the seals, the Cult and the Empire embarked upon a campaign of destruction with the stated aim of summoning the Watchers. The religious precepts were rewritten and henceforth described the seals' disappearance as the only way to prevent the world from falling into total ruin. The completion of such a process would give rise to the "Seeds of Resurrection," which were said to protect humanity by granting it access to a new form. As the three elementary seals as well as the thirteenth Goddess of the Seal, Furiae, were located in the heart of the Union's territory, the Empire decided to launch a major offensive against the alliance. Benefiting from an insane strike force, the Empire's battalions quickly gained the upper hand over enemy troops. Gradually, an army of red-eyed soldiers amassed at the gates of the allied castle protecting the Goddess. Driven by his brotherly love and blood lust, Caim, a young man with jet-black hair, joined the battle.

The Prince of Death

Caerleon, six years earlier. The kingdom under the flag of the Union prospered under the reign of the good King Gaap. In the heart of the castle, his son the young Crown Prince Caim spent his days practicing sword fighting, waiting for the day when he would succeed his father. Warmly surrounded by his friend and jousting partner Inuart and his sister Furiae, betrothed to his comrade, the blue-blooded teenager lived happily and cared deeply for his loved ones. On his eighteenth birthday, he hurried to meet his parents to receive their blessing, as was customary. The scene Caim would witness on arrival was a dreadful one. A massive black dragon sent by the Empire savagely devoured his mother, followed by his father. Although he had managed to escape with his sister, the prince would be forever changed. The news, a year later, that his beloved sister had been chosen to become the thirteenth Goddess of the Seal, therefore condemned to suffer for the rest of her life, had only added fuel to the fire. The kindness and sense of justice that Caim had inherited from his suzerain father had been completely erased by the episode of his parents' death. The emptiness in his heart filled itself with a powerful desire for revenge, a visceral aversion for dragons and a vicious passion for slaughter. As Caerleon collapsed after the royal couple's death, Caim, a deposed monarch, joined the Union forces as a soldier with the firm intention of unleashing his hatred against the Empire.

DRAKENGARD

To the Goddess's rescue

While the Union army struggled to ward off repeated assaults from hordes of red-eyed soldiers, the imperial battalions entered the Goddess's castle. A few hundred meters away, Caim, grappling with the enemy, noticed the impending danger. Cutting down dozens of Empire mongrels, the prince gradually made his way to Furiae. But in the midst of a joust, he found himself cornered and suffered a serious injury to his back. Staggering, he nevertheless continued his progress and, completely exhausted, entered the inner courtyard of the fortress. He came face to face with a red female dragon[96] captured and tortured by the enemy, Caim rushed forward without thinking, driven by his intense desire for revenge, to finish her off. As he wielded his sword over the creature's skull, Caim interrupted his momentum, realizing his looming death. The blood loss from the open wound in his back was rapidly increasing, to the extent of forming a large puddle at his feet. But his time had not yet come, Furiae was calling for his help. He then gave the beast an ultimatum: a Pact or death. The creature was hesitant; humans were, in her opinion, a sub-race only capable of bringing about their own destruction. Nevertheless, driven by the same will to live as the human who had appeared before her, the dragon put aside her pride and accepted to bind her soul to that of Caim. The latter paid the price with his voice, but could still communicate through thought with his new partner. Reinvigorated by the magical virtues of their agreement, the symbionts headed for the skies together to counter the Empire's land reinforcements and air offensive. The red dragon's incredible firepower would soon turn the battlefield into a blazing hell. But the Empire's soldiers kept pouring in by the hundreds. A large regiment thus infiltrated the heart of the castle, exhorting Caim to join Furiae, trapped with her fiancé and protector Inuart at the top of the keep. Eliminating all the imperials swarming in the castle, the older brother finally found his childhood friend and sister, both safe and sound. Unable to communicate, which he explains by way of showing them the seal of the pact inscribed on his tongue, Caim followed Inuart's recommendations and decided to abandon the fort and find a safer place in order to protect the Goddess from the Empire. Before setting off for the nearby Elf village, Inuart pulled out his precious harp and sang a ballad to celebrate the reunion of Caerleon's three comrades.

On the way to their destination, Inuart, madly in love with Furiae, expressed his dismay about not being able to marry now that his betrothed had become the Seal's guardian. As a loyal friend, he nevertheless renewed his vow to protect her against the vile intentions of the Cult. By the time they had arrived, the elves' hamlet was nothing more than a pile of ashes covered with burnt and dismembered bodies. In its search for the forest's seal, the Empire had shown no restraint. Whilst a stunned Inuart contemplated the disaster, the red dragon received a telepathic message from Verdelet, the Union's bishop in charge of

96. Angelus is her real name. We chose not to use it for the subsequent account of *Drakengard*'s events for three reasons. Firstly, it could suggest that the other characters refer to her in this way; however, it is not the case: they simply call her the "red dragon." Secondly, it would betray her role within the script: Angelus represents the dragon species more than herself. Her point of view reflects the perspective of a thousand-year-old race that judges men's vanity on the basis of its knowledge, hence the importance of anonymity, or rather of the generic name. Finally, her name is only revealed to Caim in ending A, which is not the canonical ending.

watching over the Goddess of the Seal. Thanks to a Pact sealed in his youth with a black dragon, now petrified, the old man had obtained great powers that had allowed him to rise to the Union's highest functions and, in this instance, to communicate with other creatures bound by a Pact. In his message, he bid Furiae to join him in the desert temple where he lived, so that she may receive his protection. Very much the only person concerned about the Goddess's comfort and condition, Verdelet was renowned within the alliance for his loyalty towards the precepts and respected for the zeal he displayed in his quest to defend the seals. Thus reassured, Inuart and his soul mate hastened to reach the desert plains while Caim, whose curiosity had been aroused, decided to further investigate the disaster that had befallen the elves. In the purlieus of a clearing, he discovered, written in blood, the commandments of the Cult of the Watchers.

Speak not the Watchers,

Draw not the Watchers,

Write not the Watchers,

Sculpt not the Watchers,

Sing not the Watchers,

Call not the Watchers' name.

Branch No. 1⁹⁷, first option: Leonard's regrets

A few meters away, Caim was listening to the last words of an elf at death's door, who told him that his comrades had been taken to a nearby mausoleum dedicated to the Cult of the Watchers. Ignoring almost everything concerning the function, goals and real nature of the Cult and especially of the Watchers, the red dragon and his pact partner followed the trail given to them in order to obtain more information from the allegedly kidnapped elves. However, there was no sign of life in the shrine, other than the imperials, whom Caim gladly slaughtered along the way. At the request for help from a stranger he encounters, but mainly because he perceived the possibility to further quench his thirst for torture with a few of the Empire's puppets, the bloodthirsty prince decided to pursue his investigation beyond the neighboring lands, in the Valley of the Faeries.

In the vicinity, kneeling on the ground, a monk named Leonard was contemplating the bodies of his three young brothers, lying before him and pierced by arrows. The intense light of the flames consuming the hut where they had lived in peace swept across his face. Painfully, the man brought a dagger to his neck. Life had become meaningless to him.

Orphaned by war, Leonard had miraculously protected his siblings, whose education he had taken care of. He had secluded himself in the woods, in order to isolate his family from the world and its unbearable violence. However, this voluntary exile was also a way for this seemingly virtuous man to conceal his own vices. His lustful appetite for the soft and tender skin of children aroused the most amoral desires in him. That night, passion had consumed his body. Thus, he had escaped into the woods for a few moments to satisfy his sexual urges. When he returned to his brothers, the Empire had killed them. With his family destroyed, he had lost everything.

Leonard dropped the dagger, then collapsed, face down, devastated. He could not resolve to take his own life. A Faery then appeared, a mocking and malevolent

---

97. Due to its complex narrative structure in which the story is closely interconnected with the range of possibilities offered by the game, *Drakengard* offers a few alternative paths on which it is impossible to express an opinion as to whether or not their inclusion in the canonical structure is valid. We therefore chose to list them and specify that their presence does not alter the overall arc of the script, but is rather aimed at better characterizing the characters and increasing the narrative's density. The "first option" is the traditional path, while the "second option" is part of an alternative branch, although the outcome of the two options always leads to a common aftermath. As in many games, especially Japanese ones, the *Drakengard* script is divided into different missions which the player can access from a menu. In this instance, the novelty lies in the fact that making the characters accessible after certain scenes unlocks alternative versions of these episodes including the aforementioned characters before their first appearance. Hence certain anachronisms such as those found in the second option: although Caim had not met Leonard before having visited the mausoleum of the Cult, he was accompanied by him in the devastated elf village in the secondary branch.

spirit who had come to afflict him. The taunting fairy used this opportunity to force her prey, whose mental state was shattered, to form a Pact with her. In this moment, out of pure fun, or rather pure malice, the evil spirit condemned the pitiful man to blindness—and to endure its venom forever.

Warned by the telepathic voice of this new recipient of the Pact magic, the red dragon and Caim headed towards his position. A man with blinded eyes and a friendly face introduced himself before saying a prayer for the souls of the Empire's soldiers slain by Caim. Then, he decided to join the prince in his quest. Leonard had only one goal when he embarked on this dangerous path: to die in order to absolve himself of his sins. The group was now hurrying towards the desert to find Furiae.

Branch No. 1, second option: child soldiers

Alongside Caim and the red dragon in the elf village, Leonard received a premonition: the Empire, with its war machines, was devastating the forest surrounding the precious seal of the region. Without further delay, the trio went to the scene to attempt to bring this madness to a close. In the purlieus of a clearing along the way, Leonard suddenly collapsed. His heart could not bear what he had just glimpsed, or rather sensed: the youngest conscripts of the Empire had been dispatched to the battlefield by the Cult of the Watchers to burn the forest and destroy the seal. The vicious Faery took advantage of this moment of weakness to verbally abuse Leonard, and at the same time allude to his secret inclination which had undoubtedly provoked his indignation. Caim, on the other hand, did not seem to care. Despite Leonard's countless pleas to spare the little darlings, Caerleon's butcher slaughtered them all—dozens and dozens—down to the very last in a concert of agony and tears. His heart was dark. Leonard's torments, depressed by this vision of horror, only intensified when he noticed how much the children laying on the muddy ground looked like his little brothers. In a surge of pity, he undertook to bury them with dignity. At that moment, he noticed that one of the children was still breathing. He approached him to try and comfort him. And the trap was triggered. Suddenly, the child soldier rose and summoned a horde of demons that Caim quickly eliminated. Conscripted children or not, war dictates its death logic in all circumstances: no matter the device's morality, as long as it enables murder. Burdened by his own naivety, Leonard brooded over the world's sad fate, while Caim progressed in the woods, insensitive to the recent events. In the depths of the Forest of the Seal, the prince and his companions met the Faery king, keeper of the premises. Sarcastic and tormenting like the vast majority of his congeners, the monarch made fun of the red dragon for his partnership with the race of men, then warned Caim of the precarious situation in which his friends, who had taken refuge in the desert, found themselves.

Impossible love

In the Desert of the Moon, Caim found Furiae, alone. Inuart and Verdelet had been captured by the Empire and presumably imprisoned not far from where they stood. At his sister's request, Caim decided to set out in search of them, convinced he would find new heads to impale with the tip of his sword. The red dragon chose this one-on-one moment with Caim to underline the obvious feelings that Furiae had towards her brother. Had he not felt the loving passion that drove her? She was a Goddess, but she was also a woman. Her inner fire burned, not for Inuart to whom she was betrothed, but for the one who shared her blood.

This had begun during her adolescence, before she had even been chosen by the mark to protect the world from the Watchers. Naturally, she had never been able to talk about it, or even admit it to the person she loved most, for fear of being rejected. Already contained, this unnatural feeling had been buried even deeper within her, ready to explode, ever since her duties as the chosen one had greatly restricted her ability to live with her loved ones. Drowning in an ocean of guilt and frustration, alone in her castle, Furiae did not know what to do. Completely blinded by his quest for revenge, the subject of her affection was unaware of the sorrows of love afflicting his sister. Caim still did not seem to understand, although he had been warned by the dragon. But if anyone knew anything, it was Inuart.

Prisoner in the jails of the Empire, wrapped in chains, the eternal runner-up lamented. If only he had the strength, like Caim, to protect Furiae, he could earn the admiration of his heart's desire.

His father had broken the news to him when he was fourteen. He, the son of a vassal, would marry the daughter of the great king Gaap. What an honor! However, he had already noticed the signs of his own weakness while jousting against Caim in the garden of Caerleon's castle. No matter how much will or effort he would put into it, he was systematically knocked to the ground. His arms and legs were weak, his skin too white... To be worthy of the upcoming wedding, he had to become a man and match the prince's standards. But it was pointless. Full of rage towards himself and his puny body, he consumed himself from the inside. His father, sympathizing with his distress, then offered him a harp. In an overnight flash, the adolescent had managed to run his virtuoso fingers over the instrument, tuning the pinching of the notes to the strength of his voice. That's when Furiae had caught him playing. On that day, through the gaze of his idyll, he had discovered the intensity he was looking for, the intensity reserved for a man. Even if this fire burned more ardently when she contemplated Caim, he was satisfied with this. But at this moment, arms and legs tied, what use would ballads and serenades be to him? The harp had become useless. As if to answer his lament, a dark figure appeared before him. Manah, the High Priestess of the Cult, aware of the conflict consuming Inuart, had come to torment her prey. She made fun of his impotence and his love, but eventually showed him the path to follow in order to satisfy his ambitions: a Pact with a dragon.

Branch No. 2, first option: the desert's Seal

Released from the Empire's prison by Caim, Verdelet informed him that Inuart had been taken to another place, in enemy territory. But there was more. The man of faith exposed the Empire's true intentions: to summon the Seeds of Resurrection through the destruction of all the seals. Verdelet then implored the prince to prevent this horrible calamity. But in the desert, a few leagues from the prison, the Empire was already busy breaking the first seal. Despite their swift intervention, Caim and the red dragon failed to push back the massive influx of soldiers converging towards the magic device. Incapable of stopping the Empire's plans, they chose to retreat and regroup with Furiae. At the Union camp, Verdelet and the dragon picked up a disturbing voice originating from a prison further to the south. Alarmed by the power and madness emanating from this clamor, Caim and his companions began to move. From between the smoking ruins and the cell bars twisted by the explosion of the red dragon's flames, a magnificent elf emerged and approached Verdelet and Caim. Floating above her were two spirits of water and fire, Undine and Salamander, her pact partners and the sources of disruption. Arioch, as the woman introduced herself, explained that she was searching for her beloved children. She had crazy eyes and a deranged gait. Unexpectedly, she brought her mouth to Caim's neck with the intention of devouring him. But Verdelet intervened. Temporarily soothed by the priest's magic, Arioch joined the group.

Branch No. 2, second option: the elf genocide

While Verdelet begged Caim to protect the seals on the front steps of the prison from which the ecclesiastic had just escaped, Arioch silently approached with bad news. Undine and Salamander had sensed it: the seal of the desert was no more, no need to try and save it. This was a hard blow. But the group had no time to wallow, the Cult was already planning on breaking the seal of the ocean and had gathered its forces around the sea temple protecting it. With a southward flap of her wings, the red dragon and her companions reached the sea, packed with Empire warships. The worst scenario had occurred. The cries of women and children in agony reverberated in the air. They were being thrown overboard. Taken hostage and persecuted by the Empire, the elves were suffering a drowning genocide. From the sky, with little thought, Caim began the carnage. His companions' efforts to calm his bloody rage had no impact on his determination. The Empire would perish at his hands, regardless of the collateral damage. Once again faced with the torments of war, Leonard fell into despair. Arioch, for her part, seemed delighted with this unfortunate sight. Which one would taste better? Crouching on the riverbank, leaning over the corpse of a toddler thrown into the sea, the elf enjoyed the tender flesh she brought to her mouth. Horrified, Leonard witnessed the unspeakable. He who was so fond of these precious little angels. How? Why? The Empire—once again.

When it had destroyed Arioch's village, the once ordinary, loving and sane housewife had lost her son and husband in a horrible bloodbath. She also lost herself that day. No one could bring her back from the abyss of despair into which she had fallen. Little by little, her awful cries of grief became intertwined with her laughter, until they were completely indistinguishable. During violent fits of madness, she began to devour children, convinced that it was the only way to keep them safe in her womb; to somehow become "one" with them. Her soul, her conscience, her sensitivity, everything that made her human: all of it had vanished. Only a primitive, animal instinct remained, which drove her to eat human flesh, if possible as delicate as the flesh of a baby.

After sinking a fleet of imperial ships, Caim entered the sea temple only to discover that the seal had already been destroyed. As the Empire broke the magic locks preventing the arrival of the Watchers, Furiae was forced to carry a little more of the weight of the world on her shoulders. At this rate, the enemy would soon reach her too.

Inuart's revenge

Gathered around a campfire on the road to the next seal, Caim and his party sensed an evil presence. A threatening shadow was flying over them: a dragon. Inuart landed a few steps away from Furiae. With blood-red eyes and a triumphant demeanor, he no longer looked like the timid boy Caim once knew. The High Priestess's brainwashing had worked: Inuart had gained power. But henceforth, he was nothing more than a pawn. To find favor with the dragon, the harp maestro had sacrificed his musical and singing skills. Such was the price of the Pact. But now, he was convinced he could protect Furiae by turning her over to the Empire. And he would succeed by will or by force. Caim rushed forwards in disagreement. A flash of sparks appeared. He crossed swords with Inuart, who had no difficulty in knocking his rival to the ground. As he rose, Caim noticed the red dragon grappling with Inuart's creature. The dragon's skin had an abyssal black glow. His eyes opened wide. This was his parents' murderer. All the hatred he had built up, condensed and fostered over the past six years had finally exploded. Ignoring Inuart, the orphan rushed like a madman towards his nemesis, carried away by a terrible rage. Before Caim could reach his target, the black dragon had soared into the sky and released a massive fireball that struck him and seriously injured the red dragon. Nailed to the ground, the warrior and his mount were forced to watch as Inuart forcibly kissed Furiae and fled away with her. The Goddess of the Seal had now fallen into the hands of the Empire. Surely, the world would soon sink into chaos. Unless someone intervened. After a few days of recovery, Caim and the red dragon entered the imperial territory. Furiae must live.

Seere's prayer

In the mountains forming the natural border between the Empire and the Union, a very young boy with blond hair named Seere was panicking. His sister Manah had disappeared, kidnapped by the Empire. His father was no longer moving. Neither was his mother. He called to her. Shaking her corpse. Why wasn't she answering? He gave her a kiss to wake her, like in the tales she used to read to him at night. Nothing worked. The Cult had slaughtered them. But Seere was alive. Not out of luck, but out of love. Before dying, his mother, descended from a line of magicians, had forced him to form a pact with Golem, a stone giant who was able to protect him during the assault. In exchange, the boy would never grow old, trapped forever in this childish form.

His village had been destroyed. Golem kept him company, but he still felt terribly lonely among the rocks that spread as far as the eye could see, he who only existed through his mother's love for him. The opposite was also true: his mother only lived and had eyes for him. Seere felt guilty, sometimes, for hogging all her affection, leaving absolutely no tenderness for her sister, Manah. He believed that she was probably still alive. But naturally, he was unaware of what had actually happened. He did not know that she was now leading the Cult of the Watchers and trying to destroy the world. When he last saw her, their mother was taking her into the depths of the mountains, on a steep path which did not seem to lead anywhere. She had been abandoned there, but Seere was unaware of that. This was the logical outcome of Manah's tragic childhood, during which beatings and verbal abuse had replaced the maternal love that the little girl had yet longed for. Seere had noticed the brutality with which his twin sister was treated by their mother. He greatly feared these outbursts of hatred. It was as though the person he loved with all his being was turning into someone else during these fits of anger. But although he had witnessed his mother's harshness with his own eyes, he did not want to believe that on that day she had left Manah in the hands of the Empire. Thus, when he came across Caim, who was on his way to the Empire, Seere begged him to venture into the valley where he had last seen his sister. The prince agreed to the detour. But obviously, there was no sign of Manah. They met nothing more, in truth, than an army of goblins, giants and other atrocities recruited by the Empire which Caim was more than happy to chop up. Another carnage to his credit. The more blood soaked the prince's blade, the more his vengeance grew and the deeper he sank into an abyss of darkness, wrapped in a deafening silence—soon torn by a distant cry. The Faeries, guardians of the forest, had failed in their task. The last seal on earth had just been broken. Only Furiae remained now, Goddess of the Seal, on whom the fate of the whole world rested. Taking Seere with him, Caim headed for the Empire. Time was running out. Any minute now, the Goddess could perish at Manah's hands. Without further delay, the Union assembled all its forces at the Empire's gates, in a final attempt to turn the tide of war.

Caim versus the Empire

The armies had gathered on either side of the vast undulating plain that divided the territories of the two sides. They were about to wage the battle of their lives. The assault had begun. But halfway towards the imperial block, the Union's infantrymen came to a standstill, astounded. They had caught sight of a new threat. Crossing the mountain ridge as if it were a low wall, three titans had joined the battlefield to sow death on behalf of the Empire.

As the only one capable of facing them, the red dragon ridden by Caim engaged in a long and difficult battle. Their weakness appeared to lie in their eyes. But the dragon's flames were systematically absorbed by the magic emanating from them. Nonetheless, nothing seemed capable of resisting Caim's cold determination. The window was small, but for a brief moment, the colossi lowered their barriers, while recharging the energy beam they used as a weapon of mass destruction. One after the other, the cyclops fell under the fire of the red dragon. The Union army was now free to regroup and launch a new assault on the Empire. Joined on the ground by Caim whose feats matched those of a thousand men, the alliance could win. A true slaughter took place. Decimated by Caim's wrath, the imperial battalions covered the green plain almost entirely in their metallic gray armor stained with blood.

At last, the Union had triumphed. Gathered around the hero of this historic success, the victorious troops celebrated their sworn enemy's defeat. The Empire was no more. Caim, with his sword brandished towards the sun, exulted in response. When suddenly, the sky turned crimson red. Then hell broke loose. Launched from a mysterious flying fortress that had just appeared, a swarm of huge balls of energy descended upon the earth. The impact triggered a massive explosion. In a disintegrating burst, several flame tornadoes engulfed any form of life for miles around them, so abruptly, so rapidly, that not a cry of pain was heard. Then the ground soiled by the explosions began to shake. By the hundreds, countless dead on the battlefield sunk into the earth and came back to life in a putrefied form. Transformed into pandemonium, Midgard was in danger of being engulfed by chaos. Had the Goddess of the Seal died? Leonard could still feel her presence in the south, concealed in the heart of a water citadel. Caim traveled there hurriedly, but only to find a magic passage that led him inside the previously encountered flying fortress. In this maze of stones, Caim and Seere finally faced Manah, the High Priestess of the Cult of the Watchers. Her brother barely recognized her. Her glowing blood-red eyes, her strange and disturbing attitude, her masculine voice, her indecipherable words: besides her resemblance and her blond hair which betrayed their kinship, she was no longer the Manah he had known.

She was no longer quite human. The Watchers' brainwashing prevented her, despite reconnecting with her brother, from coming to her senses. Love, love, love: this was all she had ever desired, everything she now possessed and everything she wished to keep. Scared by the fanaticism and corruption of his sister's soul, Seere left her to Golem. With one hand, the stone giant crushed the child, reduced to a pile of flesh and bone. The fortress immediately trembled. Previously maintained in the air by Manah's magic, the flying ship was now destined to collapse. Caim and his group managed to escape in extremis. However, stuck in one of the fortress's rooms, Inuart and Furiae shared their last moments together. With no available means to escape, the building's collapse proved lethal to them. And thus the final seal disappeared. The cohesion of dimension, time and space ensured by magic had been destroyed. The apocalypse had begun.

The end of Dragonsphere

In the menacing Cathedral City sky, three halos of light pierced the blood-red thunderstorm clouds. From the empyrean, a legion of giant babies with electric wings descended to earth. The Watchers had arrived. In this theater of horror, everyone had a role to play. Arioch, lured by this godly feast, feasted on the lifeless bodies of some of the Watchers killed in the confusion, before she herself was cruelly devoured by a horde of these gargantuan infants. Verdelet, on the other hand, unveiled his genuine cowardly nature and sought shelter. Rider of the apocalypse on his red dragon, Caim reveled in his favorite hobby: killing. Time and again. Relentlessly. But no matter how many of these creatures he destroyed, new ones endlessly appeared until the firmament had been completely obscured by these terrifying beasts. A different kind of threat then emerged. The Grotesquerie Queen, leader of the Watchers, a giant with the naked and hairless body of a young woman, with intense milky white eyes and skin, appeared above the tallest buildings in the city. According to legend, God's creature, the Watchers' leader was capable of absorbing and twisting time at will in order to destroy the entire universe.

Cornered by a cohort of levitating Watcher babies, Caim, Leonard and Seere faced death. One of them, precisely, needed to take his revenge on life and absolve his cowardice. Thanks to the Faery's magic, Leonard self-destructed to open a passage for Caim and Seere in the hope that they could reach the Grotesquerie Queen and dispel this sordid nightmare. Fueled by the essence of time, the queen's stomach kept swelling like the abdomen of a pregnant woman. The end was nigh, Verdelet predicted in a final telepathic farewell message. The queen would destroy the world as soon as she reached her critical size. Eaten away by the grief of having killed his sister and thus precipitating the world's downfall, leading furthermore to Leonard's death, Seere mourned, resigned. Hovering over the Grotesquerie Queen, Caim and the red dragon, the only worthy fighters, gathered their last forces, then dove towards their target.

Flash.

Shinjuku, Tokyo, June 12, 2003. Undisturbed azure sky, birds singing, nature humming. Suddenly, the celestial dome is torn apart spewing forth the Grotesquerie Queen. Her huge body falling backwards onto the skyscrapers of the business district. Caim and his mount also crossed the dimensional portal, continuing the fight in the middle of the Japanese capital. Inexplicably deprived of the power of her flames, the dragon and her master fought the beast in a magical duel. Eventually defeated by the prince and his partner, the Watcher disintegrated into an infinite number of small particles in Tokyo's sky.

"It is done! At last...," whispered the red dragon. The creature barely had the time to savor her victory when two fighter jets from the Japanese Self-Defense Forces shot her down with several missiles. Killed instantly, Caim and the dragon collapsed. Impaled on the antenna of the Tokyo Tower, in the district of Minato, their epic had ended.

White Chlorination Syndrome and Project Gestalt

The 6/12 events, as they were named in reference to the collapse of the twin towers, killed fifty-six people and injured three hundred and twenty others. The total damage was estimated by the Japanese government at over 60 billion yen. On the Internet, despite the authorities' censorship, many conspiracy theories were emerging as to the true nature of the battle between the "Giant" and the "Dragon." The latter's body was recovered and then transferred to a secret laboratory by the authorities in order to study its nature. Meanwhile, the international community and public opinion, in a state of disarray, were trying to understand the nature of this event. To this end, Japan held a summit which included the United States, China and Russia. As a result, the decision was made to increase the military budgets. A few months later, a strange disease that became known as White Chlorination Syndrome (or WCS) struck a part of Shinjuku's inhabitants. It caused the sufferer's body to calcify entirely, transforming him into a salt statue. The world's scientists had begun studying this new type of disease. At first sight, the mortality rate of the infected subjects seemed to reach one hundred percent, but it was later discovered that the WCS could also lead, in contrast to calcification, to the appearance of extremely violent behaviors similar to psychotic madness. As the epidemic escalated within Shinjuku and transformed an increasing number of people into threats to the public order, the government put an end to mobility in the district and declared the entry into force of martial law. Nevertheless, unable to completely contain the outbreaks of violence, the authorities created a plan to isolate Shinjuku from the rest of the world. Despite protests from the international human rights community, a huge wall was built all around the district, the Wall of Jericho, to contain the threat. In order to cover the situation from inside the wall where operations to contain the WCS were still being conducted, a few journalists voluntarily decided to remain in the area. In December 2004, however, all communications with reporters were lost. The last video capture to have crossed the barriers of quarantine had ended with a cry and the mysterious appearance of a giant white creature.

Three years later, satellite images of Shinjuku revealed that a huge black spot had formed in the heart of the confined area. Nonetheless, its origin was unknown. Barely three months after this discovery, the Wall of Jericho was breached from the inside. A stream of raging white creatures poured over the surrounding areas, spreading death and despair. These were actually former humans infected with the WCS, and later became known as the Legion. Among them, a blood-eyed monster named Red Eye was spotted coordinating Legion assaults. Distraught by the attacks of these new types of enemies and handicapped by the inefficiency of their traditional weapons, the Japanese Self-Defense Forces suffered many casualties. To make matters worse, the fall of the Wall of Jericho caused a resurgence of the WCS epidemic in adjacent regions. Honshû, Tokyo and the rest of the Kantô region were severely affected, while Legion forces grew stronger as the disease spread. In a matter of days, the situation had grown out of control. Many refugees fled to territories that were less afflicted by the virus, driven out by the chaos caused by the Legion and the staggering rise in crime that followed. In the light of these accumulated dangers, it was decided that the Japanese government's headquarters should be relocated to the Kyûshû region, still relatively untouched by the unrest. In a severe situation of weakness, Japan accepted a military alliance with the United States, eager to conduct research on the corpses of the Legion. But despite the efforts of the two great forces to repel the creatures with carpet bombing, the Legion's forces were barely shaken. No operation, even on a large scale, seemed capable of containing their proliferation. With their backs to the wall, the United States and Japan were considering the nuclear option, greatly supported by the international community. On August 6, 2009, sixty-four years to the day of the Hiroshima disaster, the first atomic bomb was finally dropped on Shinjuku, the original home of the Legion. Over the next few days, more nuclear warheads were dropped on strategic areas occupied by the enemy, until most of Japan was devastated by nuclear fire. According to initial reports, the bombing campaign was a success, and all traces of the Legion had vanished. But very quickly, cases of the WCS began to break out in the rest of the world: first in China, then throughout Asia, and finally all over the globe. The Legion appeared in large numbers on all five continents, led by their leader Red Eye who had survived the Japanese nuclear winter.

In the aftermath of this global disaster, research to uncover the Legion's secrets was intensified. Studies conducted on the body of the Dragon allowed the scientific community to shed some light on the causes of the WCS. Evidence had indeed shown that, according to the parallel universe theory, the Dragon and the Giant had entered this dimension from a different world. Thus, when the Grotesquerie Queen disintegrated, an infinity of particles foreign to this reality was disseminated throughout Shinjuku. Maso, also known as the demonic element, was the pathogen of the White Chlorination Syndrome. It was highly infectious and could be transmitted through body fluids, feces, cough or even through the respiratory tract. Above all, Maso was immune to heat or explosives, even nuclear. Thus research had demonstrated that the multiple atomic raids on Japan, ironically enough, had only resulted in dispersing Maso particles all over the planet. At the same time, researchers realized that the energy was equally stored across the multiple parallel universes. Taking advantage of the fact that the demonic element had come from a different dimension and had consequently disrupted this balance, scientists managed to use the particles extracted from the Dragon to break the law of mass conservation and thus, in a total repudiation of the Lavoisier principle, create from nothing. This process was called "magic."

However, the WCS's true nature and the cause underlying the duality of its symptoms remained unknown to the gray eminences and humanity. In reality, when humans came into contact with Maso, which we could consider as a Watcher atom, God offered them a Pact. If they agreed, they would become members of the Legion, bloodthirsty creatures in the great Maker's service. If they refused, however, they would die of calcification.

Unaware of the superior forces involved, yet greatly influenced by this series of unprecedented discoveries, savants decided to explore new trails to restrain the proliferation of the WCS. Through the use of the Dragon's Maso properties, they notably managed to extract a human's soul and then reinsert it into his body with no consequences. And so began the Gestalt Project, which was intended to immunize humanity against the WCS by dissociating the carnal envelope from the spiritual being–while keeping both intact.

The pressing need, nonetheless, remained to repel the growing number of Legion troops. A new drug was created, the Luciferase, with properties allowing to slow down the virus infection. The strategy was clear: gathering elite soldiers, force-feeding them with Luciferase, then sending them to the front to annihilate the Legion. The first contingent of mercenaries, under the name First Crusade, was formed and sent to Brazil. None of the soldiers survived. After checking the causes of the failure, it turned out that the effects of Luciferase only worked properly on children. The Hamelin Organisation, an international consortium, was then founded to recruit (and in some cases, abduct) and then train teenagers with great physical abilities and naturally predisposed to combat. They would then be dispatched to the different areas of operation where they would fight the Legion. But despite the effectiveness with which successive Crusades contained the enemy, the conflict fell into a stalemate, as none of the belligerents seemed capable of gaining the upper hand. The war dragged on and the economy collapsed. Forced into exile and poverty, millions and millions of people affected by the conflict lived in huge slums on the outskirts of major urban centers. Eventually, the Thirteenth Crusade members, at the cost of their lives, managed to overcome the Red Eye in Jerusalem, from where the intelligent creature guided its troops. With no Commander to lead them, the Legion's ranks were broken and the threat it represented significantly decreased. However, the WCS continued to spread rapidly, and the development of a vaccine did not appear to be in progress. Japan was also conducting experiments to contain the Legion's threat. While the international Hamelin Organisation benefited from a virtual monopoly on the military use of magic, the archipelago's authorities, who did not want to depend on foreign aid to defend themselves against the hordes of the Legion, decided to set up the National Weapons Laboratory, concealed beneath a huge mansion. Its objective involved the local development of magic weapons that would provide the country with a strategic advantage. Like its direct competitor, the Laboratory rapidly started experimenting on children. In 2025, seven young people were subjected to atrocious torture in order to turn them into weapons. At first, the operation was a success. Number 6, previously known as Halua, had become the "perfect" weapon capable of annihilating just about any enemy. But overwhelmed by the pain of physical transformations, the creature became enraged and attacked its human creators. The magic weapon Number 7, or Emil, Halua's brother, which the scientists had endowed with the power to petrify, helped them lock Number 6 in the depths of the Laboratory. After this bitter failure, the funds were cut and the structure closed. Emil, for his part, took up residence in the mansion, and forgot about his origins–for over a millennium.

Following the Luciferase and Laboratory failures, Project Gestalt received a resurgence of interest from institutions. For the first time, scientists had succeeded in reintegrating a soul, or Gestalt, into a physical copy of the individual, or Replicant. The Replicant System was therefore set up: on the basis of genetic data stored in the Gestalt, it was possible to clone artificial bodies at will. The

Gestaltization process–extracting the soul from the body–and Replicantization process–reinserting the soul in a body identical to the original one–were presented to the public and a roadmap was drafted. All of humanity would be transformed into Gestalt and put to sleep, while the Replicants, who would be endowed with minimal consciousness and immunized against the WCS, would be in charge of traveling across the Earth and purifying it of all traces of Maso and the Legion. To this end, androids would be placed at strategic locations around the globe to monitor the progress of operations and ultimately return the Maso particles recovered by the Replicants to their original dimension. Once the entire planet had been purged, the Gestalts would be able to safely join their corresponding Replicant. Thus, mankind would be saved. In order to ensure this massive return of the Gestalts into their envelopes when the time would come, a great power was however necessary. After many years spent studying magic, scientists successfully transferred the Gestalts into book-like vessels equipped with the necessary ability to perform Replicantization: this was Project Grimoire. Among the thirteen Sealed Books which had been created, the Grimoire Noir and Grimoire Weiss released a sufficient quantity of energy, when simultaneously activated, to perform the transfer of souls. Everything was therefore ready. The wealthiest citizens among the upper classes were the first to take part in the Gestaltization process.

Nevertheless, the World Purification Organization, the public face of Project Gestalt, had discovered that over long periods, or sometimes because of technical errors, Gestalts had a tendency to gradually lose consciousness and become violent (despite the loss of their carnal envelope, Gestalts had a physical form and could interact with the physical world). Ultimately, this so-called "relapse" phenomenon resulted in the permanent death of the Gestalt. A series of analyses revealed that in order to stabilize the souls' consciousness, solid and pure Maso had to be extracted from a Gestalt who had managed to preserve his sentience and physical integrity after the Gestaltization, in order to distribute it to the other Gestalts. At the same time, it was established that to produce this special individual–the "Original Gestalt"–, the soul extraction process had to be achieved by means of the most powerful magic book, Grimoire Noir. With the support of the Hamelin Organisation, the World Purification Organization had begun mass producing copies of Grimoire Noir and distributing them to the poor in slums or areas devastated by the WCS under the authority of humanitarian operations, in the hope of finding the Original Gestalt.

Original Gestalt

In Tokyo, in the Shinjuku district devastated by years of war and bombings, a father and his daughter entered one of the rescue centers which served as facades for the Original Gestalt hunt. Nier, a 40-year-old with broad shoulders, mid-length white hair and a hood over his head, was searching for a cure for his sick child, Yonah. But he found the shelter's situation strange. All around him, other underprivileged people who had come to ask for help would come into contact with copies of Grimoire Noir and, overwhelmed by the book's power, would instantly transform themselves into relapsed Gestalts. These things no longer had flesh, or even a truly human presence. But their bodies made of a translucent pulp of yellow and black matter could easily be distinguished. Sensing the danger, Nier fled with his daughter while the furious Gestalts, driven mad by the book, chased him through the streets of the Japanese capital. Trapped in an abandoned supermarket, with the threat only a few steps away from him and his offspring, Nier saw no other way to save himself than to use the copy of Grimoire Noir recovered from the reception center. Fortunately, nothing happened. Or rather, it did: Gestaltified, his soul had managed to preserve the material appearance of his body, and his conscience was intact. Nier had become the Original Gestalt. Assisted by the Grimoire Noir and its magic, he easily eliminated the pests. But when he returned to the supermarket to check on his daughter, the latter showed the first signs of a failed Gestaltization. Convinced that she could protect her father, she made the mistake of coming into contact with her own copy of Grimoire Noir, and now risked death. In exchange for the World Purification Organization's promise to save Yonah at the end of Project Gestalt, Nier agreed to provide Maso to the worldwide Gestalts in order to preserve their consciousness until the Replicants had purged the world. Gestalt Yonah undergoing relapse was then placed in a deep and long sleep, while all of humanity entered the Gestaltization process, assured of preserving its sentience.

Several centuries, then a millennium passed. As was expected of them, the Replicants, under the leadership of the androids, had purified the world of Maso and the remains of the Legion. In the year 3287, the androids completed the ultimate ceremony to send the last particles that had come from a different dimension back to their original universe. Project Gestalt had come to an end. All over the world, dormant souls began to awaken in order to integrate their Replicants. However, what they discovered was not going to make their task any easier. No prognosis had anticipated this. In response to their environment's stimuli, the Replicants had acquired their own consciousness and developed a civilization, currently at the medieval stage. Even worse, through their eyes, the Replicants perceived the freshly awoken Gestalts as bloodthirsty monsters whom they called "Shades" and proceeded to eliminate them all. Instead of the Replicantization, which was supposed to reintegrate the Gestalt into their flesh and bone vessels, war had broken out all over the globe between the two factions. Simultaneously, the Gestalts, although treated by Nier's Maso, were relapsing and experiencing fits of extreme madness. It appeared that the birth and development of consciousness in a Replicant provoked a relapse of the corresponding Gestalt. Caught between the Replicants' assaults and the inevitable relapse of all the Gestalts as their alter egos were awaking to the world, humanity was once again threatened. In the castle from which he had ruled over his congeners for over a thousand years, the Original Gestalt was concerned about the situation's evolution. If nothing was done, Project Gestalt would be doomed, and he would never be able to save Yonah. However, one hope remained: Project Grimoire. Activating the capacities of Grimoire Noir and Grimoire Weiss would provide the Gestalts with the ability to force their mass integration into the Replicants. Without further delay, Nier obtained the original Grimoire Noir. Stationed in a small country village where they supervised the Replicants, two androids, Devola and Popola, were in charge of retrieving Grimoire Weiss. To do so, they sought the help of Nier's Replicant, who, like his congeners, knew nothing about his true nature, Project Gestalt, or even the administrator role played by Devola and Popola.

NIER

The sun was rising. Nier said goodbye to Yonah, bedridden and weakened by a cough, before heading to the library where Popola had convoked him. For some time, the father had used his warrior skills to serve the village leaders in order to earn money to treat his daughter. However, nothing very dangerous awaited him today: a simple errand entrusted by Popola during which he would have to deliver a few mutton legs to the local merchant. He returned home at dusk once he had completed the task. There he found Yonah lost in thought. She tried to describe her dream from the previous night, filled with clouds and pink animals, but lost track and coughed. To comfort her, Nier told her the story of the legendary Lunar Tear, a magical flower which granted wishes. Even the one to heal. Soothed by this tale, the fair-haired girl peacefully fell asleep. The next day, Nier returned once again to the library in search of work. Shades, Popola informed him, seemed to be attacking the carpenters who were busy rebuilding the bridge at the edge of the northern plain which bordered the village. Initially fearful and steering clear of lively places, the Shades had gradually become more aggressive and no longer hesitated to attack the villagers. Nier was naturally worried about them, due to his concern for Yonah, and therefore had no qualms about eliminating them—as many as necessary. When he returned to the village, the one he had promised to protect was nevertheless nowhere to be found. Panic overwhelmed him. According to Popola, Yonah, in her father's absence, had asked the leader about the Lunar Tears, who had informed her that some could be found in the Lost Shrine located to the east. Convinced that his daughter had ventured there, under the illusions of the little story he had told her the previous day, Nier set out in pursuit of her. Making his way through the crumbling old building and the horde of Shades assailing him, he had finally reached the last hall. Sleeping behind a magic barrier with two huge statues at each end was Yonah. At the heart of the protective shield was a strange object which appeared to power the device: Grimoire Weiss. As he intensified his fight against the Shades which had by now overrun the room, Nier also attempted to deal a few sword blows to the barrier's weak point to tear it down. The obstacle eventually yielded to the repeated blows and vanished. While the mysterious object that had been embedded in it fell to the ground at the same time. A book. Its brown cover was set in its center with an iron face. It flew. It spoke. However, Grimoire Weiss seemed to have lost its memory. It informed Nier that everything it could recall was related to its so-called great reputation and to the secrets it contained—even though it claimed to have forgotten their true nature. But the conversation came to a sudden end when the two statues—actually the guardian Shades of the book, Hansel and Gretel—awoke. Together, Weiss and Nier engaged in combat. Whilst the warrior was struggling to pierce his opponents' thick armor, the book, as if it had partially recovered from its initial torpor, had suddenly obtained new magical powers. The duo now had the upper hand. Weiss produced a massive magic spear and threw it in the direction of the first guardian, Gretel, who was hit right in the face. Liters of blood spurted through the air before falling back down as scarlet rain on the rocky ground. The enemy collapsed, lifeless.

Witnessing the death of his partner, Hansel fell into a terrible rage. But, in a matter of seconds, Weiss's spears had overcome his anger. Impaled from all sides, the second guardian collapsed. Nier hastily retrieved his daughter and, together with Weiss, escaped from the shrine. Once outside, Yonah had to stop. She was suffering: strange black runes began to appear on her arm. It was the Black Scrawl. Nier knew only too well what awaited his daughter, as this deadly disease had taken the lives of so many villagers. Back to the hamlet, desperate, he tried to sound Devola and Popola out on possible solutions. But the sisters were more intrigued by the companion levitating above his head. Popola then told him the myth of Grimoire Weiss, the legendary white book that would stand against the terrible Grimoire Noir, the black book which, according to prophecy, would plunge the world into chaos by spreading the disease. That was all it took for Nier to convince himself of Weiss's ability to annihilate the Black Scrawl. But according to the fable, Popola added, the white book could only fulfill its destiny while in possession of the "Sealed Verses." These verses were in reality fragments of Weiss's power which Devola and Popola had to recover to trigger the reintegration of the Gestalts into the Replicants, but their true origin was concealed thanks to this myth that had been entirely invented. Weiss noted that this was probably the source of his sudden rise in power in the Lost Shrine, where he had absorbed two Sealed Verses. The more the elements were consistent throughout the discussion, the more Nier became convinced of the legend's legitimacy. Without stopping to think, he swore an oath to recover the missing Sealed Verses so that Weiss could save his beloved daughter. Reluctant at first, Popola yielded to Nier's perseverance and finally indicated the location of the next Sealed Verses: to the north, in the village of Aerie. Meanwhile, Nier, galvanized, set off on his path, convinced of his future victory over the Black Scrawl... The plan was working perfectly.

A web of lies

Of course, it was all a vast web of lies. Although Grimoire Noir truly existed, the prophecy was nothing more than a trick aimed at exploiting Nier's credulity and his attachment to Yonah. Devola and Popola in truth had to find a way to recover Grimoire Weiss and restore it to its full power in order to reunite it with the black book—all without arousing suspicion. They had thus voluntarily sent Yonah into the depths of the Lost Shrine where they knew that Grimoire Weiss had been guarded for more than a millennium by the two Gestalts Hansel and Gretel. Naturally, Nier would rescue her and recover the book at the same time. All that remained was to invent a reason for him to venture in search of the Sealed Verses. A piece of cake for these androids, who knew the real reason behind the appearance of the Black Scrawl. No evil epidemic was concealed in these runes, it was merely the mark left on a Replicant when his corresponding Gestalt had entered the relapse phase—although it was true that it would eventually lead to death. Without the genetic data stored in a Gestalt, the Replicant System could no longer create a body. But Gestalt Yonah found herself trapped in a near-relapse state, every Replicant Yonah who succeeded each other for more than a thousand years would inevitably be affected, without necessarily being condemned. Nier, in his Replicant version, was therefore the perfect target. Exploiting his fatherhood was enough to lure him with the hope of a miraculous cure causing him to rush headlong in search of a pipe dream.

Encounter of the third kind

Suspended between the two faces of an enormous ravine several dozen meters above the ground, the village of Aerie resembled a spider's web: fragile and not very respectful of the common laws of gravity. Its houses were connected by a network of wooden walkways, ladders and bridges perched in the void. Nier began to explore the premises in search of the next Sealed Verse. The village chief probably had more information. In front of the latter's house, Nier introduced himself. But before he had even been able to express his request, a voice on the other side of the door indicated that strangers were not welcome. The Shades who had taken up residence in this improbable village had apparently forced the inhabitants to isolate themselves in their houses and to fear any external influence. Nier would not find the help he had hoped for in this recluses' refuge. As Weiss suggested, it would be best to turn around and regroup with Popola. Back at the Aerie's entrance, Nier's gaze dwelled upon a dazzling necklace of white flowers suspended from a makeshift bungalow made of rusty sheet metal. Lunar Tears: they really existed. Nier extended his hand to touch them when, behind his back, a voice coarsely ordered him to step back. A young woman, Kainé, approached.

Her face was severe but graceful, she wore a succinct outfit and held a serrated sword in each hand. Her left arm and leg were completely wrapped in bandages. She continued to approach and came face to face with Nier. She did not say a word, but clenched her fist. An evil aura began to surround her. Was she a Shade? She did not look like one. Suddenly, she rushed towards Nier, who was forced to retaliate. Both fighters exchanged a few blows, before a giant Shade interrupted the joust. Its long front legs slid on the battle ground with its massive and deformed body crawling behind them. Kainé dashed towards the creature which she seemed to have already met. Her words betrayed a certain grudge: "Die!" she bawled at her enemy. "Die, die, die! I'm gonna pull out your teeth and cram 'em up your ass!" Also threatened by the giant Shade's attacks, Nier joined the fight. With Weiss's help, he managed to knock the creature to the ground. But it immediately rose and violently kicked Kainé. Stunned by the attack, she endeavored to contain the pain that overwhelmed her, then fired a magic missile which pierced the Shade's eye, before finally giving up and fainting. Seriously wounded, the Shade retreated, leaving behind a Sealed Verse. The book absorbed it. Nier recovered Kainé's unconscious body, then lay her down on the makeshift bed nestled in the shelter where he had spotted the Lunar Tears. Weiss had no doubt: this woman's powers were proof of the fact that she was possessed by a Shade. She woke up precisely at that moment. Kainé told Nier her first name before advising him to leave. She especially instructed him to stay away from the Shade they had fought against: it was her prey. Nier followed her instructions and headed back to the village, without, however, renouncing to destroy this Shade. He thought it surely contained another legendary Sealed Verse.

In his childhood, Kainé had been abused by Aerie's inhabitants. Stones and insults were indifferently thrown at her face. The villagers believed she was a monster, a pariah, because of her hermaphrodite nature. Orphaned, she would have willingly given up living if her daily life had been limited to harassment and discrimination. But the, sometimes harsh, love of her grandmother, Kali, had given her a reason to keep going. The old woman, however, wore herself out daily caring for the household, and Kainé soon had to learn to carry out the maintenance tasks in her place. One day, when Kainé had returned home after collecting stones to secure the pile of sheet metal which made up their house, she came face to face with a giant Shade threatening to kill Kali. She unsuccessfully attempted to stab the beast. Her grandmother was slaughtered before her eyes. Full of rage, she attacked the Shade, which did not waver and, on the contrary, inflicted atrocious wounds on Kainé. She was left for dead, her left arm and leg torn off by the monster. Nearing her final moments, a small parasitic Shade named Tyrann entered her body to take possession of it. Kainé resisted with all her might. Her hatred for the Shades, and for the giant Shade in particular, had sparked a powerful desire for revenge. Sensing this, Tyrann proposed a Pact. Provided that Kainé supplied him with hatred and blood, he would lodge himself in her heart, without interfering, and lend her the necessary strength to carry out her revenge. However, at the slightest sign of weakness, he would take possession of her entire body. Kainé agreed. Her lost limbs were replaced by those of the Shade. Now she only lived for revenge.

The family workshop

As soon as he had reached the village, the father rushed to check on his child who had stayed at home. But unfortunately, all Nier could see was that Yonah's condition was worsening. He prepared a palliative remedy for her, then once again sought Popola's wise advice. She informed him that the piece of scrap metal he used as a sword would not be sufficient to defeat the monster he had encountered in Aerie. A blacksmith capable of upgrading his weapon could be found at the foot of Junk Heap to the northeast. This would be his destination should he wish to improve himself. Still accompanied by Weiss, Nier traveled there. Jakob, the young blacksmith, welcomed him. In the back shop, his little brother Gideon was whining. Their mother had not returned from her last trip into the mountain to collect materials. She had left a week ago. Deprived of its supplies, the shop could not do business, and Jakob could not upgrade Nier's blade. In addition, no one knew how to operate the machines in the old industrial area embedded in the mountains. What was certain, however, was that it contained many useful materials for a blacksmith. Yet one must nevertheless be able to face the machines swarming in there. Too scared, Jakob dared not venture there. No matter, Nier offered to go himself and find what he needed. Without delay, the warrior rushed into the cold corridors of the factory in search of titanium alloys. After having taken a few robot carcasses to pieces, he returned to the shop laden with the necessities. While Jakob fulfilled his end of the bargain by upgrading Nier's arsenal, Gideon's intense crying filled the forge's already suffocating hot air. The poor little boy was lost without his mother. Touched by the situation, Nier offered to help by looking for the missing parent. According to Jakob, his mother had ventured far into the mountain using the elevator located in the heart of the factory. While demolishing a few robotic chassis along the way, Nier scrupulously followed the route indicated by the blacksmith all the way into the depths of the complex: no hint of life on the horizon. However, he was fortunate enough to recover a Sealed Verse from the remains of an enormous machine which protected the building. Along with those of the Lost Shrine and the Aerie, he now possessed four of them, although he did not know exactly how many existed. The prophecy was not clear on this point. Following the destruction of the device, a new bridge had just appeared. Nier entered through the door at the other end. And waiting behind it was something that some might have foreseen. The corpses of Jakob and Gideon's mother and her lover, probably killed by the defense system which Nier had just destroyed, lay on the ground. Judging from the contents of their luggage, they had attempted to flee.

Back at the shop, Nier told both children the truth. Gideon could not believe it. But Jakob, for his part, knew that his mother was irritated by her duty to her children—after all, he was the one who had taken care of the family since she and her father had separated, not her. She wanted to start a new life without them, beyond the mountains. Her firstborn understood this—she was his mother, but she was above all human. All things considered, it was probably preferable for her to end her life in this way together with her chosen one, he philosophized. Nier, puzzled, withdrew. He hoped that honesty had been the right choice. Weiss had no doubt about it. Before he left for the Aerie, Jakob and Gideon saluted their good Samaritan one last time. With a smile on his face, Nier vanished: seeing them full of enthusiasm, he knew that the blacksmith brothers would take care of each other.

Kainé's fight

Back in the suspended village, Nier came across Kainé grappling with a swarm of Shades. He rushed to her rescue and without a word, Kainé accepted his providential help.

The creatures did not last long under the combined blows of these two experienced fighters. But the real trial of strength awaited them a little further. The giant Shade had returned. It had just leaped from the ravine's wall onto the village's central platform. Kainé threw all her strength into the fight, closely followed by Nier and Weiss. As the battle raged, voices rose from the surrounding huts. They called Kainé a cursed hybrid, accused her of attracting Shades to the village, and expressed their disgust for the young woman, suspected of not being human.

The people of the Aerie repudiated Kainé, even as she fought to prevent the destruction of the village. Impervious to her peers' hatred, the pariah redoubled her efforts in her battle against the beast. Soon, the latter would show its first signs of weakness. Victory was near. When suddenly, the Shade spoke directly to Kainé. That husky voice was her grandmother's. Moved, Kainé lowered her guard, as if suddenly bewitched by a spell. The voice was trying to convince her to stop fighting. Or rather to let go. So much pain, so much despair, what was the point of staying alive? But Kainé snapped out of it and flew into a rage. The blast of her aura's explosion swept away the moaning Shade, she then burst into laughter. Its poor attempt to manipulate her mind had failed. Kainé would carry out her revenge at any cost. She would honor her grandmother's memory. In the background, Nier took advantage of the confusion caused by the altercation to build up Weiss's power into two prodigious magical fists, which he slammed heavily into the giant Shade. The platform collapsed under the violent collision and exploded into a volley of wood. When the dust from the impact had cleared, only the monster's corpse impaled on the platform support post remained. Weiss recovered the fifth Sealed Verse from the creature's heart. Blown away by the attack, Kainé lay on one of the suspended bridges, half conscious, uncertain of the path to follow. Her only purpose in life, her grudge, had disappeared with the beast's death. She let herself go. But a voice forbade her to give up. Nier's voice. She followed it and came back to life. Now, she had to find a new purpose. Meanwhile, she would accompany Nier in his quest to heal Yonah. In fact, she knew someone suffering from the Black Scrawl. A king to be precise. He ruled over the city of Façade in the desert. Kainé explained that ever since the monarch had become ill, all of his kingdom's apothecaries had been striving to find a cure. A godsend for Nier. Even the slightest possibility that the desert people might know more about the plague afflicting his daughter was a blessing. He set out towards the south.

Masks and rules

His feet scoured by the hardened sand of the desert, Nier arrived at the gates of Façade. Two men with strange wooden masks covering their faces were guarding the entrance. At Kainé's sight, the two individuals began to dance and talk in a foreign language. Then, they opened the door. Ever since she had rescued one of the village's small children from the claws of a pack of wild wolves, Kainé had been welcome in Façade.

The whole city was embedded in a rectangular crevasse. The houses made of mud were connected either by an incomprehensible maze of stairs, or by a strange system of rolling sand which irrigated all the districts. To move about, one would climb into a floating gondola and the sand propelled by huge wheels would carry the boat forward. The king's residence was located at the very end of the network, on the other side of the city. But how did one find his way through this jumble of streets and mechanisms absolutely devoid of logic?

They happened to run into a young native girl named Fyra, precisely the one who owed her life to Kainé, who offered to help Nier and Weiss familiarize themselves with her city and the local language. She was mute, or rather bound by a Rule forbidding her to speak, though she still managed to communicate with the book through sign language. Weiss thus learned that Façade was subject to more than a hundred thousand rules, including Rule 106, which prohibited citizens from living on level ground. This explained the eccentricity of these deformed buildings and the profusion of steps. After having shown them around, Fyra ended the guided tour in front of the palace. She then informed Nier that the king had not survived the Black Scrawl. The prince now ruled in his stead. Maybe his advisor could teach him more. Henceforth capable of fluently speaking Façade's language thanks to Fyra's teachings, Weiss demanded a hearing with the prince from the advisor who was waiting in front of the residence. But none would be granted at that time. With no invitation to enter, Fyra, Nier and his flying brochure headed back to meet Kainé, who preferred to wait at the entrance. The young native was astonished when she met with once again the face of the woman who had saved her. Weiss could not believe it either. This precious child had been rescued by this deviant? No way, thundered his majesty–his bindings falling apart. But the bickering was stifled when, not far away, Nier heard a small group of soldiers panicking: the prince had disappeared into the Barren Temple! The only problem was that, even though Rule 83,348 ordered them to go to his rescue, Rule 50,527 forbade commoners from venturing into this sacred place. Complying with one rule inevitably lead to the violation of the other. What to do? Full of ardor in spite of her small size, Fyra appointed herself to enter the premises, before Kainé outwitted her by invoking Rule 1,024: "the request of any foreigner to whom the inhabitants of Façade were indebted must be granted." Kainé thus demanded that she be entrusted with the prince's rescue. With this legislative sleight of hand, Nier and his companions headed towards the Barren Temple.

Sand Prince

At the heart of the temple, the small rescue team came face to face with a young boy, who was none other than the prince of Façade. But before Nier and the others even had the time to express the reason for their presence to the heir, a flying cube appeared behind the prince and kidnapped him with an immobilizing ray. Kainé tried to follow him, but was also captured by one of these curious objects in the process. The boy and the woman were taken to the temple's depths, where Nier and Weiss joined them. A heap of blocks forming a giant appeared: the temple's guardian.

Kainé, who had unexpectedly escaped from her attacker's clutches, struck the first blow. Struck on the head, the guardian lost a part of the blocks composing him. He immediately replaced them with new ones. It might take a while, but the supply of blocks would eventually run out, thought Weiss. Cube after cube, tirelessly, the trio thus proceeded to bring about the giant's complete elimination. Once the area had been secured, the prince emerged from the ravine where he had been held prisoner. He recovered a kind of mask from the ground, then was escorted to Façade by Fyra and the others. In front of his residence, he revealed the purpose of his getaway to the Barren Temple. Without the royal mask he had just recovered, symbol of his country's power, Façade was unable to negotiate with its neighbors for water and food supplies. Thanks to this totem, he could now accede to the throne and thus convey an image of strength and stability to his partners, and thereby restore the glory of his nation. Indebted to his foreign friends, the new king rewarded their exploits with a Sealed Verse, then left them after they swore an oath: that one day his benefactors would return to visit Façade. Nier agreed, then returned to the village where Yonah was waiting for him, while Kainé preferred to vanish.

Those who dream

For the first time since he had begun his quest in search of the Sealed Verses, Nier had spent the night with his daughter. He was dreaming. A boy with silver hair appeared. His lips were moving, but Nier could not hear him. He endeavored to decipher the movements of his mouth.

"S-E-A-L-E-D V-E-R-S-E"

Where? He was eager to learn more and attempted to decipher what the boy was trying to tell him.

"F-O-R-E-S-T O-F M-Y-T-H"

The next morning, Nier kissed Yonah and then set out to ask Popola about the content of this strange vision. But before he could even explain the situation to her, the librarian handed him a troubling letter from the mayor of the Forest of Myth, a small village located in the Northern Plains. A perfect coincidence. Nier readily agreed to investigate the source of this missive. It could be related to his dream from the previous night.

The place was practically deserted, and there was little sign that this was actually a forest. Barely a few scattered trees, shrouded by a fine mist, broke the horizontal monotony of the plain. As a matter of fact, the Forest of Myth was home to Sleeping Beauty, a wide computer network used by the inhabitants of the ancient world—humans—to study the demonic element, Maso, as well as quantum physics. The site was also used as headquarters for the creation of Replicant bodies based on Gestalt data. Naturally, the latter were not aware of this. Sitting still on a log, the mayor seemed to be waiting. Nier questioned him.
Be...ware...the wor...ds..., the old man painfully articulated. His message sounded like a warning.
Contagious...words... Those...who...dr...eam...

But it was already too late. Nier and Weiss were now trapped in the mayor's dream, prisoners of his drifting conscience. The village chief informed them that, like all the inhabitants of the Forest of Myth, they had just been severely affected by the Deathdream. Those who contracted it were thrown into eternal slumber, ensnared in their own dreams. Their only means of communication was therefore the superimposed text on the player's screen. And indeed, the world began to crumble around Nier. The characters faded away, followed by the scenery. All that remained were the white words scrolling on an ink background.

Weiss took a moment to think of a way of escaping from this prison made of letters, then raised a hypothesis: since they were trapped in a dream, all they needed to do was imagine a way out for it to appear before them. This one oddly took the form of a riddle submitted by a mysterious character, to which Nier gave the right answer. Soon the Deathdream would evaporate, but first the group rested.

When they woke up, images returned and the scenery slowly reappeared. Nier, standing in front of the mayor, had not moved an inch. The latter rose from the log which had held him captive, then staggered towards the Divine Tree in the middle of the village. The old man prayed to it, completely unaware of the fact that this tree contained all of mankind's memories and the data of Project Gestalt. "According to legend" he said, "the tree contains a magic word: a Sealed Verse." Weiss demonstrated the myth's accuracy as he extracted the verse from the tree. However, the flying book was becoming suspicious of something. Acquiring this verse had been too easy, too predictable.

The mayor generously thanked his saviors, who headed back to the village. On the way back, Kainé joined the group and they visited Popola together. Nier recounted his adventures to her, not suspecting for a single moment that absolutely everything he had achieved so far had been schemed by the woman he regarded as his friend and confidant. Nor did he suspect that she was about to cunningly send him to find the last Sealed Verse, because Popola had been discreet, using intermediaries to do the work for her. Once again, she used Yonah to manipulate Nier. She informed the warrior that his daughter had a strange request to submit to him.

Emil's secret

Back home, Nier probed Yonah, who revealed that she was corresponding with a young boy. In truth, it was not Emil, the boy who had been turned into an experimental weapon by the National Weapons Laboratory, but his butler who was impersonating his master. In his last letter, the fake Emil told Yonah that he was ill and in serious danger. Unable to come to his rescue, the young girl begged her father to go and inspect the mansion to the south of the village where the boy lived. Although disturbed to learn that his offspring seemed to be discovering love, Nier accepted the request.

The boy's residence was monochrome. In fact, it was also the case of the entire area surrounding it. The grass, the trees and the sky: here the common rural environment was colored in shades of gray. Hope, love and laughter had been sucked out of this place long ago and for all eternity.

On the front steps of the huge building, a butler greeted Nier and his companions and then led them to a dining room where he asked them to wait. Unsurprisingly, the gloomily luxurious interior turned out just as bleak as the exterior had suggested. Weiss, usually so arrogant and reckless, was paralyzed by fear. Time passed, but no one showed up. Kainé soon became bored and was planning on taking a nap on an extra couch. As for Nier and Weiss, they decided to explore the building to stretch their legs (and bindings), but discovered nothing more than empty rooms and a few sinister portraits. When they returned, Kainé had disappeared. Something was brewing. They therefore retraced their steps in search of a clue that would help elucidate this mansion's mystery. In the corridor they had used earlier, Shades suddenly appeared from the ground and attacked them. Nier made short work of them and then continued on his way. The residence's corridors all looked alike, with interchangeable doors at their ends. Nier pushed one of them, almost randomly. A young boy was sitting on a bench facing a grand piano. Emil was dressed like the nobles of the Victorian era. His eyes were covered by a blindfold made from a common piece of cloth. He introduced himself to Nier as the mansion owner. He had voluntarily blocked his eyesight long ago, he explained, to protect people from his terrifying petrification power. However he was ignorant to the true nature of this curse. Nier asked whether this was the illness mentioned in the letter that Yonah had received. Emil argued that this could not be the case, for the simple reason that he had not written any letter. But according to him, his butler, Sebastian, would probably have more information. From what the concerned person had to say, it turned out that Emil's servant and the sender of the mysterious letter were indeed one and the same.

Worried about his master's isolation and the suffering caused by his self-inflicted blindness, Sebastien had actually sought to summon Nier, whose exploits were on everyone's lips. But it was Yonah who received the letter and the young girl misinterpreted the simple request made by Sebastian in his letter: for Nier to attempt to heal Emil. The cure was inside the mansion, but a horde of Shades prevented anyone from getting close to it. Nier's mission was therefore simple—one could even say that he was beginning to develop a certain degree of expertise in the slaughter of Shades.

Both embarrassed and flattered by the fair amount of trouble his butler had gone to, Emil apologized to Nier and offered to help him defeat the creatures. The group set out with the intention of obtaining the cure, but also of finding Kainé, who was still missing. After having savagely chopped up a mob of Shades, our heroes' small escapade led them to the entrance of the mansion's library. According to Emil, the antidote's formula should be there. He approached the book containing it, Grimoire Rubrum, but it escaped from his grasp and flew towards the center of the room. Rubrum began to cast multiple spells against Nier and Weiss when Kainé, who had finally returned, stepped in. Gradually, and painfully, the trio gained ground on their opponent, until Grimoire Rubrum burst into a magnificent grand finale, scattering its pages to the four winds. Nier caught one, then read the caption: "Annulling a petrification curse." Weiss recovered the final Sealed Verse that was ejected during the explosion. Killing two birds with one stone. Or almost. Emil got cold feet as soon as he realized that the rest of the method to cure his illness was written in a coded language. It would take years to decipher the message—so he might as well give up.

Before leaving the premises, Kainé took Emil aside to reassure him. With an unusual tenderness revealing her true nature, she taught Emil that his eyes, like her arm made of Shade, were his own, and that despite the scars and defects, he should not feel ashamed of his existence. From his garden, Emil sensed his new friends leaving, hoping they would soon return.

Outcome

Crouching down by the bed, Nier tucked Yonah in. The little girl was at her worst, overcome by the disease. With her aching reedy voice, she asked her father not to hate her, not to resent her for the burden she was carrying. Nier swept away her fears with a simple assertion, a self-evident fact from his point of view: a father could never hate his daughter. He stood up, then headed for the library in search of a remedy to ease Yonah's pain. Unfortunately, Popola told him that her supplies were empty, and that they had to be replenished.

She therefore sent the warrior to collect a particular type of moss near the village's southern gate. There, Nier heard someone moaning in pain. Emil was holding himself under the arch, out of breath, his legs shacking. Nier rushed towards him. His friend wished to warn him of the brewing surge of Shades, but collapsed from exhaustion before he could pronounce a single sentence. Nier brought him to Popola so he could rest. He recovered after a short time. And then explained that he could feel the air vibrating behind his eyes. The Shades were almost upon them.

A first explosion occurred, followed by a second one. The ground was shaking. The south gate had been knocked down. A legion of Shades, small and large, armed to the teeth, invaded the village. Nier rushed towards the shopping street where the local militia had already engaged in combat. He hurtled down the slope separating the library from the city center. Devola intercepted him on the way. Nier entrusted her with Yonah's safety, while he would send these creatures to hell.

Nearby, two guards succeeded in lowering the large gate to impede the advance of the incoming enemy flow. However, as soon as it was lowered, the thick wooden plank was violently smashed to pieces. A massive black colossus entered the battlefield. It was heading towards the library, where the inhabitants and Yonah had taken shelter. Despite Nier and Weiss's repeated attacks, the creature inexorably continued to advance. Weiss tore its arm off. Blood spurted abundantly while the Shade screamed in pain. But the arm grew back, unscathed, as quickly as it had been amputated. The enemy was now only a few steps away from the library. Kainé attacked from the sky and knocked down the giant, who immediately got back on its feet. Eventually, with a final combined attack launched by Nier, Weiss and Kainé, the colossus crashed to the ground. Nier hastened to open the doors of the library. Inside, Emil was grappling with a regiment of Shades that he was trying to petrify. He was now living up to Kainé's creed: his eyes were a source of pride, and he had decided to use them to protect the villagers. Unwilling to allow his young friend to put himself in danger, Nier finished cleaning up the area. Nevertheless, they had not heard the last from the colossus. Its head had been severed from its body, and it was now facing the group inside the library. Since it seemed to be immortal, Weiss suggested locking it up in the building's basement. Nier pushed it in while Kainé rushed to the door panels to hold them closed. Before Nier had the time to give her the key to lock the door, the Shadowlord—in other words the real Nier—appeared accompanied by Grimoire Noir. He was carrying Yonah in his arms. The health of Yonah's Gestalt was deteriorating from day to day and the Shadowlord could no longer afford to wait in the hope that the androids would succeed in triggering the forced reintegration of the Gestalts into their Replicants. The real Yonah had to merge with her alter ego's body immediately, or she would be lost forever. In order to ensure his owner's retreat, Grimoire Noir cast an electric paralyzing spell on Nier and Weiss. The latter briefly conversed with Noir, who attempted to revive Weiss's lost memories, as well as his allegiance to the Original Gestalt. Confused by these revelations, Weiss was stricken by panic. Kaïné lost her temper.

"Weiss, you dumbass! Start making sense, you rotten book, or you're gonna be sorry! I'll rip your pages out, one-by-one! Or I'll put you in the goddamn furnace! How can someone with such a big, smart brain get hypnotized like a little bitch? Huh? Oh, Shadowlord! I love you, Shadowlord! Come over here and give Weiss a big sloppy kiss, Shadowlord! Now pull your head out of your goddamn ass and START FUCKING HELPING US!"

Kaïné's tirade brought Weiss back down to earth. Although he did not understand everything Grimoire Noir had just told him, Weiss decided that he would choose his own fate, with his comrades in arms. With Nier back on his feet, he led the assault against the black book in an attempt to rescue Yonah. But the duo was forced to recognize its helplessness: Noir's magic was too powerful. The Shadowlord ran off with the girl. In the background, Kaïné was still struggling to keep the basement door closed. The creature's countless attempts to break through had significantly weakened her. She thus asked Emil to petrify her, so that her stone body would seal the entrance. After some hesitation, Emil removed his blindfold. Kaïné said her goodbyes. Soon, she would be nothing more than a common rock.

Beginnings

Five long years had elapsed. Nier had spent every second searching for Yonah, but to no avail. The world was no longer the same. Or rather, it had become a more sinister, violent and decrepit version. The previously contained conflict with the Shades had flared into a merciless war driven by the Shadowlord. Between the repeated assaults of the creatures and the propagation of the Black Scrawl, there would soon be no one left. Nier had to toughen up to rise up to the challenge. The eye patch which covered half of his face bore witness to the intensity of the battles he had fought and the expertise he had acquired in handling the blade. That very morning, he had once again eliminated Shades that were attacking a villager. He still trusted Popola, whom he was now visiting. Weiss was still unable to remember his true nature despite his encounter with Grimoire Noir, and the android was careful not to reveal her identity during the intervention of the Original Gestalt.

In the library hall, Kainé's statue stood in the exact place where Emil had permanently immobilized her. But this could soon change. Popola handed over a letter from the boy to Nier indicating that there may be a way to cancel the spell. The warrior headed to the mansion for more details. Emil showed him a note dated 2026 suggesting that the residence's basement contained a means to control any kind of magic, and thus to reverse the petrification.

At first sight, the basement only seemed to contain relics of the old times: computers, industrial waste, archives, etc. Yet, strangely enough, Emil's growing discomfort led him to believe that this was the right place. Soon, his instincts would be confirmed. In the last room of the underground complex, he discovered Number 6's body firmly chained to one of the walls. The figure was roughly the size of two men. Her face resembled a gloomy funfair mask. At that moment, Emil recalled the experiments he had endured in the National Weapons Laboratory. The creature screwed to the wall like a vulgar animal was none other than his sister Halua. They were both weapons designed to kill.

Once again, Emil was faced with his monstrous nature. Nevertheless, it made no difference to Nier and Weiss. He still remained the same altruistic boy they had always known. And he would prove it once again. He turned to his two comrades, and then informed them of his intention to allow Number 6 to swallow him so that he could acquire her abilities. At that moment, the creature immediately broke its chains and swallowed the boy. A bitter fight thus ensued from which Nier emerged victorious. A figure rose from Number 6's remains. It was crying. Absorbing his sister's powers had turned Emil into a skeleton, clad in a simple ragged loincloth. Scared of his new appearance, he dreaded his friends' rejection. Nier approached, and then embraced his miserable body, as if to welcome him. For the first time, Emil looked up and saw his partner before him. He was exactly as he had pictured him: cool. More united than ever after this ordeal, the group headed to the village, where Kainé was waiting in her stone prison. Emil then began the healing process.

The library hall was surrounded by a halo of magic light. Emil held Kainé's unconscious body. The basement doors immediately flew open. Free at last, the sprawling Shade threw itself on Nier. More skillful, tougher and stronger after the five years he had devoted to perfecting his art, the warrior made short work of the monster. Emil, for his part, was begging out loud to Kainé to come back to life. She finally opened her eyes. In spite of the change in appearance, she immediately recognized her savior. Nier, Weiss, Emil and now Kainé: the group had been fully reconstituted. From this point onwards, the Shadowlord was in their combined sights. Popola had precisely informed them that a clue about his location lay in the depths of the Lost Shrine, where Nier had first met Weiss. It was also there that he had taken a brother's life.

Change in perspective

Gretel was crying, his brother Hansel was dead. Only he had managed to survive Nier's assault. What was the point of living now? Grimoire Weiss, whom he had the ancestral duty of protecting, had fled, and all he had left to keep him company was solitude. Yet, he had been proud of the guardian role he had been assigned. So proud that he had even despised the relapsed Gestalts who had found refuge in the Lost Shrine. After all, they were nothing more than human failures on the verge of extinction, unlike him, a healthy Gestalt. For many years, his brother and he had made fun of them. Nevertheless, in his new prison of isolation, Gretel had begun to reconsider his opinion. The loss he had experienced helped him understand their situation. Their presence began to comfort him, and he had started to consider them as his friends, his equals. But their friendship would soon end. A muffled sound resonated.

Once more in the last room of the Lost Shrine where he had freed Weiss and Yonah, Nier recognized his enemy. The guardian stood firmly between him and the small Shades. He made sounds, but no one could decipher them. Except Kainé. Her merger with Tyrann had granted her the ability to understand the Shades' language, although she was nonetheless convinced of their evil nature. At that very moment, Gretel was simply begging them to spare his helpless friends. In the depths of Kainé's soul, the parasite was chuckling, as if this lament would somehow change the slaughter he was calling for. In unison, the group attacked the guardian, who fought back even harder as his anger escalated. Nevertheless, the damage he had sustained five years earlier had irreversibly weakened him, and he was about to succumb. However, he would not perish before he had given his all to protect his companions. Before passing away from Nier's blows, the guardian hurled his spear into Kainé's chest, who collapsed into a pool of blood. For ages Tyrann had longed for this moment, the famous "weakness" that would allow him to fully possess his host. Under the parasite's influence, Kainé metamorphosed into a raging Shade. Weiss managed just in time to stop his friend with his magic before she could cause irreparable damage. Coming to her senses again, Kainé surfaced, full of remorse. She had failed to contain Tyrann, and that could not be allowed to happen again. Her presence endangered her comrades. She sensed that she had to keep away from them. But Emil refused to see her leave. He convinced her that if the parasite resurfaced by any chance, they would just have to incapacitate it once again. After these reconciliations, Nier finished inspecting the premises to find the clue Popola had told him about. On the floor, in the middle of the room, lay a mysterious fragment of stone encrusted with inscriptions. He retrieved it and returned to the librarian. The latter revealed to them that this was one of the five pieces of the key to the Shadowlord's Castle. According to the inscriptions, the scholar predicted that at least two of the other pieces were located in the Forest of Myth and at the heart of Junk Heap. As for the other two, Nier stated that all it would take to come upon them would be to travel the world and tear all the Shades he encountered to pieces. Radical.

The dreamy tree

Five years after the Deathdream epidemic, Nier and Weiss once again entered the Forest of Myth. The mayor informed them that a strange presence was emanating from the Divine Tree to which the inhabitants prayed. At the foot of the large trunk, a sparkling light drew their attention. They were propelled into a world of words, dark and blind, like they had been during their last visit. The memories stored by the thousand-year-old tree engulfed them. They explored in turn the life of a young boy condemned by a disease, of a fierce warrior and finally of the tree itself.

Long ago, its branches had remembered everything there was to know about the world and humanity. That was its goal. But years and then centuries went by. Its silence caused it to forget speech, and loneliness to forget emotions. As a result, it was pleased to see the man and his companion enter the room.

All Nier could find were a few strange scattered gems—actually the tree's memories—suggesting that the place had once been much richer. A Shade then suddenly appeared, grabbed a handful of these gems and brought them to its mouth. And here was the culprit: the creature was hastening the broad-leaved tree's deterioration by stealing its memories. But most surprisingly, it could speak. Weiss exclaimed, shaken by the mere idea that Shades could be endowed with emotions and a conscience. Nier immediately answered the tree's pleading to rid it of the pest. The thief's open stomach released a shiny object: the key fragment. As soon as the warrior seized it, the world of letters fell into ruins and reality reappeared. Only three left.

Beepy and Kalil's friendship

At the heart of the factory, the young Shade Kalil had just lost his mother, killed by their pursuers. Devastated, the child had no idea what to do. A giant robot resembling a figurine entered the room where he was hiding. Usually, the certified P-33 machine would eliminate the intruder, but Kalil became friends with him. He renamed his new companion Beepy. The latter swore to protect the boy from all who threatened him. Both lived happily in the factory until one day, during one of their strolls, they noticed two silhouettes.

Jakob and Gideon, the blacksmith brothers from the mountain, were marveling with loud cries at the rare materials they had just discovered. At that moment, a copper pipe fell and caused a wide structure to collapse. Jakob dashed to push Gideon away from the danger zone, and was buried under the rubble in doing so. The younger brother could do nothing but witness his brother's death. He then looked up and saw the robot and the Shade watching the scene: Beepy and Kalil. He immediately blamed them for the tragedy which had just occurred. Beepy's analysis, as he shared it with Kalil after having witnessed the tragic event, was quite different: the brothers' noisy enthusiasm had actually weakened the already precarious structure, causing its inevitable collapse.

At the foot of Junk Heap, Nier and his companions learned from Gideon, now a teenager, the news of Jakob's death, who had passed away four years earlier. The young brother was now running the forge. Not because it was his vocation, but rather because his secret objective involving the creation of a weapon powerful enough to kill the robot that had stolen his only family. Touched by the boy's grief, Nier, in addition to providing Gideon with the required materials, accepted the sword and agreed to carry out his revenge. Nier faced Beepy and Kalil at the exact spot where he had fought the factory's defense system. The duo was quickly overwhelmed. The young Shade thus begged the robot to stop fighting so that they could escape. But Beepy refused. He had but one mission, the one he had assigned himself: to protect his friend at all costs. Kainé picked up the conversation, but did not react. Tyrann, for his part, was jubilant—he relished absurdity and carnage. At the end of his rope, the machine went for broke. He magnetized his carcass to attract pieces of metal girders and other surrounding debris. The pieces of scrap metal clinging to his back formed two large wings, used by the robot to soar into the air, so high that he violently hit the ceiling. He came back down. And then started again. Relentlessly. He was attempting to break through the rock. Before dying, he was determined to show the world to Kalil; the inseparable comrades had promised this to each other. But Nier interpreted this differently as he could not understand the Shade's words. And with a heavy sharp blow, he cut Beepy down. Defenseless, Kalil suffered the same fate. Side by side, the improbable friends said their goodbyes before leaving this world. Gideon barged in like a maniac and started repeatedly hitting the burned pile of scrap metal. He roared with laughter. His hatred, fueled for so many years, had driven him mad. Nier seized the key fragment that Kalil had dropped, then returned to the village. There was a letter waiting for him in his mailbox. Façade's regent had invited his old friend to attend the royal wedding which would soon be celebrated.

The wolves' retaliation

A Shade in the shape of a wolf stood at the top of a dune. During his lifetime, his owner had forced him to go through the Gestaltization process. He listened to the complaints of the members of his pack. They had had their fill of humans and their habits. Their nature and corruption had turned the lush forests of yesteryear into a desert. But the Alpha knew that it was too dangerous to attack men head-on. Moreover, he was convinced that coexistence was still possible. The illusion lasted for a time. Until the day Façade's soldiers killed several of his brothers with their spears. In the minds of the sentries standing guard, the imminent royal wedding had justified the pure and simple elimination of any possible threat. A dozen dead wolves run through by blades lay in a pool of blood, barely soaked up by the sand. A butchery. The alpha Shade tried to save one of his congeners, who was still breathing, but to no avail. Wrath swept over him. It was payback time.

Celebrations were well underway outside the royal palace, with villagers dancing and throwing confetti. Emil was enjoying every moment. Nier and Weiss were having fun, while Kainé pretended to grumble. The wedding was timely for Façade. Poor harvests and the escalating conflict with the wolves had caused the inhabitants to lose hope. The king wanted to believe that his union would lift the people's spirits a little. All in white, the future queen stood at his side on the square. He had chosen Fyra, now a beautiful young woman. Nier was naturally delighted with their union. Finally, under Rule 904, the advisor instructed the engaged couple to seal their marriage with a kiss. King and queen, bound for eternity, then paraded briefly before the crowd. At one end of the square, a conscript came to meet them. He was covered in blood. The wolves had entered the city. Fyra was lifted off the ground and sent crashing into the wall, mowed down by the Shade. The pack overran the square which had been cleared of onlookers scared off by the attack. Nier retaliated and managed to drive the enemy away. Kneeling on the ground, the king was holding his wife as she bled to death. Fyra had no regrets. Once an outsider, she was leaving with the feeling of having finally been accepted by Façade's citizens—and even by its king. The monarch rose slowly and demanded revenge. His advisors failed to deter him. He would go alone if necessary. But the people shared their monarch's grief and joined him. Nier and the others also chose to accompany him in order to honor Fyra. As Façade prepared to storm the wolves' lair, the Shade counted his troops. The successive human assaults had drastically reduced the desert wolves' numbers. Only a large handful of them could still fight. And they would not run away. Even if it meant dying, they would leave with their honor intact, fighting off the invader. Façade's soldiers broke into the beasts' lair and then spread out. The masked people's fighters led the assault on the young wolves, while the king and Nier focused their attacks on the Shade. The pack was soon decimated, but its leader somehow kept on fighting. On his own initiative, Weiss stunned the canine with a magic punch. Taking advantage of the opening, the king jumped into the air and violently threw his spear at the enemy, cutting right through him. A piece of key—the fourth—slid to the ground, before being intercepted by Nier. As he passed away, the Shade saw the good and loving face of his former master again—the face of a time when men and animals lived in harmony. Pleased with the success of the offensive, the sovereign withdrew to Fyra's grave. Nier offered his condolences one last time, then returned to the village to visit Popola. Once again, she seemed to possess a clue regarding the location of a key fragment—the last one. The secluded inhabitants of the Aerie had sent him a peculiar letter mentioning the opening in the village of a huge supermarket ready to welcome customers from all over the world. The letter stated that the construction of this complex was part of a radical revision of the city's isolation policy. The sender also added that one of the villagers had heard about a piece of key, and would be more than happy to talk about it with Nier. Weiss could hardly believe this sudden turnaround, and neither could Kainé. The xenophobic veil that surrounded the Aerie could not have disappeared so easily. Nevertheless, it seemed obvious that something strange was happening over there.

The ultimate weapon

At first glance, the village appeared as quiet as five years ago when Nier and Kainé had freed it from the giant Shade's oppression. Nonetheless, upon closer inspection, a small handful of residents had indeed set up several stalls and shops on one of the platforms. Half a dozen people, at most, were strolling among the stalls. Nothing comparable to the large mall promoted in the letter. Nier mentioned the letter to one of the passersby, in an attempt to learn more. The passerby did not actually answer the question, but in turn asked him about the Shades. Nier therefore revealed his intention of killing them all. At that very moment, the man and most of the villagers in the area transformed into

Shades. A curse had struck the entire city. Husbands, who had metamorphosed into creatures, were attacking their wives, sisters were turning against their brothers—chaos had engulfed the Aerie. Somehow, Nier, Kainé and Emil had cleared a path to the narrow footbridges in order to rescue the remaining healthy villagers. But it was pointless. The life force of every resident was absorbed by a kind of mini black hole located in the heart of the canyon. The mass expanded as it sucked up the inhabitants' lives until reaching its final form: a gigantic black sphere wrapped in protective petals and inlaid with a giant eye.

While dodging the creature's magic missiles, Weiss and Nier positioned themselves to strike the enemy's weak spot. Once they had reached the right angle, the book generated a formidable magic spear that Nier sent right into the Shade. The contribution of Emil's total omnipotence allowed the javelin to pierce both the armor of petals and the sphere, which succumbed. But suddenly, the boy's skeletal body expelled purple energy rays. The increasing number of rays merged into a gargantuan energy orb which engulfed and pulverized the entire city and what remained of its inhabitants. Driven into a corner by the intense battle against the Shade, Emil had lost control of the "ultimate" weapon lying dormant in him ever since he had merged with Halua. Fortunately, Nier, Weiss and Kainé had managed to escape from the area hit by the explosion. When he regained consciousness, Emil was horrified to discover that he had taken the lives of many innocent people. Nier consoled the weeping boy with a few comforting words. After all, if it had not been for his intervention, all his friends would have died. The fifth key fragment lay on the ground, abandoned by the spherical Shade. Soon, Yonah would be free.

The Shadowlord's Castle

Sealed in a recess of the room where Hansel and Gretel used to guard Weiss, an elevator led to a completely different part of the Lost Shrine. Using the completed key, Nier lifted the magic barrier, and then entered the iron cage with his brothers in arms. As he stepped out of it, he discovered another part of the world which he had never seen before. The ruins and general state of disrepair of the world he had lived in throughout his adventures had made way for beautiful plots of well-cut greenery, perfectly tended tree lines, statues and polished marble structures, as well as a splendid fountain. Finally, at the end of the path, stood a large double door. Nier pushed it. Two familiar faces surrounded by the atrium's light welcomed him. Devola and Popola demanded that he turn back. Their attitude was no longer the same as in the village. A sardonic and haughty tone had replaced their usual benevolence. They revealed to the group the true nature of the Sealed Verses and their allegiance to the Shadowlord. Completely confused by the situation, Nier refused to step aside—his daughter was waiting for him at the end of the road. With no other choice, the sisters reluctantly raised their magic scepters and attacked their protégé. Most likely out of pity, they withdrew after a few exchanged blows, inciting Nier to seek the truth in the castle's bowels. Still shaken by this betrayal, the father followed the twins' advice and crossed the next threshold. In pairs, some twenty ghostly figures were waltzing on the dance floor of a huge ballroom. Suddenly sensing the presence of an aggressor, they mutated into Shades one after the other and threw themselves at Nier with all their might. In their eyes, the Shadowlord's Castle constituted their last bastion, in other words: humanity's sanctuary. If it fell and dragged the Original Gestalt to his downfall, mankind would be doomed. Unaware of the true stakes of his personal vendetta, Nier cut down each and every one of these creatures until almost nothing remained of them but pieces. In a concealed closet, Kaïné discovered a multitude of young Shades, which had been hidden by their parents. Panic-stricken, the little children gathered around their mother who had managed to escape Nier's violent outburst, and all merged together. The creatures, harmless separately, turned into a terrifying giant boar. Nier and his group hurled themselves at the animal. But no matter the violence or the method they used to strike it, the monster systematically got back to its feet. Even more worrying, the animal was releasing poison into the air, seriously disabling whoever inhaled it. Fearing that they would be completely incapacitated by the gas, the group fled to the next room. The enraged beast immediately chased after them. The race ended in a room with locked doors. Once again, the poison was contaminating the atmosphere. Just as the Shade was about to charge at Nier, spears materialized and cut through the beast's muzzle, breaking its momentum. Led by their king, Façade's soldiers surrounded the abomination, ready to fight, while some of the troops were busy opening the next door. The monarch had gotten wind of Nier's intentions. For obvious reasons, the Shadowlord hardly inspired confidence in him, so he therefore decided to supplement his friend's assault. After unlocking the door, the masked fighters grabbed Nier and forcibly dragged him out of the room to join his friends who were still waiting for him. The warrior tried to resist—he knew that the king could not compete alone against this mastodon—but he was abruptly shoved into the corridor with the doors closing behind him. Nier pounded the metal plates, but it was pointless. For the sake of friendship, and for Fyra, Façade's king was determined to put his life on the line during this battle.

The joust was fierce. Every single Façade soldier perished, without exception. Inevitably wounded, the sovereign raised his spear in anticipation of the final assault. Facing him, the Shade was preparing to attack. It cursed these fake humans for having slain so many of its own, for having massacred so many of its children. And then charged at him. More skillful, the king managed to drive his spear into the boar's head, which collapsed on its side. Victorious, but fatally wounded, the man sat down, at peace. He would soon join Fyra.

Emil's farewells

Devola and Popola received the intruders' visit for the second time. Since Nier and his group still failed to understand their true nature, the androids revealed to their visitors the truth about their existence and the goals of Project Gestalt. Nier, Emil, Kaïné and Weiss found out that they had been nothing more than tools at the service of true humanity: the Shades. Despite these revelations, the group's determination remained unchanged: the Shadowlord must die. Once again, the two sisters stepped in. But this time, they would not flee. On one side, the androids who had remained loyal to humanity, and on the other, the artificial bodies that had become independent: the fight promised to be tragic, but it was unavoidable. Devola was the first to fall. Popola hurried to her side and tried to help her, but the intensity of the bleeding made it impossible. On the brink of death, with her eyes locked on the eyes of her sister, Devola understood why humans had designed them as twins. The world was simply too hollow and cruel for a single soul to endure the burden of years.

—I love you, Devola whispered to her sister before passing away.

Witness to the scene and its absurdity, Nier begged Popola, his lifelong friend, to stop this madness. Fulminant, the android recovered with the firm intention of resuming the fight. Why would she renounce her revenge after Nier had struck down the being she loved most in the world? Little by little, her anger turned into madness, a dangerous and terribly destructive form of madness. She roared. Similar to the ultimate power which pulverized the Aerie, an intense orange wave of magic was unleashed in the air, threatening to destroy everything in its wake. Popola was determined to get it over with, even at the cost of her life. In order to avoid combustion, Emil generated a protective magic bubble in which the group took refuge. The magician guided the floating globe and its passengers towards the next building. However, as they moved away from the danger zone, a magic ray fired by Popola took hold of them, preventing them from going any further. Immobilized in the air, they were at the mercy of the explosion. Thus, Emil turned to his comrades. He promised them that everything would be fine.

Even though he had once hated his eyes, and now hated his body, he explained that in the company of Nier, Weiss and Kainé, he had developed a sense of pride: he was proud of being their friend. He said his goodbyes.

Taking on the pull of the magic ray on his own and despite the objections of his companions, Emil allowed himself to drift out of the bubble, then thrust Nier, Kainé and Weiss towards the last section of the castle. His shattered body was absorbed by the massive black sphere emerging from Popola's hatred. Darkness surrounded him, as if he had gone blind again. In his newfound solitude, he wished he could see them again, just one last time. He was scared. He did not want to die. A muffled blast filled the air with silence, then a blinding light absorbed the landscape. When the colors returned, everything had disappeared.

In the wide corridor where they had landed, devastated by the loss of their friend, Nier and Kainé mourned in silence. Kainé suddenly got up and kicked Nier in the stomach, then brought her face closer to his. Her expression softened for a moment before hardening again. Finally, she turned to their objective at the end of the corridor.

Behind the next door lay the fate of humanity.

The end of humanity

Although it had wide windows on each side, the curtains had been drawn and the room was lit by projectors mounted on the ceiling, as if to keep away onlookers. At the end of the huge room, Nier spotted Yonah, asleep on a canopy bed. He rushed towards her. But rising from the ground, the Shadowlord and Grimoire Noir blocked his path. Replicant versus Gestalt, the battle could begin. Nier fought with all the rage and pain he had accumulated over the five long years during which he had, in a way, been deprived of his daughter. Kainé joined in the fray. Supported by Grimoire Noir's infernal magic, the Shadowlord furiously defended himself. However, before an outcome had been reached, Yonah emerged from her slumber and imposed a truce by entering the battlefield. Her first words were addressed to her father—the Shadowlord. Neither Replicant nor Gestalt, the Yonah who was now expressing herself was fully human.

Upon returning from the library, the original Nier had reintegrated his daughter's soul into the Replicant he had kidnapped. The result of this operation, however, had caused major problems. This Yonah was constantly hearing the cries of her alter ego, whose personality had remained. The inner voice was calling for her father, Nier's Replicant. There was nothing fair and good, Yonah told the Shadowlord, about preventing this girl, who loved her father as much as she loved hers, from enjoying a family life. Despite the Original Gestalt's desperate groans, as he besought his daughter not to leave him, Yonah's decision seemed irrevocable. She moved closer to one of the huge windows and allowed her Gestalt–her soul–to escape into the daylight. Her body collapsed. Kainé rushed to her side to attend to her. The Shadowlord, overwhelmed by the thousand-year-old despair of not having been able to save his daughter, released his resentment by attacking Nier. The fight resumed with renewed vigor. But without warning, an utterly exhausted Weiss crashed to the ground. From the day he had first met him in the Lost Shrine to this day, Nier had drained all the magic supply stored in the book. Thus, the time had come for His Highness to say his goodbyes. Weiss accomplished his ultimate achievement by using his remaining strength to destroy Grimoire Noir. Henceforth deprived of a great part of his magic, the Shadowlord was at Nier's mercy. The Replicant, standing in front of his opponent who was down on his knees, hesitated for a moment, then swung down his sword. Somewhere far away, most likely in some afterlife, a father and his daughter were finally reunited. In turn, Nier's Replicant joined his own Yonah, who had been purged of the Gestalt which inhabited her body. Together, they gazed at the bright daylight. Kainé was watching them in the background. Somewhere along the way, ever since Nier, a perfect stranger, had helped her fulfill her dream of revenge, the positions had been reversed. Nier's battle had become her own. She had saved herself by saving Yonah. For the first time in ages, alongside this reunited family, she felt hope. A hope of love and belonging. Tyrann, however, hardly felt this emotional turnaround. Overwhelmed by Kainé's sudden and overflowing kindness, he had involuntarily entered the relapse phase. Infected by gangrene, the host's body began to metamorphose into a Shade. Taken by surprise during his reunion, Nier reacted too late and could not contain this evil. Kainé therefore made her last request: asking him to kill her before it was too late. Tyrann, on the other hand, transfigured by the kindness contained in the heart he shared with his symbiont, suggested an alternative to the executioner. If Nier sacrificed his soul, Kainé could become fully human and continue to live. Of course, the process would cost him his life, but more importantly it would erase all memory of his very existence. Yonah would forget about her father and Kainé would never know her savior's identity: total annihilation. Nier picked this option.

The breeze gently lifted the curtains infiltrated by rays of sunlight. Kainé awoke to the blinding afternoon daylight. She inspected her hands, arms and legs: she was alive. She surveyed the huge room as if she were looking for something or someone, but only found Yonah. The young girl embraced her benefactress and thanked her for having freed her from the Shadowlord. Kainé wept. She claimed to have found something special, something unique.

Somewhere in the far off distance, Emil's head landed in the desert. The rest of his skeleton had gone up in smoke, but this part of his body had survived Popola's attack. Emil, or what was left of him, began to roll across the dunes. His first objective: find a body, or at least legs. Then, he would rejoin the others.

Reunion

Kaïné was constantly having nightmares. She was unable to shake off this strange feeling that haunted her, the feeling of having lost something important that day in the Shadowlord's Castle. All she knew was that Tyrann no longer parasitized her, and that she felt inexplicably close to Yonah, the girl she had rescued. Frustrated by her failure to find any meaning in these remanences, she decided to go out and let off steam on a few Shades she had spotted lurking in the Forest of Myth. When she arrived, the decorum was not what she had expected. The trees' roots were intertwined with a multitude of power cables. The forest had merged with the machines. Or rather, it was displaying its true form. When Kaïné stood before the most impressive tree, the wires merged to form the silhouette of a young man. The heap of cables introduced itself as the "overseer." Before Kaïné could even ask anything, the overseer started to give an explanation. At this very moment, the overseer pointed out, the system was entering its final phase and had already initialized its shutdown sequence. Therefore, it could not allow a stranger to interrupt the smooth running of the procedure. As if it had just given an order, a battalion of robots suddenly appeared and attacked Kaïné, who retaliated. Despite this, the silhouette continued its explanation. His goal, as overseer, involved maintaining the distribution network of the purified Maso provided by the Original Gestalt, or Shadowlord. In short, it was responsible for the smooth running of Project Gestalt. Nonetheless, now that Grimoire Noir and Grimoire Weiss, which were essential for the reintegration of the souls in the Replicants, as well as the Original Gestalt, the Maso's source, had been destroyed, Project Gestalt's failure was undeniable. Without purified Maso, the Gestalts were condemned to relapse and, ultimately, to die. The last Shade's demise would mark the end of humanity. The Replicants' future was under the same unfortunate auspices. Unable to reproduce, their very existence in this world was only the result of the Forest of Myth's body production system. Which, the overseer coldly pointed out, had no more reason to create Replicants in light of the failure of Project Gestalt and the death of the android observers Devola and Popola. Thus, threatened by the Black Scrawl and restricted by their life expectancy, the Replicants would also soon cease to exist. This world had no future.

As she cut down the robots sent by the overseer, Kaine's memories were brought back. The acronym P-33 on their carcasses reminded her of the battle she had fought in the Junk Heap with Emil and someone else. But who? The overseer had the answer. He promised to give it to Kaine if she overcame the next challenge. He thus summoned a robot which looked very much like Kaine. Then totally out of the blue, Emil stepped in. Not only had he managed to restore his body, but he also had an extra pair of arms which he had accidentally added during his self-repair. The two comrades had no time to celebrate their reunion: facing them was Kaine's doppelganger who was about to attack. During the fight, Emil noticed that the energy source which powered the robot and the entire structure was located at the heart of the Divine Tree. The boy thus suggested targeting it with their attacks. As a result, the energy core yielded to their concentrated assaults.

The scenery, the trees, the ground, the overseer, etc. Everything dissolved and blended into a large and shapeless puddle. A strong white light filled the space. Emil protected Kaine with his magic as she cut through the photons to find her way in this blinding pool of light. Silence returned. Kaine sensed she was approaching something important. She reached out her hand, vaguely making out the figure of a person.

...ine... don't...

Tears ran down Kaine's cheeks.

...go back... do not... come here...

She tried to grab hold of it, but it slipped away from her again. Anger overwhelmed her—she would not tolerate being told what to do. Not this time. Her tears got mixed up with her outbursts of rage fueled by her visceral fear of losing that important thing again. Someone[98] pushed Kaine in the back. She used the movement to propel herself forward.

GET BACK HERE YOU BASTARD! she yelled into oblivion.

The white light faded away. The blue sky was back. The Forest of Myth vanished. A gigantic techno-organic flower resembling a Lunar Tear had taken its place. At the base of the stamen, Kaine was holding the one person she cherished the most in her arms. She had found "him." Nier[99].

98. A priori, it was Weiss, given that Kaine heard a voice calling her a "slut," the book's favorite insult for her. But it remains questionable since his presence in the Forest of Myth system is not explained. It could very well have been Kaine imagining something.

99. Again, here Nier's reconstitution seems difficult to justify. We understand that the Nier whom Kaine was trying to get back could remember her, which would mean that his memory had been stored in the Replicanti-zation system. Yet, this possibility as well as the new Replicants' ability to retain the memories of their old models' lives has never been mentioned. It is worth noting that the Nier whom Kaine meets again is the one from the beginning of the game, before the five-year ellipsis, which suggests that it is the Replicant's original model, and not the one at the end of the game who chooses to sacrifice himself, which only adds to the confusion. In short, Nier is alive again, with memories concerning Kaine, but we don't know exactly how this is possible.

The other Devolas and Popolas

Following Devola and Popola's failure to protect Project Gestalt, virtually all the androids sharing the same model and supervising Replicant operations around the world were put out of service. Other than those in charge of Nier's Replicant, only one other pair were kept alive for the sole purpose of being turned into a control group. Their memories had been erased and, most importantly, they had been reprogramed to constantly feel a strong sense of guilt for the actions of their fellow androids.

These twins, although they could no longer recall it, had therefore known humanity, made of flesh and blood. They had been responsible for its fate and took great pride in it. Then they had endured the recrudescence of the Black Scrawl and the countless cases of Gestalt relapses. In the space of a few hundred years, they had witnessed the collapse of mankind's future. Once a blessing, their mission as observers had become a burden. But a shared burden. Because the humans, in their great indulgence, had created androids in pairs, so that they could support and console one another. Otherwise, the sisters could not have endured their fate. One day, they found out that another pair of observers based in a remote city had torpedoed Project Gestalt. Deprived of their purpose, Devola and Popola gathered the data they possessed on the world of men and sent it to the Moon. Protecting humanity was their instinct, imprinted deep within their being by humans themselves. The very same instinct that drove other androids to despise their models, considered to be the gravediggers of men. Both sisters suffered discrimination, contempt and marginalization. And later persecution. Even though they were held accountable for actions they had not committed, they accepted the hatred directed against them. As expected, they felt responsible. After all, they believed that since they were also involved in the supervision of Project Gestalt, they should at least share some of the blame. Nevertheless, they tried to avoid harassment, traveling from town to town whenever the situation made it necessary. Until the day the inevitable happened: an android physically attacked Devola. On that day, they fled and did not set foot in another village for some time. They could no longer tolerate the violence of their fellow androids. The desert welcomed them for a while; and in this vast infinity of nothingness, they adopted a resolution to continue sharing their common destiny.

Extraterrestrial invasion

A few centuries later, humanity finally came to an end with the death of the last Gestalt. The Replicants also disappeared, as predicted by the Forest of Myth's overseer. Emil, who had become immortal by virtue of his magic, found himself traveling the world alone.

In the year 5012, Emil came across a UFO. He approached to welcome it. Far from sharing the boy's pacifism, the spaceship attacked him. The magician retaliated with his entire range of techniques. But the invader resisted. Determined to protect the land once inhabited by his comrades in arms, Emil created four hundred and thirty copies of himself and won the battle against the intruder with their support. However, the war had only just begun. All over the planet, aliens were landing with the firm intention of subjugating Earth to their dominant reign. Over the next hundred years, Emil pursued his fight against the aliens, going so far as to produce an army of more than eighty million clones.

One year after the beginning of the invasion, and spread all across the planet, the androids–who were once responsible for overseeing the Replicants– retaliated. They gathered together under the banner of the Army of Humanity in order to stop the alien's advance and to preserve the old world, out of loyalty towards their former masters. Factories were built to produce combat models capable of forming a decent armada that would hold back the invader.

About a decade later, aliens designed machines, complex biological life forms they used as weapons of war. During the following centuries, their mass production proved to be a decisive asset in their fight against androids and enabled them to conquer an increasing amount of territory. In the face of this dangerous threat, the androids secured every piece of information related to the old world on a server installed on the Moon. Concurrently, the Army of Humanity built a network of twelve orbital bases from which it organized assaults–called "descents"–to reclaim the Earth from the machines' clutches. However, despite their persistent efforts, the androids suffered many defeats. Eventually, the machines succeeded in conquering eighty percent of Earth's territory. For thousands of years, they did not increase their presence but simply repelled the androids' attacks. During that time, the machines developed into superior organisms, when compared to the aliens, due to their ability to adapt and evolve. The intelligence resulting from their perpetual interconnection through a "network," which linked all the machines together, allowed them to surpass their progenitors. In their opinion, this was reason enough to eliminate them permanently. Nevertheless, once rid of the aliens, the machines still remained defined by the fundamental command that their creators had imprinted deep within them: "destroy the enemy," in other words, the androids. Except, to continue to obey this command, the machines had come to the paradoxical conclusion that they could not entirely triumph over and destroy their opponent, the androids. In order to solve this existential conflict, the mechanical life forms sabotaged their own network by diversifying the evolution vectors of different population groups, thus giving birth to individuals considered outside the mold such as Pascal, the peaceful machine. The latter and some of his peers, who founded a village, preferred to cut themselves off from their fellow machines a few centuries after the aliens stopped sending orders, because they could no longer bear to see their friends die one after the other in the conflict against the androids.

In the year 11932, the Army of Humanity began designing anti-machine android units with incredible potential under the name YoRHa. Several prototypes were developed under the leadership of the android scientist Zinnia, who was working in the sixth orbital station, the Labo. But the development of the real combat models, which would be deployed on the battlefield and could turn the tide of war, was slow. The exorbitant production costs of these units were slowing down the manufacturing process. Zinnia's main problem was the power supply. The YoRHa units' cores, their "black boxes," had to be made from high quality machine cores, which entailed astronomical operational costs. And delayed the Army of Humanity's counteroffensive. As he helplessly witnessed the android's being defeated, worn out and demoralized by an eternity of fighting, Zinnia came up with a great idea. If the androids were to once again believe in their creator, Humanity, the troops' morale would inevitably skyrocket, and the hope of winning the war would be restored anew. Strongly convinced of his intuition's relevance, Zinnia devised a secret plan to spread the rumor according to which humanity had in fact not been wiped out, but was exiled on the Moon. For this purpose, he installed a communication server alongside the data server already present on the natural satellite. The trick was therefore to invent an entire organization that would represent men, the "Council of Humanity," and to use the communication server as a relay to broadcast audio messages emitted by this phantom entity to all the androids on Earth. Thus, the fighters would believe once more in the existence of their gods, mankind. In addition, a thirteenth orbital base was built to host the future elite YoRHa unit, which would be introduced as the armed wing of a resurrected humanity, the androids' benefactor. Zinnia's plan was a success. The news of the Council of Humanity's existence was spreading among the entire android population. The fake organization was henceforth in charge of coordinating and federating the forces of the Army of Humanity, more galvanized than ever. However, one of the YoRHa prototypes manufactured by Zinnia, Number 9, rebelled against its creator when it found out that its black box had been made from machine cores, the android species' sworn enemy. Seeking revenge, it implanted a backdoor[100] in Zinnia's lunar system through which the machines could access humanity's data and the system of the YoRHa base. Then, it instructed the server to automate the production of YoRHa units according to a particular pattern. Since the machines would use the backdoor to enter and destroy the YoRHa network and its members, Number 9 programed the server in such a way that it would recreate a new generation of units each time this happened. Thus, when sufficient data had been collected on one generation of models and it was time to transfer it to the next, a backdoor was deliberately opened in the orbital base server so that the machines could rush in and destroy the base, with a virus, for example. This way, all units and documents related to Project YoRHa were destroyed and the lie concerning human life on the Moon remained—as well as the war. By gaining access to the YoRHa and human servers, the machines acquired new intelligence allowing them to evolve and adapt to the opponent's creations. So that neither the androids, constantly enhanced by Project YoRHa, nor the machines, constantly informed of the said project's progress, could definitively prevail over the opposite faction. This constant confrontation constituted the prerequisite for the fake Council of Humanity's control over the androids throughout the world. After all, who or what would androids live for should the war come to an end? Thus, Number 9 triggered an endless cycle of destruction and creation: as long as the backdoor existed, the machines would be able to destroy the YoRHa units, and the latter would automatically be rebuilt, condemned to die as soon as they were created.

After murdering Zinnia and setting fire to the Labo out of sheer revenge, Number 9 was defeated by another prototype, Number 2, who died in turn, engulfed in flames. And the truth about "Project YoRHa" disappeared with its instigators. In the eyes of the world, humanity was safe, and the YoRHa units were putting an end to the everlasting conflict between androids and machines.

Following the machines' self-sabotage, the network initiated a self-repair process which incorporated elements from its environment. With the backdoor opened by Number 9, the network rebuilt itself in part through the human memories and data found by the machines on the lunar server, including those related to Project Gestalt and the Original Gestalt. While accessing the human archives, the network's structure evolved into a meta network, or concept,

---

100. In a computer program, a "backdoor" is a feature unknown to the user and used to secretly access the software in order, most of the time, to exploit it.

resulting in the birth of the ego N2, which took the form of girls dressed in red. In a way, they embodied the machines' collective consciousness. In the following years, the network's hybridization with human history would drive the machines to reproduce humanity's way of life. They therefore experimented with several types of governance: absolute monarchy, the republic system and democracy. They tried exploring scientific studies: mathematics, philosophy and sociology. But unlike humans, they never managed to invent new cultures or values. They only ever imitated them. As a result, they reproduced their failures, endlessly, without ever learning from their mistakes. Except when it came to combat.

The 14th Machine war broke out in 11939 and lasted until 11945. For the first time, a range of YoRHa androids was officially deployed on the battlefield.

A2's story

The android A2 belonged to the first generation of YoRHa models deployed to assist ground resistance in their fight against the machines during the Pearl Harbor descent on December 8, 11941. On the ground, she made contact with a group of resistance fighters, including a certain Anemone, the resistance's future leader. Their objective was to capture an enemy bastion: Mount Ka'ala in Hawaii. But the operation soon went downhill. Several members of the battalion were infected by a virus which jeopardized their circuits and drove them mad. Others were killed by the machines, which had come in large numbers to maintain their position. Despite the YoRHa and the resistance's multiple requests, they were outright refused reinforcements by Commander White of the orbital base, who was in charge of the YoRHa forces. In short, White abandoned the squadron on the battlefield, condemning it to certain death. As expected. At the heart of the enemy positions, A2 actually met the N2 machine network embodiment who, after having taken the lives of her remaining android friends, informed her that the YoRHa command had designed her generation of models with the sole intention of sending it into the firing line. Her comrades in arms and herself were expendable prototypes whose sole—but secret—purpose was to be tested in real combat conditions. The data recovered in the process by the orbital base was used for the development of the next generation of YoRHa androids, from which models 2B and 9S would later originate. The manipulation was orchestrated by the Commander, following orders from the lunar server set up by Zinnia and Number 9. A2 realized that evolution and programed death were an integral part of Project YoRHa. YoRHa units were born to die in battle, while their legacy improved the performance of those who would follow them. Ever since she learned the truth, A2 felt nothing but hatred, both towards those who had betrayed her and towards the machines that had murdered her only family. There were sixteen of them at the beginning of the Pearl Harbor operation, but A2 was the only one in the YoRHa division who had managed to survive. Furthermore, Anemone was the only remaining member of the resistance.

On March 10, 11945, the two hundred and forty-third descent began, with the objective of destroying a Goliath class machine.

NIER: AUTOMATA

The descent

In the ruins of an abandoned factory, a young machine contemplated the remains of one of its fellow machines. From the outside, machines looked like cans on legs. Their half-sphere shaped head with two luminescent round eyes was mounted on a cylindrical trunk[101], which was in turn fitted with two scrap metal arms and legs. Standing before the corpse of its counterpart, whom it called "brother," the little machine came up with an idea. It hurried to fill a bucket with oil in order to rehydrate it. But it stumbled, fell and knocked over the bucket because of its spring-loaded legs. From a higher position, the android YoRHa No. 9 Type S(canner), or 9S, was watching the scene. No matter how much oil it poured, he thought, this machine was dead, and it was certainly not its brother. In his opinion, machines had neither brothers nor family.

In the sky, six white lines indicated the beginning of the mission. 9S began to move. The flight units with the YoRHa Type B(attle) androids on board had begun their descent towards the objective. According to the base's intelligence, the factory was likely to shelter one of the most ferocious Goliath class machines. The Council of Humanity had made its elimination one of the war's top priorities. However, as soon as it had entered terrestrial airspace, the YoRHa contingent was almost entirely annihilated by flying machines before it could even reach the ground. Only the android 2B survived, who appeared as a young woman with white hair dressed in a short black dress. On site, she made contact with the 9S support unit responsible for providing assistance and information. The teenage-looking scout, accustomed to working alone beyond enemy lines, was delighted to finally collaborate with a partner. However, 2B immediately dampened the enthusiasm of her new acquaintance by informing him that emotions were

---

101. A theory based on the resemblance between the faces of the machines and that of Emil suggests that the machines had been created in the boy's image. But nothing can confirm this.

forbidden according to the YoRHa code. Following this exchange of courtesies, the two androids split up to search for their objective. 2B explored the factory on foot while 9S used a flight unit, with the two nevertheless maintaining contact through their communication devices.

In addition to an array of cutting-edge built-in technologies transforming the YoRHa units into ultimate androids, each unit was systematically paired with a pod, a small rectangular flying robot which provided advice as well as combat support with its offensive abilities, such as a machine gun. Helped by her Pod 042, 2B swept the factory, without finding the slightest trace of the Goliath. Ditto for the cheerful 9S and his Pod 153. 2B emerged on the other side of the facility where a path to another site, which may conceal the objective, had materialized. She had barely began to move away from the building when it began to move. Two huge cranes with impressive saws attached to their arms broke away to attack her, then once more merged with the factory which turned out to be, as a whole, the Goliath machine. Standing up on its gigantic legs, the enemy propelled itself towards 2B's position. Still in his flight unit, 9S joined the battle that had just broken out. Thanks to his unique hacking skills, he infiltrated the opponent's system in order to take control of the missiles fired by the Goliath, which he turned against the sender. Visibly stunned by the attack, the giant appeared to turn off for a moment, but suddenly slammed down his huge arm on 2B's position. 9S appeared out of nowhere and managed to shove the limb away before it struck the ground. In the process, the colossus swung an uppercut with his other arm and struck 9S. Hurled into the air, the android landed on the roof of the Goliath's structure. 2B, visibly less apathetic than at the start of the mission, let out a cry of concern. She leaped onto the opponent's body and, climbing stairs and ladders, reached 9S's mutilated body, still alive, but unable to keep on fighting. Utterly overwhelmed, 2B ordered her pod to patch up her partner, but it was too late to have any hope of healing him, especially in the heat of battle. Invoking the YoRHa soldiers' duty, 9S thus entrusted his flight unit to 2B, so that she could complete the mission. She accepted the task without hesitation, entered the vessel and resumed fighting, while 9S hacked the enemy from his position. In doing so, the boy managed to remove the Goliath's arm. Pod 042 overrode the computer protections protecting the limb and placed it under 2B's control. Henceforth, both the android and the machine were on equal footing. Meanwhile, fearing that the mission would lead to death, 9S transferred 2B's memory data to the orbital base, their headquarters. For androids, losing a body was irrelevant as long as their memories were securely stored in digital form. The YoRHa units' bodies were mass-produced, and reinserting memories into them was enough to ensure the individual's continuity. In an ultimate effort,

2B finished off the Goliath with a swift sword blow to the face. The explosion's blast propelled her onto the platform where 9S lay. The enemy had been vanquished. But three other Goliaths, identical to the previous one, immediately emerged from the aquatic depths surrounding the androids' position. In the face of imminent death coming from all sides, 2B and 9S congratulated each other on the success of their mission, and then both blew up their black box, their primary energy core.

In the bunker, the YoRHa units' orbital base, 2B was equipped with a new body—and her memories. In a hallway, she met 9S, whom she thanked for having taken care of her data. But this 9S was not the same. His physical envelope was certainly identical, or rather brand new. Yet, he could not recall any of the events that followed his meeting with 2B at the factory. 9S had run out of time to transfer his own data. Their relationship, erased; shared moments, forgotten. But 9S hardly cared. The mission remained a success, the Goliaths had all been swallowed up by the explosion. Thrilled by this victory, bending his left arm and placing his hand over his heart, he chanted loudly the YoRHa watchword: "Glory to Mankind." 2B reluctantly imitated him in response. She had experienced this situation dozens of times before. Her real denomination was 2E, for Executioner, a series of YoRHa models in charge of eliminating other YoRHa units, designed on the basis of the A2 prototype's combat data. 2B's true role was to accompany 9S in his reconnaissance missions, and to kill him every time he came too close to the truth about Project YoRHa. Given his talent as a scout, 9S would definitely discover the YoRHa units' hidden face sooner or later. Therefore, 2B was constantly assigned to his side by Commander White with the sole order to kill him as soon as he would jeopardize the project. She had already put this into practice. Over and over and over again. Countless times. And each time, 9S's memories had been reset so he could be redeployed on the battlefield, fresh and operational. But even though she knew that she was condemned to eliminate every 9S unit with whom she collaborated, 2B could not help but grow attached to him. Her role was her burden.

In the base's command room where the android operators who coordinated the ground units were crammed together, 2B and 9S received their next mission from Commander White: a tall android with long blond hair, the only person in direct contact with the Council of Humanity. She was also the only one to know the truth about Project YoRHa and the end of humanity. She entrusted 9S and 2B with the task of establishing a connection with one of the pockets of android resistance on Earth and gleaning any intelligence in its possession. Partners once again, the scout and the fighter were headed for the base hangar.

Adam & Eve

The resistance camp was located on the outskirts of a large City Ruins. Vegetation had long since reclaimed its rights and wildlife had conquered over the concrete titans. There were also a few machines. However, those encountered by 9S and 2B on their way showed no signs of hostility. They just wandered around, staring into the void. An anomaly, according to 9S's analysis. Machines were and would remain a threat to humanity. This observation was confirmed by Anemone, the resistance leader, who warned the pair that dangerous mechanical life forms could be found in the desert to the west of the camp. Encouraged by their superiors, the duo visited the scene to defeat the enemy contingent. But something was amiss. The desert machines, which did not usually wear clothes, were all dressed in odd patched ponchos. Stranger still, they were speaking, or rather jerkily uttering words such as "android, kill, enemy, why?" The androids executed their natural enemies without giving much thought to it.

"Help me," a machine appeared to be begging.

2B was speechless. 9S immediately reassured her: the machines were randomly uttering words, their speech was inconsistent. After all, why would they ask those they attacked for help? The pair pursued the last target which had fled towards an abandoned residential area located below the dunes, in the midst of the desert. The pursuit led them into a clearing surrounded by rubble. What they witnessed there was beyond comprehension. The ground was strewn with android corpses, presumably transported to this precise location for some unknown reason. Surrounding them, in pairs, masked machines were frantically mimicking the human mating process, swinging the lower part of their cylindrical body towards their partner's lower structure, resulting in nothing more than the metallic sound of the impact.

Love. Life. Love. Life, said one machine.

Together. Forever, said another.

One of them was standing above a cradle, which it gently swung, and repeating at the top of its voice, a kind of mantra: "Child. Child. Child." When 2B and 9S's target finally appeared, the machines, as if awakening from a hypnotic state, interrupted their activities and hurled themselves at the androids. After a few exchanged blows, the machines began, this time all together, to repeat another mantra: "This. Cannot. Continue." At first slowly, then frenetically, more and more quickly, until they entered a collective trance that drove them to agglutinate in groups of ten, forming one unique body between them, or rather a huge cocoon. A vulva slit opened. A naked adult body fell from it. Its name was Adam. Painfully, it stood up straight. Despite its appearance, 9S could tell it was definitely a machine. And must therefore be eliminated. 2B and 9S launched the assault, and it turned out to be a very strange fight. Indeed, as the androids struck their opponent, the latter learned from the fight and adjusted in real time. First dodging, then parrying, and retaliating. However, nothing insurmountable for two YoRHa models, who managed to pierce the machine's artificial flesh with their swords. The carcass collapsed. Shortly after, a bright light emanated from it. Another body completely identical to the previous one emerged from its chrysalis. Another machine had just been born. Adam lay on the ground. And Eve was the creature made out of the original. Standing firmly on its legs, chest forward, Eve uttered a terrifying cry of anger at 9S and 2B. The sound wave caused entire sections of the walls to fall, forcing the androids to leave the area and turn back to the desert.

Once they had transferred the data of their battle against Adam to the base for analysis, 2B and 9S were assigned their next task by the Commander: an old-fashioned search and rescue mission. Several YoRHa units had recently disappeared from the radars following their descent.

Simone's obsession

The signal of the units' black boxes emanated from an abandoned amusement park, a vestige of human civilization. However, the machines had reclaimed the place, as if to bring it back to life. Wearing clown makeup and dressed in bow ties and colorful pants, they scattered confetti and balloons on 9S and 2B's path, without ever attacking them. As they scoured the area, the pair of androids encountered a battalion of machines operating a tank from the old world. But once again, the odd life forms did not seem ready for the battle, instead using the vehicle as a parade chariot from which they spread joy and happiness. Once they had finished exploring the premises, 9S and 2B ended up in a theater. On stage, the curtain was drawn back. A machine called Simone about three meters high appeared, dressed like a diva. Her dress was adorned with android corpses.

Simone was trying to seduce another machine by the name of Jean-Paul[102]. She was desperate for his love. Despite her efforts, her jewelry, her songs, he did not look at her. She was not beautiful enough. It was rumored that eating androids could help, so she embraced this practice. She even swallowed a few machines. But to no avail. All this was in vain, she could not win the love of her

102. A reference to the romantic relationship between the French philosophers Jean-Paul Sartre and Simone de Beauvoir.

soul mate. All she hoped was that someone would finally look at her. But clearly, despair and anger had taken hold of her before this could happen.

She let out a strident cry, then rushed towards the intruders. With no other choice, 9S and 2B engaged in combat.

"Beautiful... I must be beautiful"

Obsessed, the machine repeated these words as she deployed her lethal arsenal. Suddenly, she withdrew to the stage and made an attempt at hacking. 9S retaliated in the same manner. By accident, he accessed the machine's memories and witnessed Simone's unsuccessful attempts to seduce Jean-Paul. In the end, Simone's hacking attempt failed. She screamed. In despair? A hail of wooden crosses poured over the area where 2B and 9S stood. Dozens of crucified android corpses lay at their feet. 9S could still pick up the signal from their black boxes: they were alive, but obviously reprogramed to serve as Simone's weapon. The electromagnetic waves they emitted threatened to scramble the duo's systems, so they quickly put an end to their fellow androids' torment. Simone was sinking deeper and deeper into madness. Her attacks intensified. Finally, 2B ordered 042 to destroy the enemy with its laser beam. Simone exploded. In her final moments, she saw her loved one again. He was reaching out to her.

As he left the building, 9S questioned his certainties. Did machines have emotions? More sure of herself, 2B referred back to what he had said in the desert.

The aliens' discovery

Back at the park's entrance, the pair met a flying machine carrying a white flag. First, it thanked the androids for killing the "broken machine," then it offered to guide them to its village. Skeptical, but curious, 9S and 2B decided to follow it. The machine led them through a hidden passage in the amusement park, then through a series of suspension bridges all the way to the edge of a forest dominated by a massive tree. On the platforms surrounding the trunk, machines of various sizes and shapes were waving white flags. Pascal, the community's pacifist leader, greeted the androids, who were more suspicious than ever. His first intention was to convince them of his wish to live in peace with them. To demonstrate his good faith, the leader invited 2B and 9S to mingle with the machines and witness their commitment to peace for themselves. Here a loving family, there a troop of harmless kids, and further away a heartbreaking seducer: the hamlet appeared to be safe. In order to convince his guests, Pascal mentioned the friendly relationship he had allegedly established with Anemone, the resistance leader.

He entrusted them with a fuel filter that Anemone had supposedly requested, and expected that by handing it over to her, 2B and 9S would definitively be reassured. Back in the resistance's refuge, Anemone corroborated everything. The give-and-take relationship with Pascal's village, she argued, was not only risk-free, but also profitable. In turn, she gave the duo an item to bring to Pascal. After another conversation with the latter, 2B finally admitted that getting to know the village machines could be an asset for the war. Suddenly, a very loud noise echoed. From the base, Operator 210 assigned to 9S informed him that two Goliath class enemies, similar to those fought at the factory, had just landed in the City Ruins, accompanied by a horde of bellicose machines. All YoRHa units were summoned to the scene to take part in the battle. 2B and 9S urgently joined the two flight units that had been prepared for them and headed for the air. The giant machines were no match for them and quickly succumbed. But as it was about to die, the second Goliath resonated with something in the ground, and exploded. The explosion damaged the landscape, carving a huge hole in the middle of the City Ruins, not far from the resistance camp. Simultaneously in space, the base's screens all turned red: the sensors reported the presence of aliens in the depths of the abyss. The Commander took the opportunity to broadcast a message to all YoRHa fighters. It was time to launch an offensive. If the androids managed to get their hands on the aliens and annihilate them, the machine's mastermind would be destroyed. She predicted that this would mark the beginning of the end of war. Following orders, 9S and 2B rushed into the freshly opened passage. At the end of a narrow rock tunnel infested with hostile machines, a door opened onto a large dome-shaped room. A footbridge led to the central device, probably the controls of what appeared to be a cockpit. A dozen alien corpses circled the structure. Behind a window, 9S also identified the remains of destroyed alien spaceships.

Adam and Eve, who had become the machines' leaders, welcomed their visitors. With his sword drawn, 2B attacked the former, while 9S took care of the latter. As they fought, the two humanoid machines recounted the aliens' downfall at the hands of their creations. But this event was ancient history for Adam. His interest in the humans living on the moon, however, continued to grow. How could men kill so many of their own kind and yet love them so passionately? The two twins had now set their sights on solving the human enigma. And what better way to do this than by receiving the help of androids, created in the image of men and women? All 9S and 2B would need to do would be to visit the moon and bring the humans to Adam and Eve for dissection and analysis. Naturally, the pair refused to take part in the machines' lugubrious project, and continued to attack. But at that very moment, claiming that time was running out, the brothers vanished.

The king is dead

After having informed the Commander of their recent discoveries, 9S and 2B were instructed to collect information on Pascal. Understanding the reasons behind these unusual machines' pacific attitude could prove crucial in winning the war. Pascal opened up easily, when questioned by the androids in the machines' village, and revealed the existence of machines disconnected from the network, such as himself. In the forest to the west of the City Ruins, a kingdom had even been founded by a community of machines attempting to create a nation. Intrigued, 9S and 2B headed there to better understand the behavior of mechanical life forms disconnected from the network. But a group of machines intercepted them at the edge of the forest. Unlike Pascal's village, androids were not welcome here. Covered in chain mail like knights and riding mechanical mounts, the woodland machines shouted a battle cry to the glory of their king and their kingdom. Galvanized, they assailed 9S and 2B.

256 years ago, a conscious machine by the name of Ernst declared the independence of the forest territory. He gave his own parts to his fellow machines, in the hope that they would also discover their free will. He was therefore made king by the machines of the forest who were touched by his kindness and nobility. Newly endowed with egos and empathy thanks to the king's sacrifice, the kingdom's subjects made a point of developing a haven of peace in the forest, in accordance with their sovereign's vision. Over a century later, the king passed away as a result of having distributed all his parts. His final wishes were placed in a baby machine, with the hope that one day this future king could once again guide the woodland people.

2B and 9S eliminated the knight machines and continued on their way through the forest, pushing back wave after wave of soldiers defending their lands. Increasingly troubled by the behavior of his so-called natural opponents, the scout 9S could not help but try to analyze the situation. How could machines, mere weapons, understand a concept as complex as loyalty? The more he cogitated, the less sense it all made; although he was still convinced of the danger they represented.

On the other side of the bridge, overlooking the chasm which divided the forest in two, was the king's castle. 9S and 2B crushed the last pockets of resistance that had taken refuge there, and eventually reached the throne room. The room was empty, or almost. An infant was nestled in a baby carriage, all alone, abandoned by the soldiers who had left to protect the kingdom on its behalf. In a crash, a blade emerged from the rooftops and struck the baby, skewered like a vulgar steak. Thrown back a few steps by the shock wave, 9S and 2B received information from the base about the individual who had just appeared. Code name A2, this YoRHa type android with long white hair had been wanted for a long time by the command for desertion. The issued order was formal: to eliminate the target, before she went on the offensive. The soldiers followed their orders, but the altercation came to a sudden end when A2 decided to flee. Before losing sight of her, 9S could not help but inquire about the reason for her betrayal. She whispered in response that if anyone was guilty of treason it was the YoRHa command. With these disturbing words, A2 disappeared. Tormented by this event, 9S decided to call upon Pascal's knowledge. But the machine could only confirm that A2 was a threat. Caught at an impasse, 2B therefore suggested retreating to the resistance camp, while waiting for the next orders.

Naval battle

Anemone informed the YoRHa duo of the imminent docking of a supply carrier on the Pacific shore. 9S and 2B were designated to clean up the coast occupied by a battalion of machines. Just as their mission was coming to a spectacular end, the androids received an emergency message from the base. Offshore, the ship was under attack from enemy fire. The entire YoRHa contingent was being rallied to defend it. Once again, the pair jumped into their deployed flight units and headed for the sea. While hovering above the aircraft carrier's position, 9S and 2B attempted to repel the armadas of flying machines bombing the submersible's wide surface. After a series of chaotic scuffles, 9S's sensors went crazy. A huge enemy was nearby. Grün, a titanic machine, emerged from the depths and devoured the aircraft carrier, crushed as if it were candy. Since the YoRHa flight units could not defeat this monster on their own, the orbital base launched a satellite laser strike. But it failed, pushed back by the machine's electromagnetic field. 9S thus urged 2B to use a cannon located on the shore: according to him, the explosive power should damage Grün. Yet another failure. The machine rose. Extracting itself from the water as if the vast ocean had given birth to it, its Dantesque body rose until the mountain serving as its skull skimmed the clouds. It attacked 2B and 9S, saved in extremis by Pascal and the village machines who had come to help them. 9S finally decided to take drastic action. He clung to a nuclear missile that he steered right into the colossus's mouth. The explosion spread within a radius of several hundred meters. All communications with the base were down.

Humanity's mimes

His conscience was intact, but not his body. 9S's mind wandered, lost in a digital space composed of a complex entanglement of paths: a data maze. Little by little, the android recovered his memories. He thought that the machine network had most likely tried to protect itself during the impact, and that the defenses against intrusion had therefore briefly come down. Or maybe the electromagnetic pulses had interfered with it. In any event, 9S was now drifting through the mechanical life forms' network. He might as well take the opportunity to investigate. While browsing through the machine archives and the way they had tried to imitate humans, 9S discovered that failure appeared to be their goal. A voice called out to him from the network, Adam's voice. He claimed that hatred was the only real purpose of life, because it was driven by the desire to die, mankind's prominent characteristic. His opinion shook 9S, who began to question himself about his own urges, and his feelings towards 2B. Adam tormented 9S, until he could no longer stand it and begged for everything to stop.

The remains of countless YoRHa units who had fallen in battle washed up on the shore, and 2B was struggling to stand up. Immobilized on the horizon, as if it had always been part of the scenery, stood the smoking enemy who had cut down all these bodies. But 9S was nowhere to be found in the heap. Worried, his partner set out in search of him. Although barely perceptible, Pod 042 managed to locate the signal of his black box, not far from the crater created by the destruction of the Goliath in the City Ruins' center. 2B followed the trail into a strange underground town. It was one of Adam's creations, stemming from his fascination with humanity. Although clearly shaped to reflect human civilization, no one would ever mistake it for one of mankind's actual creations. Instead it looked like a forger's work, a carbon copy lacking the original's authenticity. Everything—the facades, the walls, the streets—was creamy white, as blank as a canvas waiting to be painted on. In the square near the bell tower, 2B met the forger, Adam. The humanoid machine welcomed the android like a hunter catching his prey.

Immortal by virtue of the network which allowed them to reincarnate themselves, machines remained incapable of grasping the concept of death. Yet death was what enabled humans to truly exist and to thrive. It gave them a reason to live. To achieve this state, Adam had therefore cut himself off from the network and organized the conditions for this meeting by capturing 9S, crucified against one side of the bell tower. When she spotted her teammate's injured body, 2B exploded with rage—as expected. Determined to risk his life in order to experience the thrill of existence, Adam had staged the dramatic circumstances of the upcoming duel. And of his own demise. With a clean blow, 2B pierced her opponent with her katana, rotated the blade, and then disemboweled him. Adam collapsed into a puddle of red liquid resembling blood, as an eternal mimic of humanity. He had longed for it: death awaited him, dark and cold. Relieved, 2B retrieved 9S and sent him to the headquarters so that he could recover his functions. Meanwhile, she stayed on Earth and received a call from the Commander. The latter informed her that Adam's death had caused half of the deployed machines on the planet to lose their connection to the network. Furthermore, the loss of one of their leaders had seriously damaged cohesion among their ranks. Soon, the androids could possibly win the war. But for the time being, the command needed to collect more information. So once again, 2B was ordered to investigate the machines' activities. She contacted Pascal, who informed her of the existence of a community outside the network, who had taken refuge in the abandoned factory. Their representatives wished to sign a peace treaty with the machines' village. 2B agreed to join Pascal on site.

Perishing in the name God

Hidden away in his quarters on the orbital base, 9S initiated a self-hacking procedure to repair his damaged circuits. As a technical support, his Pod 152 was concerned about potential corruptive elements that could have infiltrated his system during Adam's visit. However, after a quick check of his sensory systems and memory, 9S ruled out the likelihood of any virus having infected his program. Everything was running perfectly. Nevertheless, when he logged into the base server to download his data, he detected a failure. The computer distortion turned out to be quite serious. Enough for 9S to feel the need to search for the cause directly in the command's data center. By following the trail, he accessed the archives of Project YoRHa. A document caught his attention. It seemed to indicate that the Council of Humanity had been designed within Project YoRHa's framework. But, he wondered, was it not the opposite? 9S unfortunately did not have time to dwell on this. 2B had sent a distress signal from Earth.

Instead of a community, 2B found herself confronted with a sect worshiping God. As she entered their hideout, the machines lost their minds and started to attack indistinctly allies and enemies alike, yelling their mantra: "We shall become gods." As they delivered every assault in their power, they proclaimed that they would find salvation in death. And all must discover this—and therefore die. Grappling with hordes of fanatics swarming from all sides, 2B waited for someone to answer her call.

Using the base's state-of-the-art technology, 9S directly hacked the factory's systems and managed to clear a secure path for his teammate.

The prodigious hacker caught his breath for a moment, then set off to meet the Commander. He only had one thing on his mind: the Council of Humanity had been invented by the YoRHa units? And forced to acknowledge her subaltern's insight, the Commander confessed everything.

Eve's grief

Lying on his bed, 9S was thinking, confused and dubious. The human race, annihilated? How would he announce this news to 2B? The red alert rang out in the base. All YoRHa units were requested to join the battle stations. The machines had stormed the resistance camp. They had arrived in large numbers, driven by a fury more ferocious than usual, and had begun to devour the androids. It was a way for them to further their evolutionary process as their natural enemies were gaining ground in the war against them. In short, they were fulfilling their original function: killing androids. On site, 2B was struggling to contain the assault of a Goliath class enemy. Already on his way, 9S was approaching the area aboard his flight unit. Drawn to the battlefield by the signal from his ally's black box, he spotted her opponent and ejected himself from his vehicle in mid-air. The metallic mass crashed into the machine, completely destroyed by the impact. 9S plummeted heavily to the ground. 2B hurried to his side. He did not seem injured.

A silhouette rose from the machine's smoking ruins. Eve was furious. Sorrow was eating away at him. Androids had murdered his brother—his only brother, his only family. They would all die for this affront. From all sides, dozens of machines flocked towards Eve. They reacted to his emotions. The rusty carcasses coagulated around their leader, magnetized by his rage. Something was taking shape. A kind of loose sphere resembling an atomic particle, made of countless pieces of scrap metal gravitating around Eve similar to electrons revolving around an atom. 2B and 9S attempted an unsuccessful first assault. As long as machines protected him and gave him their life force, no physical attack would harm Eve. 9S initiated a hacking attempt. If he succeeded in disabling his ability to control objects, Eve would lose control of the machines. Once he had infiltrated the enemy's circuits, the android had a front-row seat. Eve's entire psyche, exposed, was revealed to him. His grief. His loneliness. His lack of understanding. Why did his brother have to die? He was everything to him. He had collapsed in a heartbeat. 9S made progress in this maze of emotional data, breaking down security barriers, avoiding traps that were laid for him. Time was running out. His pod warned him of a contamination risk from the environment. He kept going and reached his target. Contamination was confirmed. But he had succeeded. Eve could no longer regenerate himself. Back in the physical world, 9S and 2B combined their attacks. But Eve unleashed a powerful salvo of electromagnetic pulses which completely short-circuited 2B and 9S's combat abilities. Their pods took over. Burst after burst, they eventually brought Eve to his knees. He was defeated. 2B wielded her blade over the machine's neck. Eve whispered the following word, or concept, like a prayer: "Brother." The steel cut right through his head. His body collapsed. 2B sighed: "It's over." Absolutely not. A few steps away, 9S was dying. Contaminated by a mechanical virus during the hacking procedure, he only had a few minutes left. Uploading his memory to the base was not an option: it would infect all the androids. In any case, he could reload a previous backup. But his present self, the 9S at this very moment, in this very place, would disappear forever. He knew it. So did 2B. The executor's hands gently stroked her companion's cheeks. Her fingers moved down and settled on his neck. He allowed her to go ahead. She clenched her hands and tightened her grip. He tried to catch his breath, by reflex, but did not panic. Her choking sobs were tearing her apart. 9S arms dropped. His eyes were closed. 2B's wails were accompanied by abundant tears.

—It always ends like this, she moaned.

She embraced the lifeless body, while nearby the eyes of hundreds of machine remains began to flicker simultaneously, as if they were resonating. One of them extricated itself from the rubble not far from her. 2B was about to release all her grief onto the can when a familiar voice stopped her. 9S had managed to retain his data by overwriting the memory of nearby machines. Regenerated by the surrounding network, his conscience was miraculously intact. 2B dropped her sword and staggered towards the envelope containing her partner, relieved and happy to know he was alive. And together, their mission continued: to defeat the machines.

2B's requiem

In the base's command room, the Commander was delighted with the elimination of the two main units Adam and Eve. As a result, the machines' hierarchy was clearly damaged. A golden opportunity that the Council of Humanity chose to seize by ordering a large-scale attack to definitively repel the machines. 2B and 9S met in the City Ruins' center, the nerve center of the recapture operation. In their earpieces, a transmission from the Council of Humanity ordered the YoRHa units to do their utmost to complete this ultimate mission. 9S knew that it was nothing more than a smoke screen. But the rapid redeployment did not really give him time to reflect, or even reveal the truth to his teammate. For the time being, he must simply carry out orders. And they were simple. Both he and 2B would travel the city and provide assistance to the other YoRHa units in charge of eliminating the machines. From one area to the next, the guerrilla warfare led by the duo gradually allowed the android armada to establish its domination over the city. But during a skirmish, the machines radically changed their strategy and began to use electromagnetic pulse attacks. 2B and a few other androids were hit hard. The impact instantly deactivated their circuits and completely exposed them to attacks. Outside the impact zone, 9S rushed to push back the enemy offensive and protect the battalion. Temporarily rid of the machines, he tried to assess 2B's situation. But immediately all the surrounding YoRHa units entered into a trance. The electromagnetic pulses had triggered the dissemination of a logic virus in their brain. Worse yet, it had affected all the troops on Earth. 9S hurriedly hacked 2B to restore her circuits, but was unable to save the other infected androids who had suddenly turned against their comrades. Henceforth devoid of allies or even of the possibility of joining the base, the pair decided to upload their data to the main server through a backdoor before blowing up their black boxes. 9S and 2B then woke up in new bodies aboard the orbital base. They were headed for the operations center. The Commander must be informed. At first skeptical about the veracity of her subordinates' report, the YoRHa leader was forced to face reality when the units on the base also fell under enemy control. Through one of the possessed operators, the machines claimed that they recognized the stratagem's paternity and swore to destroy the base. Alongside the Commander, 9S and 2B eliminated their former comrades and headed straight for the hangar: the base would not be able to resist this level of compromise. And neither would the Commander. Subsequently infected, she used her last moments of consciousness to symbolically entrust the survival of YoRHa to her last two representatives. Forced to abandon their superior to her fate, 9S and 2B seized the flight units and headed for space. Surrounded by interstellar darkness, they contemplated the disintegration of their headquarters. 2B silently raged in pain. To avoid being hit by debris, the two androids began their descent towards Earth. Upon their arrival, four YoRHa units in flight immediately chased after them. 2B took control of 9S's craft and sent him to safe ground. Alone, she faced her pursuers. She was victorious, but suffered serious damage, forcing her to eject herself from the vehicle. On the ground, hostile machines reserved a nasty welcome for her. She managed to get rid of them, but death came knocking on her door. The logic virus had infected her too. It was slowly starting to corrupt her systems.

She knew that the end was near. She painfully embarked on a long walk towards the abandoned shopping mall, not far from the City Ruins. Since there were no androids in the area, the virus could not spread there. If she was going to die, she might as well do it alone, without contaminating her fellow androids. One after the other, step by step, her motor functions deteriorated. When she finally reached her destination, her hearing and vision had been severely damaged. Her data bank was beyond repair. And she could no longer perform a backup with the base destroyed. Corrupted YoRHa units appeared. But none of her offensive functions were responding. A2 arrived just at the right moment and eliminated the threat. Nonetheless, this was the end of the road for 2B. She drove her sword into the ground; it contained her memories. She offered it to A2, and begged the fugitive to preserve the future on her behalf. The earth started to tremble. Without a word, A2 removed the blade and freed the condemned android from her ordeal. In her final moments, 2B turned around and saw 9S on the bridge a few meters away. She whispered his name lovingly. The katana withdrew, and 2B's face fell on the cold stone. In a single motion, A2 cut her hair and offered her offcuts to the deceased: she had accepted her request. 9S exploded with rage, he drew his sword and started running towards A2 with the firm intention of killing her. The tremors were intensifying. Before he could reach her, the wooden planks crumbled beneath his feet and he fell into the ravine below. The earthquake was rumbling louder and louder, as if a volcano was about to erupt. A multitude of white pillars rose from the ground to unsuspected heights, reshaping the entire landscape of the region. Peace returned. A mysterious tower now overlooked the City Ruins' center. Built underground by machines, the building was first envisioned by the collective consciousness of the N2 machines as a launching ramp to aim a missile at the Moon and the human server, in order to annihilate the resistance and the YoRHa units for good. Then N2 studied the androids, as well as Adam and Eve. They examined the way they lived and considered the meaning of life. And then changed their minds. They had decided to transform it into an ark. Thus, the tower was used, on the one hand, to store memories and data on the machines' history, thanks to three buildings called "Resource Recovery Unit" located throughout the region. And, on the other hand, to propel an ark into space whose purpose was to reach a new world and colonize it with the information that had been collected.

A2's oath

Two weeks had passed. Behind the scenes, the pods were conferring. 153 initiated a discussion protocol with 042 and informed it that the 9S unit it was in charge of had been repaired and was ready to be reactivated. When 2B died, 042 had lost his assigned unit. But just before succumbing, the android had made sure to change her assistant's affiliation so that it would accompany A2. A decision was therefore reached by mutual agreement between the pods to continue their support mission.

Temporarily deactivated following the damage sustained during the earthquake, the fugitive awoke among the rubble at the sound of 042's voice. Following the protocol procedure, it submitted a report to its new mistress and offered its assistance. A2 refused. Strong-headed and fervently solitary, she did not appreciate the company of a talking robot. All the more so as the latter was incapable of making itself useful: it was totally unaware of the nature of the gigantic structure which had just appeared in the middle of the city. But 042 persisted: A2 did not have the required authority to get rid of him. The YoRHa unit had no choice but to tolerate its presence at her side, and thus explained her intentions: killing as many machines as possible. 042 therefore informed her of the location of a powerful Goliath class enemy in the desert.

The battle turned to A2's disadvantage when the machine struck her with an electromagnetic shock that damaged her memory module. 042 infiltrated the android's circuits and guided her from the inside to repair the damage sustained. As the self-hacking process progressed, fragments of 2B's memories reappeared, intertwined with A2's memory. Only possible conclusion: the fugitive's conscience had begun to merge with the data bequeathed by her victim. At the end of her memory space, she eliminated the machine which had entered during the electromagnetic pulse assault. Then 2B appeared before her as a hologram. They were not so different, the cluster of pixels revealed to her. No one could help them. All they could do was cry and scream...

"Shut up!"

Furious, A2 threw her sword at the hologram as she left the digital realm to join the physical world. The blade ended up in the desert sand. No more machines—all defeated—and no 2B—vanished.

Reaping death

When he opened his eyes, 9S saw two twin faces with red highlights. Devola and Popola were in charge of repairs at the resistance camp, and it took nothing less than their full attention to get the boy back on his feet. As 9S sat up on his operating table, the sisters told the story of their unit model. Or at least the snippets of information they were allowed to keep. They knew nothing about Project Gestalt, erased from the archives, or almost. They only recalled that their type of units were originally created to oversee a major project. At the time, they remembered, one of them lost control of her abilities which turned the tide of events–for the worse. From their point of view, even if this was in truth dictated by their programming, working at the clinic was a way to redeem themselves for the sins of their kind.

Still dejected by 2B's demise, 9S reluctantly thanked his benefactors and headed for the mysterious tower to investigate its appearance. On the way, Pod 153 gave him a short report on the status of the building. Most likely the work of machines, it contained a main elevator in its center and had ejected three objects into the air when it emerged from the ground. Arriving in front of what looked like a front door, 9S attempted to hack into the system to open it. But, to no avail. A message preprogramed by the machines informed him that to enter the structure, he would first have to unlock each of the three sub-units dispersed a few steps from the door. Each key could be obtained from the three Resource Recovery Units scattered throughout the region–the famous objects that the tower had ejected. Without further ado, 9S set out in search of them. A burning desire for revenge drove him. Naturally, he was planning to kill A2 for 2B's assassination. But, above all, he would not stop until he had destroyed all the machines.

The first Resource Recovery Unit had landed in the woodland kingdom, not far from the king's castle. He could not miss it. The imposing metal cylinder was levitating in the middle of the forest, piercing the sky beyond the highest peaks. Its first floor remained nevertheless accessible on foot. A strange inscription in Celestial Alphabet was written above the door[103] : "Meat box." 9S rushed into the hallway. From there, an elevator took him to the upper levels. One by one, he cleared the successive floors of the mechanical life forms he could find. His conscience shattered a little more with each machine killed along the path of his revenge. He screamed to cover the agonizing complaints of the beings he was slaughtering. When he reached the top, he destroyed the Resource Recovery Unit's power core and obtained the first key. On the ground, a defeated machine begged him.

"Kill me, coward! Kill me! Kill me! Kill me!"

103. An alphabet invented by the German esoterist Henri-Corneille Agrippa of Nettesheim, derived from the Greek and Hebrew alphabets, which was used to communicate with angels. Taro Yoko uses it as a gimmick in all his games, from *Drakengard* to *NieR: Automata*, often matching the letters A, T, G, C, which correspond to the nitrogenous bases of DNA: adenine, thymine, guanine, cytosine. The Celestial Alphabet, like other nebulous elements of Yoko's universe, such as the Red Eye disease or the multiple intertextual references between his games, are part of a creative process which willingly mixes the most contradictory and remote elements possible. One should not always see this as a calculated and measured intention on the part of the director, who generally has fun forging links, and later fills in the gaps in his narrative, as he does by entrusting the writing of the novelized versions of his games to the author Eishima Jun. The latter is responsible for adding the necessary coherence to Yoko's patchwork universe.

With each atom of his being engulfed in fury and bitterness, 9S grabbed his katana and violently destroyed his enemy.

Pascal's disillusion

Sand had penetrated A2's fuel filter during the fight. Following 042's suggestion, she headed for the resistance camp where the androids were likely to have a spare part. On her way, A2 encountered a handful of machines molesting one of their fellow machines. The android ripped apart the attackers and paused for a moment, wondering how to kill the remaining machine. The machine protested and introduced himself as the eternally pacifistic Pascal. But A2 did not appear to be convinced by his nonviolent ideals. The machines had robbed her of far too many friends for her to ever consider forgiving any of them. Hearing this, Pascal renounced. If he must die to ease the conscience of others, then so be it. Troubled, A2 considered Pascal's resolution for a moment. Then chose to spare him. As the village chief returned to his people, A2 entered the camp. Anemone, the troops' leader, could not believe her eyes: her friend was alive. They had both gone through hell together during the Pearl Harbor operation. On that day, the machines tore their families away from them.

And what a surprise it was for A2 when she learned that her comrade was negotiating a give-and-take relationship with the enemy! But Anemone reassured her: Pascal was harmless, and he could provide her with the spare part she needed. Following, in spite of herself, the wise advice of her former teammate and 042's insistent requests to call a truce, A2 formed a bond with Pascal and the machines' village.

At first, it only involved mere barters. Eliminating a dangerous machine in exchange for a fuel filter. A philosophy book in exchange for a few items and a little money. Gradually, A2 broke away from her solitary existence, built relationships and ended up becoming a full member of the village. Perhaps it was the refreshing innocence of the child machines that softened her. Or because of Pascal's idealism, who was constantly going on about peace and the protection of future generations. In any case, A2 no longer showed hatred towards the village machines–instead, she seemed to feel genuine sympathy, falsely concealed behind her directness.

Once again on a mission on behalf of the village, she was heading for the resistance camp when she received a panic-stricken call from Pascal. His explanations were muddled, but one thing was clear: he was calling for help. The android turned back and ran towards the hamlet, where something unspeakable awaited her. The flames were already consuming most of the houses and had even spread to the slide A2 had built for the kids. In the chaos, she discerned red-eyed machines, villagers who had suddenly been struck by madness, throwing themselves at their fellow machines and devouring them. Pascal informed A2 that he had managed to get the children to safety. As for the rest of his people, there seemed to be no hope. A2 ordered Pascal to take shelter, while she prepared to purge the village of its troublemakers. As soon as the job was done, she searched for survivors. None. Informed by telecommunication, Pascal was devastated. A2 joined him at the abandoned factory where he was watching over his precious children. But misfortune struck again. Countless hostile machines were gathering around the building, as if they had been attracted by the children's presence. A2 went out to welcome them in her own way. Followed by Pascal. Facing the imminent extermination of his people, he had no choice but to abandon pacifism and take up arms to defend himself. The android obliterated the first waves of enemies that swarmed into the factory. A few dozen at most. But in the distance, an enormous regiment was closing in from the air, exclusively made up of airborne tanks. At least a hundred or so. Too many for A2. Suddenly, a gigantic Goliath class machine stepped in, similar to the one 2B and 9S had fought on their mission at the factory. Pascal was in control of the machine. Whilst coldly and loudly repeating his desire to kill, he obliterated the enemy squadrons one by one.

Another Goliath appeared, but its intentions were not friendly. Pascal emerged victorious from the duel and then rushed to the room where the children were waiting–for eternity. Their small frail bodies were scattered all over the room, their small hands holding the swords that had pierced their own carcasses right through their core. All of them had committed suicide. Pascal sank into an abyss of panic and incomprehension. Why? But he knew why. Fear, he explained to A2, who was equally confused. Pascal, in teaching them emotions, had taught them about fear to keep them out of danger. But instead of protecting them, fear had destroyed them. Unable to bring himself to continue living with such a trauma, Pascal urged A2 to hack his circuits in order to erase his memories. Memory after memory, A2 dispelled Pascal's thoughts, the children's laughter, the peaceful village life... until he had forgotten everything.

The essence of the Yorha units

No matter how many times Pod 153 repeated to his unit that his vital signs were low, 9S's only obsession was to destroy the tower and the machines in the process. The Resource Recovery Unit containing the second key adjoined the coastline. Like the previous one, it was adorned with a curious name written in Celestial Alphabet: Soul box. Nevertheless, this time there were no machines to eviscerate, but a series of devices to hack in order to unblock the path. A few of them revealed information about the nature of the tower's operation, including its ability to launch a missile. A building of this size, concluded 9S, could easily fire a weapon capable of reaching the Moon where the server and the fake humanity were located. Another highly classified document described the backstage of Project YoRHa. Its content was a bombshell for 9S, since it taught him that the YoRHa units' black boxes were made from machine cores. 9S refused to believe it—to believe in an ounce of similarity between them and himself. He continued his ascent and, at the top, hacked into the Resource Recovery Unit's core. In doing so, he accessed his own memory space, where an entity was trying to erase his memories of 2B. Overwhelmed by an intense fear, he butchered it. Even though it was dead, he kept hitting it with his sword, as if to continue offloading his fear. The corpse took on the appearance of 2B. He burst into tears. And then into laughter.

With the second key in his possession, 9S was getting closer to his goal. But his circuits were becoming weaker. The many recent battles he had waged had caused damage to some of his main motor functions. If he did not perform maintenance quickly, he would soon shut down. Increasingly concerned about his condition, both mental and physical, 153 guided him to Devola and Popola at the resistance camp. Repaired by the twins, 9S headed towards the last Resource Recovery Unit's location.

This one was named God box. The YoRHa 210 unit appeared on the roof. The operator previously in charge of establishing the connection between 9S and the base had succumbed to the logic virus. The confrontation was unavoidable. The boy temporarily got the upper hand, but quickly exhausted himself, while the energy supplies of his opponent did not seem to wane. As 210 was about to deliver the final blow, A2 sprang from behind and pierced her thorax. The warrior removed her blade, dropped the body and stabbed it a few more times. The operator would never get up again. A2 turned to 9S, to whom she entrusted 2B's last wishes: for him to become a better person. This was too much for 9S: how dared she pronounce the name of his former partner? He attacked his friend's murderer. A2 parried his attack. The Resource Recovery Unit started trembling. Once again, the ground crumbled beneath 9S's feet. The teenager fell without having been able to satisfy his revenge. As for A2, she found herself facing a new enemy. An adult machine had just landed a few steps away. Its arms had been replaced by two rows of machine heads, which it controlled at will with laser technology. All around, smaller machines wearing buckets provided support for the one they loudly called "big brother." With a few careful wrist movements, A2 shattered this beautiful family and headed for the tower.

153 and 042 established a confidential encrypted communication. 042 had been asking itself questions. What was it feeling? Had it developed a sense of attachment to A2, 2B and 9S? Yet, tactical support units were not supposed to acquire a will of their own. 153 agreed. The mission and their duty to their creator came first. Nevertheless, the two pods parted ways in the hope that the other would not die.

Forced redemption

9S regained consciousness near the amusement park where 153 had dragged him after the Resource Recovery Unit's collapse. In the confusion, the droid had succeeded in securing the last key. All that remained was to open the tower. 9S visited the site and deactivated the three sub-units which were blocking his path. The tower's security fell. In the process, he initiated the hacking phase for the front door. At that very moment, an armada of machines, alerted by this intrusion attempt, landed on the scene. 9S was compelled to abandon the procedure in order to ward off his assailants. But the more he eliminated, the more they appeared. 042 picked up an allied signal nearby. Devola and Popola entered the scene, armed and ready to fight. Following their suggestion, 9S focused once more on hacking the tower while they struggled to push back the machines. But the building's algorithmic defense system was too strong. 9S was hit by an electric shock that knocked him down. Popola took over the hacking attempt, allowing her conscience/consciousness data drift into madness in order to generate an overload that would temporarily weaken the barrier. Between several spasms of pain, she explained to 9S that she was taking this risk so that she and her sister could finally atone for their sins. The door opened. Devola grabbed 9S and threw him inside before it closed again. As the elevator took the boy to the upper floors, 153 detected old data related to the sisters: a file that told their story. After consulting it, the pod wondered: why would Devola and Popola prefer to die together than to live apart? 9S held back his distress. He hoped that 153 would never have to understand this.

Rise to founder

Was there actually any good reason for why the tower would have an entrance? The materials were transported by air, not through any door. 153 sensed a trap. But whether or not this was a trap, it did not change 9S's objective: killing them all. The elevator finally stopped. The doors opened onto a narrow path suspended in a huge empty white space. Like Adam's city, the scattered buildings inside the tower resembled unfinished human buildings, a pale imitation of Gothic architecture. 9S followed the only available road. Corrupt YoRHa models tried to slow him down. How had they gotten in? Never mind. He made short work of them and continued his advance. A voice broadcast inside the tower indicated that a surprise awaited him in the next room. When he entered the ersatz church, half a dozen 2B models spread out in a circle around him. He placed his hand over his mouth, as if to suppress a sob, and then guffawed. He was decidedly happy to kill them all. At the intersection between hatred and love, 9S took drastic action. As he finished off his last victim, a faint tick echoed, then the booby-trapped bodies of the 2B units exploded in concert.

On the tower's front steps, A2 ran into the twins, both in a pitiful state. Eaten away by her desire for redemption, Devola called out to her. Had she and her sister managed to help? A2 reassured her, then rushed into the elevator. She reached the room where 9S had fought the 2B models. The blast had carved a crater. And the boy had disappeared. With 042's approval, the swordswoman agreed to search the entire building to discover its true nature. During her investigation, she came across a large room in which the walls had been replaced by massive built-in cabinets standing side-by-side. Their shelves were overflowing with books. A library. It was the one from Nier's village which had most likely been duplicated by the machines. Naturally, androids, who only needed to download the required information to learn it, were unfamiliar with the cultural and intellectual function of such a place. However, it would appear that machines used it as a data center and archive room, just like humans. For what purpose? And how could machines know so much about humanity? A2 hacked into the library to find out more. To her absolute amazement, entire sections of file registries extracted from the moon's human server were stored there. A particular document caught her attention: "Operational Summary of Model Number Two in Project YoRHa." Suddenly, a huge Goliath class spherical machine smashed the roof and challenged A2.

9S regained consciousness among the rubble. The collapse caused by the explosion had thrown him one level below and severed his left forearm. Glued to the ground, he was rolling in pain when he noticed one of the 2B models he had killed next to him, partially trapped under blocks of stone. His lament stopped. He touched the android's serene face with his gloved hand, then grabbed hers, which he delicately placed on his own scared young face. He groaned softly, his teeth clenched, as if to contain a deep pain—in his heart. He crouched down while holding the hand of 2B's replica in his own. Then with a sudden jerk, he ripped off the arm from the carcass and attached it to himself. It was necessary for him to continue his fight. Immediately, the logic virus contained in the corrupted part he had just added spread to the rest of his system. 153 recommended an emergency self-hacking procedure to contain and eliminate the threat. For once, 9S obeyed and managed to restore virtually all of his functions. Nothing would stop him, not even the virus that had obliterated all YoRHa troops. His perseverance led him a little further into the tower, where he met two little girls dressed in red who manifested themselves in the form of holograms: N2. They provided him with a document from the human server that revealed to him the cyclical nature of Project YoRHa, as well as the inevitable perpetual outbreak of war between androids and machines. Thus, 9S learned that the YoRHa models had, from the outset, been designed to serve as puppets whose purpose was to fuel an insoluble conflict and establish the authority of a fake God: humanity. In other words, what was described in this file reflected the exact course of events that had led to the annihilation of the YoRHa units and the death of 2B. The little girls therefore asked the android, who was now aware of this, if he still wanted to continue fighting. 9S was in shock. But these revelations only stoked his rage. With a sharp blow, he chased away the holograms, though without causing any damage to his targets which vanished into thin air. Their existence did not require a physical presence, and they could therefore not be harmed by physical means. However, 9S did not calm down and resumed his ascent to the top of the tower, barely interrupted by an assault of contaminated YoRHa units from which he stole a flight unit.

After a few minutes of fighting and with no emerging victor, the Goliath machine withdrew, allowing A2 to resume her investigation. She left the library and entered a new area dominated by a terminal which was installed on a platform. In the process of hacking the device, she met the red girls—for the second time. During the Pearl Harbor mission, they were the ones who had wiped out A2's squad before revealing the truth about Project YoRHa. While the two mechanical entities recounted the events of that fateful day to celebrate the reunion, the android became irritated and, like 9S, wielded her blade against the holograms that were tormenting her. But the more A2 brandished her weapon in the space surrounding her, the more the red girls multiplied. And the more they proliferated, the more A2 redoubled her efforts to get rid of them. The perfect loop, eventually broken by 042's suggestion. Instead of endlessly blowing hot air, a better tactic would be to exploit the weakness of the red girls' logic circuits in order to deliver a fatal blow. In other words, to let them multiply without destroying them so as to overload their consciousness and thus create a lag[104] which could be exploited. A2 complied, put away her weapon and waited. Meanwhile, her opponents held forth on the similarities between androids and machines, bound by their will to resemble humans; on the innate superiority of machines by the virtues of the network, and the useless resilience of androids, who should accept death; on the perfect nature of their existence, both one and multiple, finite and infinite. Finally, the red girls' egos split apart through duplication. A conflict arose among them. Should A2 be allowed to live by virtue of the evolutionary principle, embedded in their system, according to which species would become stronger by overcoming crises? Or should they kill her here and now, by virtue of the preservation principle, just as essential to their identity, which dictated the enemy's elimination? Unable to decide, the red girls and their clones split into two groups and fought against each other while A2 incredulously watched on, witnessing the exact replica of human behavior. Eventually they wiped each other out, and the android was henceforth free to activate the platform. As she rose to the heights of the tower, the machine encountered earlier in the library approached the elevator.

Top-tier duel

A few meters away, on board his flight unit, 9S also encountered the machines' resistance. A Goliath of the same size and shape as the one fought by A2 fiercely opposed his progress. Throughout the confrontation, the armored machine asked its enemy: why do machines and androids have to fight in a perpetual war? Why had it been created? Why did androids exist? 9S remained silent and chased the machine to the top of the tower where he found A2, grappling with her own opponent. He exited the flight unit and landed not far from her. Their eyes met. 9S dropped his guard, ready to attack the woman he believed to be a murderer. In the meantime, behind them, the two machines merged to form a colossal opponent, forcing them to temporarily cooperate against the common threat. But as soon as the danger was eliminated, the two rivals moved face to face, with their swords drawn.

A2, with her guard down, took the floor, urging 9S to become aware of the tower's threat, which she suspected was a huge cannon aimed at the lunar server. But the boy did not care. Androids, let alone the YoRHa units, were not welcome in this world, he observed. Humanity was extinct, the lunar server, an invention. And the YoRHa units perpetuated the lie, brought into the world to be savagely slain. The Commander, him, 2B: sacrificial lambs, all of them. Now, A2 had appeared before him, the one who had deprived him of his partner,

104. Computer slowdown.

of his reason for living. This alone was enough to justify a fight to the death. Nevertheless, A2 told him the truth about 2B, or rather 2E, as she had found out in the library.

Was he aware, deep down, in spite of himself, that 2B had to kill him sooner or later? Not always, not in all his countless lives, but this time yes, he knew, as it had already happened several times before his former selves died by the hands of 2B. On one occasion, he had even made her promise not to hesitate to kill him again. Because this promise meant that he would be able to meet her again, even if he would no longer be himself.

A2 was only the messenger, but she assured him that 2B hated this murderous cycle. She suffered terribly from it. When he heard these words, 9S's anger intensified. How dared A2 claim to know anything about his relationship with 2B? How dared she still speak her name? His eyes turned red, indicating contamination by the logic virus. He would not back down. 153 tried to interfere. But 9S immediately stripped it of its rights to think and speak. It was time.

Meaningless [C]ode (Ending C)[105]

A2 rushed forward and cut off 9S's contaminated arm. The fighter took advantage of the respite caused by the injury to hack her opponent. She repaired 9S's logic circuits and thereby protected him from death, as 2B had requested of her. She entrusted the android's body to 142, who transported him out of the area, then set in motion the destruction of the tower. As she gazed up at the sky, she contemplated this world, realizing for the first time how much beauty it radiated. A chasm opened beneath her feet, she was sucked up–the tower collapsed. Following this event, the machine network was destroyed.

A Childhoo[D]'s End (Ending D)

9S could no longer tolerate feeling this need, this fascination for humans when they did not exist anymore–they had never really existed in his lifetime. This literally drove him crazy. All he cared about was 2B, and nothing more. But each time, as surely as a metronome, his love for humanity resonated silently from the depths of his soul. He thought that since this desire was inscribed in his core, all he had to do was destroy it, destroy everything. This would be the best solution.

105. Here, the paths bifurcate according to whether the player chooses to play as 9S or A2 in the final battle, resulting in two alternative endings which, in both cases, may lead to the ending E, the ultimate resolution of *Nier: Automata*.

He crossed swords with A2 time and again, but the counterattack was fierce, so much so that he was knocked down. When she was about to deliver the fatal blow, an illumination disturbed A2's thoughts: a reminiscence of 2B, reminding her of her promise to protect 9S. The latter used this moment of hesitation to drive his blade into his rival's abdomen, but stumbled and impaled himself on A2's katana. He writhed in pain and suffered violent convulsions, pitifully slipping on his own blood, until his strength gradually began to fail him. In his last moments, pain vanished and light engulfed him. He remembered his previous encounters with 2B, the distance she had maintained between them because of the mission entrusted to her. He recalled the deep solitude he had experienced when scouting beyond enemy lines in fog and flames. He remembered how happy he was to finally be with someone. Like a family.

His condition was worsening. He began to feel the cold, and the fear of disappearing. His sight became blurred, but he could distinguish a silhouette, that of the red girls, N2, whose data was embedded in the ark that was being deployed.

Adam and Eve were aboard the vessel in virtual form. The former was holding the latter in his arms. Yet, they were dead. Their presence at that moment actually reflected the traces they had left in 9S's memories during the multiple hacking procedures and the android's fusion with the machine network. Adam asked the boy if he wished to join them. And suddenly, it seemed to 9S that he had no reason to hate machines anymore. Had there ever been one? Who had he fought for? Who had he lived for? The ark was taking off. He was given a choice. First option: 9S would join the ark by transferring his data, because, in his opinion, the YoRHa units had no right to remain on this Earth. Second option: 9S would stay on Earth and chose death, because he believed that the YoRHa units had no right to be loved by this world. Before dying, he looked up to the sky towards the sun: "Ah... So that's where you were... 2B."

The [E]nd of YoRHa (Ending E)

The credits scroll. In superimposition, 042 receives 153's report. All the YoRHa units' black boxes were disabled. The pods' monitoring mission of Project YoRHa had been fulfilled. All that remained was to initiate the last phase as instructed: the deletion of all data. But, as it launched the deletion procedure, 153 detected a glitch and asked 042 to suspend the sequence. The latter came to the conclusion that the data from 9S, A2 and 2B was leaking. Faithful to its mission, 153 reformulated its request to delete the data. However, after some hesitation, 042 refused. Its droid colleague insisted: without the complete destruction of the YoRHa units, the project could not be fulfilled. 042 declined once again. It could not resolve to annihilate these three units. On the contrary, it initiated the recovery process of their data. At first, 153 was disconcerted by 042's rebellious behavior. Deep down, however, despite the many protocols and mission orders it valued, it knew that it also wanted them to survive. However, it lacked the required authority for this high-risk operation and therefore turned to the player: did he also want them to survive? The player confirmed and the credits rewound. He was about to face the system.

At the helm of a small ship, the player attacked the names of the designers and companies that took part in the game–the creators–who fiercely retaliated with a hail of projectiles. 153 attributed this resistance to a purge initiated by Project YoRHa's internal defenses. The struggle was rough. It could cast doubt, challenge its choices. But in its very soul, 042 believed it was following the right path. It recognized it was opposing the mission entrusted to it by the androids who had created the program–that it opposed its very nature as an emotionless pod, a mere subordinate. However, when all six were connected, A2, 2B, 9S, 153, the player and itself could not help but feel something. A conscience. Emotions.

One title after the next, the player pulverized the system. But the difficulty was increasing. After several unsuccessful attempts to reach the end of the credits, the player received the support of a multitude of allied ships; scattered all over the globe, other players had come to lend a helping hand. Firepower had drastically increased. As soon as the last of the CEOs, scriptwriters and other programmers had passed away, the pods took over.

All that was born had to die, philosophized 153 as he flew over the City Ruins. And the meaning of life was limited to the battle taking place between these two poles. Thanks to its efforts and those of 042 to reconstruct the bodies of A2, 2B and 9S exactly as they were and restore their memory, the trio of androids received a new chance to lead this fight. For the same result? Possibly–or maybe for a better future.

Farewells[106]

042 enabled the restart sequence. 2B awoke, numb. A2 had killed her seventy-two days ago to prevent the virus from spreading. But she was safe now. The infected program had been deactivated with the tower's collapse, as her pod informed her. 9S lay alongside her, unconscious. Despite many attempts, 153 failed to initiate the restart. An error in the loading process of his personal data

---

106. This extra ending follows ending E, which itself, in this case, most probably derives from ending D. It was presented in Japan in the form of recitals performed during a concert. There are two outcomes. One is rather tragic and follows the script that was handed out to the audience. The other, which was performed on stage, takes the opposing view of what was announced and ends on an optimistic note.

prevented the procedure from succeeding. It was likely, according to 153, that it was simply lost. 2B refused to believe that. She equipped herself, gathered some supplies, and set out to find a solution.

On the way, the pods told her about the events that had occurred during her absence: the fight between A2 and 9S, the tower's appearance and its destruction. The extensive debris had completely transformed the City Ruins' landscape. The resistance camp, however, had been spared—with the exception of Devola and Popola, who had died in combat. 2B consulted Anemone, but did not obtain any useful information. She continued her investigation, traveling all over the region in search of a way, any way, to help her see 9S again. However, with no access to the base's technology and regular maintenance, her own body was starting to suffer serious damage. She was on the verge of exhaustion.

153 received an email from Jackass, a member of the resistance, addressed to 2B. The message stated that according to some files which had belonged to 9S, one of his last communications was related to the ark deployed by the mechanical life forms. Attached to the email were the time and location coordinates regarding 9S's ultimate interaction. They pointed to the exact location where the tower had collapsed. 2B immediately headed there.

A pile of white rubble. Nothing more. 2B started digging. The coordinates indicated a position forty meters below, buried under this layer of debris. 042 warned 2B, a first time, about the precariousness of her physical condition. But she only had one thing in mind, only one goal: digging. Objective at twenty-five meters. Then twelve meters. 042 repeated its warning. But she kept on digging out rubble. In doing so, she managed to decipher the ark's composition. It was a massive memory unit made from complex crystals that were usually enabled and operational—but were now all disabled. She had to find one that was still working, a part of the ark that was still alive, to extract information from it. The bolts she had placed on her wrists to hold them in place began to tear off her skin. Each impact now caused blood to be shed. Soon, she would obtain the key to saving 9S. But like an overheating computer, she abruptly shut down.

Two days later, 042 restarted 2B. Her efforts had paid off. The pods had found a small sparkling orange crystal, a remnant of the machine's communication system. The pods had used the data it contained to create a vaccine capable of accessing 9S's memory, and thus potentially saving his personality. 153 administered the vaccine. Once. Twice. Thrice. To no avail. 2B insisted. A fourth time. Still no result. 2B was losing hope. 042 and 153 exchanged hypotheses. There was a strong chance that 9S had agreed to delete his data, or that he had made the decision to transfer it to the ark. In any case, the likelihood of recovering his memories seemed extremely low.

Script ending

Three beeps echoed. 153 detected the presence of one of 9S's memories. It played the audio track. It was the voice of 9S, clearly in pain. He was painfully explaining what had happened to him. He had decided not to board the machine's ark. He had come to the conclusion that as soldiers destined to die, the YoRHa units did not deserve to be loved by this world. Nevertheless, he did not regret his existence. Meeting 2B had brought meaning to his life. His last words were directly addressed to his partner.

"Thank you. Thank you. "

2B's silent sobs transformed into warm tears. She remained motionless, there, alongside the lifeless body of 9S. Forever.

Recital ending

Faced with the eventuality of losing 9S forever, 2B was overwhelmed by a torrent of emotions, torn by endless rage and sadness. The temperature of her black box was soaring, her vital signs were plummeting. Her grief was going to kill her. 042 recommended urgently securing the body. At that exact moment, 153's sensors went crazy. The temperature of 9S's black box was rising. A beep and a heartbeat were heard. 9S awoke, not knowing where he was. Tears of joy ran down 2B's cheeks. She was happy.

THE STRANGE WORKS OF
TARO YOKO
From Drakengard to NieR:Automata

CHAPTER IV — ANALYSIS

W ar victims afflicted by madness, a dying humanity which, in order to survive, must face its own creations, a savage criminal who attempted to save the world in a race to the death, robots seeking the meaning of existence... When Taro Yoko's games were reduced to their most basic expression, the fable the director wanted to tell became clearer: that of mankind and its torments. Often humorous, Yoko could incidentally lead people to believe (and at times he rather enjoyed playing this role) that he was merely coming out with smutty jokes about human nature. But, in reality, he took his subject much more to heart. As early as his teenage years, he had witnessed the violence of human emotions, insoluble conflicts and adamant hatred. While entertaining himself in amusement arcades, with *Dragon Quest* and other *Ikaruga*, he developed the conviction that video games could, quite simply, change the world. Too far-fetched? Yet, Yoko stood by it: he declaimed and harped on about his love for video games to anyone who would listen to him during interviews. "I am convinced that video games have the power to influence the real world," he argued[107]. Had it been someone else, the developer might have been suspected of wallowing in blissful evangelism. Yoko, however, had distinguished himself on many occasions by the sincerity of his statement, which differed from the usually smooth and polished communication of the Japanese industry. He remained one of the rare Japanese creators to tackle unashamedly topics as (stupidly) taboo as the budget allocation for a video game or the precariousness of the environment. This refreshing honesty earned the director a unique popularity among his fans. The man, it must be mentioned, was not at a loss for words, and each interview with the press gave him the opportunity to add a clever sally or to reveal a truth that other Japanese developers would rather conceal. He did not consider himself to be an eccentric, but his followers communed with his subversive creator nature. Clearly, the content of his games had promoted this state of affairs.

107. *Games*, issue 9, September – November 2015.

The *Drakengard* and *NieR* games were famous for their narrative and mechanical divergence from video game models. This, as we have already said, was a deliberate positioning and their main marketing strategy. Yoko was well aware that he could not compete in all respects with the avalanche of major blockbusters that fawned over the player with a sense of security. Since *Drakengard*, he had given up on commonness, standards and expectations in order to clear the way for strangeness. But for the director, it was also a matter of sincerity. "The world is full of lies and desires, but I am under the impression that it tends to hide and ban taboos, he explained. You can write stories about love between a man and a woman, but you cannot write about sex. Some stories are about beauty and growing up, but avoid the topics of aging and decay. I believe these are lies, and I am not very good at writing lies. I just want to be honest with myself[108]." It was probably this wish to include everything in his stories, beautiful and repulsive, good and bad, without sparing the players, without sweeping under the rug what could upset them, which enabled him to earn the respect of his fans. This clear-sightedness, or rather this openness towards the morbidity surrounding him, made it especially possible to establish a link with his goal. Taro Yoko wanted to change the world through video games, because he had witnessed the blockages, wounds and endless confrontations which each day chipped away at its harmony. His subject of study, as has been mentioned, was human nature, or rather the individual, overwhelmed by his failures, his shortcomings and his mistakes. "Why would you bring all this sadness and violence on yourself?" he kept asking us in his games. His method remained unchanged. He would position himself on a human level and put extreme pressure on his characters in order to unveil a truth about our condition, which he would then render without prudishness or artifice. His taste for strangeness was deeply rooted in our inner struggles and endless contradictions. But Yoko never sank into a sad voyeurism of the soul. His passion was pure, his ardor moderate, his intention full of humanism. How could one doubt that? The heartbreaking caress of 2B self-administered by 9S, the distress and courage of Emil as he sacrificed himself for Nier and Kaine, the peaceful farewells between Mikhail and Zero: this was by no means the work of a cynic. Because they drew their essence from the impenetrable silos of our beliefs, Taro Yoko's games explored the most diverse themes. Violence, of course, in which almost everything culminated with Yoko, but also identity, madness, neurosis or suicide. A wide range. Our aim was therefore to open a dialog with this abundant work, to explore its content in order to discover the exegesis thread, with at times, we concede in advance, personal insights as our only guidelines.

108. http://www.rollingstone.com/glixel/interviews/qa-nier-automata-director-taro-yoko-w472664

DRAKENGARD: VIOLENCE ON TRIAL

A mediocre video game

Drakengard has a special place in Yoko's gameography. Without considering this installation as his more common early work, we could however still argue that it lacks a certain essence, a certain depth. The title suffers from a peculiar marketing position, somewhere between *Dynasty Warriors*, *Ace Combat* and *Final Fantasy*, and from its excess of outrageousness. The characters are cemented in their archetypes, the *gameplay* is approximate and the storyline embraces serious features from B movies. These limitations, some creative, others due to budget restrictions, should be emphasized as they shape the game's identity.

Only in *Drakengard* could one literally slay an entire army of children possessed by demonic creatures while a pedophile is trying to save them; only in *Drakengard* could a mother bereaved by the death of her children start devouring a giant baby. At this stage, some may have thought that it was straying from the absurd, and perhaps only see a gory remake of *Kamoulox*.[109] But therein lies also the game's appeal, which could be described as regressive. *Drakengard* knows what it is and what its aim is. When Caim beats up a villager on the ground who is asking for his help[110], it is not to indicate that the hero is a scumbag (the previous thousands of murders had already let that cat out of the bag), but rather to underline that the game is becoming aware of its own absurdity. *Drakengard*'s cynicism finds its limits in the game's awareness of its own position, its own barriers.

In its perpetual self-examination, *Drakengard* calls to mind a bad movie, or rather a B movie. The game is aware that it is the bastard of a combination of genres and that it fails to convince in every respect. It knows that it was broke and that its budget was missing at least a few million dollars needed to steal the show. This kick says it all: the villager is one of the key figures in role-playing games, who usually either has to be saved or listened to; targeting him in this way meant both belonging to the genre, but also taking a step back from it through some sort of confession: *Drakengard* could not be a *Final Fantasy*, so it rejected its symbols—just as B movies are deliberately created in opposition to the codes and legitimization authorities of standard movies, which they are unable to replicate for lack of funds.

---

109. A French comedy sketch parodying TV gameshows in which two contestants battle each other by launching nonsensical phrases that include anything and everything.
110. Shortly after the elf village.

For example, to save on costs, some B movies reused the same shots at different locations on the reel. The presence of multiple branches in *Drakengard* is based on the same financial logic. Rather than drawing a longer straight line (thus more varied and more expensive to produce), the game loops on itself in order to make the player travel through places he has already visited–and which have already been designed. Role-playing games actually often use this method, as they are a major vector for broke outsiders. It is merely a trick designed to increase lifespan, often used when funds are not sufficient to produce many varied environments. And much like the identical shots of B movies, this technique has the effect of breaking the feeling of believability. How is it, indeed, possible that the acolytes Leonard, Arioch and Seere are present in the side branches during moments when the player has not yet even crossed their path? The temporal paradoxes produced by this strange editing effect inevitably shatter the suspension of disbelief. But once again, *Drakengard* is not trying to hide its sleight of hand. Instead, it reveals the game's architecture by giving the player full access to missions and showing him the path to reach additional endings. Reproduced in different ways in the sequels, this mechanic underlines the extent to which *Drakengard* does not bother with facades: it admits that the script is delivered in kit form, but it also provides the assembly manual.

Thanks to this constant back and forth between its weaknesses and its awareness of the latter, *Drakengard* manages to compensate for its clumsiness and inaccuracies. It embraces a certain form of mediocrity and transforms it into a claim. The same is true of its excess of outrageousness: cannibalism, pedophilia, infanticide, gore, apocalypse of flying babies... It is not so much a matter of nihilism as it is the subversive path taken by a small freewheeling outsider. Since it was doomed to mediocrity by the economic context (its budget, competition and its bastardized formula), *Drakengard* therefore embraced this: it is thus in perfect harmony with itself. But this does not imply that it has nothing to say, or that its aim should not be taken seriously. If truth be told, its honesty and candor, as well as the way it presents itself, humble and unpretentious, helps to open the dialog with the player. And it is clear that Taro Yoko wants to talk about violence, and even more broadly about the search for victory over others, which culminates in murder.

The fateful day

The relationship between Angelus (the red dragon) and Caim provides a matrix for this dialog. As the game progresses, Caim's personality evolves significantly. Initially driven by his thirst for revenge against the Empire and his desire to protect his sister Furiae, the antihero gradually mutates into a wild murderer whose sole purpose is to spread death in his wake. Through the virtues of the pact, Caim becomes mute and, consequently, Angelus is the only one to clearly notice this change. Throughout the adventure, she therefore worries about the darkness invading the prince's heart. Most importantly, she goes on to mock mankind and its innate belligerent nature, the disastrous effects of which she has witnessed, war after war, century after century. In ending C, she even tries to put an end to Caim's barbarism by standing in his way.

It is easy to see the relationship between developer and player in this dragon-rider relationship. The hero is mute, a relatively rare phenomenon in Japanese RPGs, so as to help the player identify with the avatar in order for them to become intermingled. And the fact that Angelus can read his mind strengthens the feeling of exclusivity which exists between the two companions, not mentioning the fact that she is bound to Caim by the pact, the very name of which refers to all sorts of agreements between the creator of a work and his audience (reading pact, autobiographical pact, etc.). Thus Caim's descent into hell reproached by Angelus's warnings and sarcastic comments could be interpreted as a *mise en abyme*. The player is indirectly scrutinized and questioned about the legitimacy of his actions: mass-murdering within the video game. This is Taro Yoko's key obsession, which he revisits in each of his games. "Most games place the player in a position whereby he must defeat an enemy, or kill an enemy, and survive this", argued the director in an interview. "In some ways, it's also come to be seen as an enjoyable thing. People have fun, and there's something fun about destroying or killing someone. And I've always wondered about that. Why do people enjoy the act of killing, and why do they do it[111]?" Take this question, turn it into a game, and you get *Drakengard*. This is the question that Caim—and us as players—is repeatedly asked throughout the game: why? What do we enjoy so much about the virtual act of killing, defeating, triumphing? With this question as the leitmotif of their game, one could be left to assume that Cavia and Yoko were rather hastily sending the player to the dock. After all, had they not themselves designed a game that made it possible to slay thousands of people? It is true: *Drakengard* does not provide any answers, yet it also does not pretend otherwise. If Caim is mute, it is also because there were no words to justify or explain his cruelty. The violence produced by the game leads to nothing. Other than, presumably, to demonstrate that such violence exists. And this is, in part, the director's goal.

---

111. https://www.engadget.com/2017/02/13/how-nier-was-brought-back-from-the-dead/

Freudian drives

According to Yoko, the violence permeating the entire video game production, but also more generally popular culture, sheds light on the dark instincts driving individuals. In his opinion, we are, in the depths of our souls, beings essentially stimulated by a collection of aggression and conquest impulses. Naturally, he concedes that they do not manifest themselves on a daily basis because we live in civilized societies, but that they most likely exist in a "dark zone" hidden within us. Like Angelus, he believes that humans repeat the same mistakes—basically waging war against one another—because of this aspect. Without our "pretentious facades," he believes, our worst instincts provoking death and discrimination would probably be revealed to the world. This perspective is clearly reflected in *Drakengard*'s pitch, but more importantly it comes very close to the Freudian intuition known as "death drive", according to which men are dominated by their death instinct.

In Midgard[112], the game's fake Europe, our modern societies are nonexistent and conflict engulfs the entire continent in such a way that social barriers are virtually nonexistent. Murder, one could say, is almost encouraged. "Pretentious facades" have never been necessary here. It was under quite similar circumstances, during World War I, that the neurologist Sigmund Freud discovered the existence of death drives among those suffering from war-related neurosis. In a nutshell, the neurologist theorized in *Beyond the Pleasure Principle* (1920) that men had a death drive which coexisted with the pleasure principle (which is meant to keep us satisfied and avoid displeasure). Freud discovered this death drive by observing soldiers who were presumably suffering from post-traumatic stress. The latter showed two main characteristics: a peculiar fixation with trauma (usually war-related) in their dreams and a tendency to unconsciously want to relive this event in the present. He called this phenomenon the repetition compulsion: an irrepressible force that constantly came back and caused individuals to relive their traumas, for them to revert to an inorganic, nonliving, and therefore dead state. Most importantly, a crucial point, although paradoxical, was that the death drive draws on the pleasure principle[113]. And it is strange to see the extent to which *Drakengard*'s characters, each more traumatized than the next, curiously fit into the Freudian mold.

Arioch, whose children had been killed by the Empire, thus seems to want to relive this loss by eating the offspring of families who had been spared by the

---

112. Originally, the term referred to the world inhabited by humans in northern mythology.

113. In Freudian metapsychology, the pleasure principle seeks a tension release (sexual, in particular) in order to reach a certain relaxation level. Yet, the lowest level of relaxation matches the nonliving state. Therefore, the death drive and the pleasure principle overlap.

raids. She is later locked up for her crimes and left for dead in a dungeon before her pact partners come to help her out. Her death is the goriest, the most joyful and the most suitable for her trauma. While feeding on the remains of a Watcher baby, she meets several of its congeners and, overjoyed by the possibility of feeding all these (fat) children, allows herself to be devoured while letting out cries of joy.

Leonard, for his part, lets his brothers die to relieve his sexual frustration and fails to commit suicide to make amends for his crime. However, he constantly relapses into rapture over the young conscripts encountered in the forest by the group. His behavior leads him to try and rescue one of the children injured by Caim, claiming the young boy resembled his brothers, as if he is trying to rectify the original trauma by reliving it. Because of the death drive, he is very nearly touched by the Grim Reaper when the young fighter, who turned out to be possessed, rises from the dead and throws himself on him. His journey is a good example of the irrepressible repetition compulsion: his desires torment him throughout the game, he tries to get rid of them, but systematically ends up revealing his true nature when in contact with children, through lines of dialog that betray his craving for sex—in which he then takes a certain pride. Moreover, he also welcomes the prospect of an afterlife with happiness, sacrificing himself for Seere, the cutest little boy.

As for Caim, his case is perhaps the most representative of all. Although he had witnessed the death of his parents, who were devoured by a dragon, he forms a pact with a representative (in *Drakengard*, dragons are asexual but choose male or female traits according to their preferences) of this species and embarked on a crazy murderous quest with her. The death drive could hardly be more obvious, in addition to perfectly overlapping with the pleasure principle as shown in ending C: after having slaughtered Angelus, Caim hurries to face off against the dragon army that just arrived, holding his sword, with a wry smile and ardor burning in his eyes. Clearly, he would not survive.

To add grist to Taro Yoko's intuition mill, in 1929, Freud published *Civilization and Its Discontents*, a book which analyzes this death drive by raising the question of whether or not humanity is condemned by this inner darkness. Did the everlasting resurgence of this death drive mean that, in a sense, we are condemned to destruction and repeated wars as Yoko seems to suggest? Naturally, *Civilization and Its Discontents* does not answer this question, carefully leaving the issue unresolved. But the book does state that, from its morals to its institutions, its culture and its art, civilization fundamentally depends on this inner confrontation between the life drive and the death drive. So, does this mean that humanity's evil is lurking in our individual destructive impulses?

Drakengard appears to adhere to this hypothesis in the apocalyptic endings B, C and D, respectively triggered by the neuroses of Inuart, Manah and Seere. After all, why not? The whole game seems to keep harping on about its death drives, with each of its narrative loops leading to a worse end for the world than the previous one. And Yoko, himself, seems to advocate the psychoanalytic thesis. But the director also regularly employs another notion to contextualize violence which falls outside the scope of this field: the norm.

The social norm questioning the entertainment norm

Yoko regularly associates the notion of violence with the norm or normativeness concept. He often uses it to question the positioning of video games regarding their brutality, as indicated in this statement: "Is it normal to reward the hero at the end of the game after he has left a trail of lifeless bodies in his wake?" In video games, we all know that the answer to that question is yes. Difficult to pretend otherwise. With the top annual sales dominated for years by shooters, the video game norm is clear. Killing, with bullets, blades or any other means, has long established itself as the most popular video game action in the world; no need to be a genius statistician to understand this. Most of the time, norm is an instinct—and what deviates from it is obvious. In rarer cases, a subversive game might blur the lines and cast doubt on our certainties. And because it examines and tests our preconceptions, *Drakengard* positions itself in this gray area. Norm here is often far from evident. It exists merely to be questioned.

Before getting into the details of the analysis, two types of norms questioned by the game must be distinguished: the video game norm and the social norm. The latter is one of the leading concepts in sociology. The social norm involves a code of conduct, either written (such as a law) or tacit (such as decency), which translates the values of a society into potential actions of the individual. Most of the time, it is used in opposition to the notion of deviance, within the scope of a purely statistical association, to describe the behavior of individuals. A deviant attitude is simply one that diverges from the generally accepted social norm[114]. Sociological literature has demonstrated that the main characteristic of deviant behaviors is sanctioning by society, either officially (condemned by law) or tacitly (social exclusion). This rectification of deviance, or its alienation, allows society to regulate nonconformists and strengthen its values, while

---

114. The first major work to focus on this dynamic was the essay *Suicide* written by the sociologist Émile Durkheim. The French intellectual demonstrated that suicide was a deviant behavior resulting from the limited influence of social norms on individuals.

reasserting the supremacy of its social norms. In *Drakengard*, the video game norm, social norm and deviance interact in a circular way, so that its fictional universe and our real world can question each other. Through this dialectic, the topic of violence is once again examined.

To put it mildly, killing is at the center of *Drakengard*. At the end of the adventure, there is a high probability that the death count will reach thousands, even exceeding tens of thousands. Without really being the norm, this orgy of violence is far from exceptional in video games. For example, *Dynasty Warriors*, from which *Drakengard* drew its inspiration, comes to mind, but also many wargames (strategy games). Killing is generally the precondition for victory in these games. Murder is a standard means to an end, it is the matrix of the player's progress, perfectly incorporated by him. *Drakengard*, for the most part, is no exception to this rule. The red dragon and Caim gain experience by killing, weapons become stronger based on their use, etc. On the other hand, unlike most violent titles, in *Drakengard* the mound of corpses building up does not serve as a pedestal for the player. It is rather the very element which hastens his or her downfall, in ending E, during the encounter between the game's universe and reality.

Ending E brings about a sudden return to reality for the player. Caim and Angelus are literally transported into our world; and all of a sudden, the game becomes part of reality. The following must be understood: the transposition of the duo of heroes is obviously physical, but also symbolic. Caim and Angelus embody the normalized violence of video games. When they enter the Tokyo sky, they bring with them the many thousands of casualties and hectoliters of blood spilled in Midgard. The player, responsible for these acts, then finds himself facing his own world and social norms. This arrival in Shibuya changes everything. The paradigm has shifted. We shift from the video game's universe, where murder is tolerated, even encouraged, to our own universe, where the maxim "thou shalt not kill" is the rule. Caim, Angelus and the player are therefore suddenly thrown into the deviant position. And as mentioned above, the main characteristic of deviance is punishment. Thus begins the player's ordeal, condemned to death for his actions.

At first, it implies dispossession, with the protagonists losing all their powers, hard-won by the player throughout the adventure. The extent of the humiliation of this moment, which teeters on the verge of castration, must be recognized. To reach this outcome, it is necessary to laboriously collect all the weapons of the game, often to the point of tearing out one's hair. Hours and hours of wandering and trial and error, endless empty plains, countless gray castles and illogical riddles are required to reach this point. Finally in possession of

Drakengard's sixty-five instruments of death, the player shows up at the gates of the epilogue, more powerful than ever... only to end up stark naked. For the weapons are unusable during the atrocious, vicious and merciless punishment that is the fight against the Grotesquerie Queen, a sort of reinterpretation of the last judgment via a rhythm game[115] –without the possibility of being saved. The only purpose of this confrontation, it should be emphasized, is to punish the player. And finally, those who succeed in defeating this final boss, are destroyed by the fighter planes of the Japanese self-defense forces that await them. The murderers have no way out. What the player has acquired through blood–his weapons, his powers, his survival–is taken away from him by this world that does not tolerate his attitude.

Could *Drakengard*'s epilogue therefore be interpreted as a regulatory process, a powerful exorcism of video game violence through its uprooting? The real social norm rectifies the player's highly deviant trajectory, as if to restore a natural order to things. The death of the barbarians Angelus and Caim marks a return to common sense with the end of the game, and confirms that everything which had preceded–crime and savagery–was an anomaly. The message is a little coarse, but *Drakengard* raises at least one issue that most games chose to ignore: the glaring inadequacy between our morals and the torrent of death in violent games.

Where does craziness lie?

This dissonance becomes crystallized in the characters' psychology. Indeed, in video games, violence offers an aspect which strongly contrasts with reality: the fact that it rarely affects the characters who perpetrate it. In most games that involve mass killing (shooters, RPGs or action games), the protagonists inflict pain, often for fun or entertainment, without ever being affected mentally. But killing or being in combat usually results in serious consequences for the mental state, as Freud had demonstrated with his cases of war-related neurosis. So imagine for a moment the mental affliction from which Nathan Drake would normally have suffered for taking the lives of more than two thousand people in the four *Uncharted* games. Caim's actions are certainly nothing to be ashamed of in comparison. However, he is explicitly depicted as a bloodthirsty barbarian.

---

115. In this fight, the dragon ridden by Caim circles around the Grotesquerie Queen. The latter produces magic black or white circles that gradually spread towards the dragon, who will die with a single hit. To counter this attack, Angelus—therefore the player—has to cast his own circles and make sure that the color matches the color of the circle fired by the Grotesquerie Queen when the patterns meet. Otherwise, it is game over. The high output of circles from the queen requires from the player a strong anticipation ability and excellent reflexes to reach the end of the fight.

Unlike *Uncharted* and countless other games, in the treatment of its characters *Drakengard* takes into account the social norm that, in our modern societies, introduces into the collective consciousness the notion that murder constitutes, reflects or generates trauma. As a result, the madness that strikes Caim and his companions wraps the violence of the game in a layer of believability. It enables the player's action to be connected to a message and establishes it in credible terms. More prosaically, the thirst for blood, pedophilia and cannibalism belongs in *Drakengard*'s hell, because the atrocities of war, the processions of traumas and the end of the world unfold all around the characters. The characters' mental deviances represent an element of reality (and not of strangeness) with respect to the game's brutality.

Obviously, the trait is exaggerated (not all cases of war-related neurosis turn into cannibalism or pedophilia). But in principle, *Drakengard*'s question remains: can violence really leave anyone indifferent? The interrogation, therefore, also focuses on the plausibility and coherence of other games with violent universes: why didn't their heroes go mad, or at least become a little disturbed?

In a way, *Drakengard* sets the record straight. Through a clever redirection of this strange burden, its small subversive act manages to draw a veil of suspicion over mainstream games. In short, contrary to what one might think, *Drakengard* is not the crazy one; the others are. For which is stranger? A soldier sinking into a bloodthirsty fury at the dawn of the apocalypse, or a treasure hunter shooting hundreds of people and staying sane (and starting a family!)? But the game's goal is not to teach a lesson. It simply provides an overview of the players' and industry's habits by illustrating a glimpse of the social and psychological reality of violence. *Drakengard* is clearly playing its mediocre video game role, as an outsider on the fringes of (and therefore defined in comparison with) mainstream production. A production in which the chronic inability to articulate a reflexive questioning of the symbolic violence it portrays remains, even today, one of the aspects which partly holds back the medium in its stasis adolescent crisis. With admittedly much clumsiness and some awkwardness, *Drakengard* tried as early as 2003, before the emergence of independent games, to examine the motives behind this fascination of video games–and of humanity–for violence. In doing so, it laid the foundations for future iterations in the series.

NIER: THE CANCER OF OUR CERTAINTIES

Casting doubt brings peace

NieR initiates a paradigm shift in Taro Yoko's approach to violence. As mentioned, after examining the consequences of 9/11 and the American invasion of Iraq, the director revisited the reasoning in *Drakengard*: one does not necessarily have to be crazy to kill, but simply believe one is right. *NieR*'s narrative arc, the story of a sane father with good intentions who destroys monsters to heal his critically ill daughter, derives from this observation. The character Nier is unidimensional: he does not feel remorse, does not question his own intentions yet clings all the while to the certainty of acting within his rights. His loving father (or brother in Japan) role defines him completely. And it is not important, as he repeats many times, if to fulfill his mission, he must exterminate all those who would stand in his way, including Devola and Popola, his closest friends. The actions of such a character, cemented in his convictions, will eventually cause the extinction of humanity.

Violence, in this case, is no longer perceived as a deviance as is the case in *Drakengard*, but as a natural result of competition between men. Both sides have conflicting ambitions and one of them has to triumph over the other to achieve its goal. The solution to this conflict, Yoko noted, often consists in inflicting violence and death, such as in wars between nations. But the director does not stop there and extrapolates his reasoning to include the need to conquer, which affects other aspects of society, even traditionally nonviolent ones, such as sport, money, even love. For Yoko it is always a matter of differentiating through domination: winning against another team, putting corporate competitors out of business, denying love to strangers because family love is more important, etc. Murder, however, remains the extreme expression of this domination impulse. Yet, Yoko observed, men rarely have the opportunity to kill in a justified way in today's society. Therefore, in a sense, they cannot fully grasp what the fundamental demonstration of their desire for triumph represents. For Yoko, this is where games came in.

The freedom of action provided by a violent video game, in a way, allows the individual to experience without consequence the implications of what killing entails. In this case, the debate is neither about catharsis, nor therapy, but simply about the fact that bringing any action into play, in this instance killing, helps transform it into a harmless subject for analysis, which can be examined from every angle, with no repercussions. The video game's ability to defuse reality is crucial for Yoko, since he believes it opens up the possibility of changing it. His goal is to use this virtual space as a catalyst to demonstrate fake violence and deter real violence. To this end, the process he uses in *NieR* involves instilling doubt in the player. "If we do not have doubts, we may find some 'reason' and actually kill someone in reality," he wrote in *Famitsu*[116] *magazine.* His discovery therefore involved materializing within the game the abysses of perdition and violence into which our convictions plunge us, notably through the character of Nier, an infallible death steamroller controlled by the player. By revealing the desolation caused by the hero's desire to triumph, especially during the final revelations, Yoko wanted to challenge our preconceptions, our sense of justice and our view of the world. But none of this would have any meaning without the contribution of a particular theme that runs throughout the entire game: perception. The masterly branch B, in which the Shades' voices are revealed to us, illustrates the idea that certainties do not withstand the analysis of their disastrous consequences.

During ending A, the player learns that the Shades are actually humans, that his quest for vengeance only leads to ruin, and that the Shadowlord had every reason in the world to rescue Yonah. But his experience does not really lead him to question himself. He simply takes in the information, without attaching too much importance to it. It is only during the second run, with the introduction of additional scenes and subtitles attributed to the Shades, through this process of humanization, that the player is confronted with his own cruelty. It is only when he must once more kill Gretel, who has only just recovered from his grief, or the defenseless child Kalil or the Wolf Shade who witnessed the slaughter of his companions by Façade soldiers, that the player's heart begins to waver. Without perspective, without confronting visions, without asserting the existence of multiple points of view, doubt cannot exist. The question of relativity, based on the maxim that there is always more than one version of the same story, is crucial in *NieR*, since it casts doubt on the legitimacy of violence.

Thus, throughout the game, a kind of maieutic method unfolds through the rupture and convergence of perspectives, with the aim of reaching an aporia, in the Socratic sense of the term: an intense dilemma stemming from a deep examination of the nature of things. Violence, of course, can be found at the very heart of reasoning: is it justified, even when it appears motivated by good principles? But the game does not stop there, also going on to question different lifestyles and prisms—which are further detailed below. Through its polymorphous nature, the game strives to convey the diversity of the world and

116. http://nier2.com/blog/2014/01/10/yoko-taros-bad-thought-process-1-of-4/ Translated from Japanese to English by Rekka Alexiel.

human nature, to demonstrate the vanity of our certainties and prove that there is more than one truth, and more than one reality. As its purpose, the game seeks only to illustrate this, because for Yoko, who sincerely believes in the good that video games can bring: to cast doubt is to bring peace.

Patchwork

NieR constructs its ambition to restore the world's plural truth on the basis of its entertainment foundations. The cornerstone of its demonstration involves borrowing mechanics from other video game genres to open up its action and thus give the impression of a multidimensional universe. In other words, *NieR* diversifies its viewpoints by deliberately forming hybrids.

The genre, in literature and cinema, as in video games, carries a vision. A vision that can at times turn out to be monolithic, frozen by the codes governing it. If *NieR* had been satisfied with its simple action-RPG role, it too would have run the risk of being trapped in one genre. Instead, by drawing its inspiration from survival-horror, shoot them up or text adventure games, it avoids adopting a definitive and rigid form and multiplies the player's entry points.

This method of displaying all the diversity of a video game is used to support the perception theme: each genre reshapes the experience and gives it a different demeanor. Thus the game constantly eludes us, refusing to be limited to one category. Its reality does not really exist, as it can only be perceived through the deforming and successive prisms of genres. Just when you think you have figured it out and have exhausted its potential, the game surprises you by disintegrating itself in the interactive fiction dream of the Forest of Myth or by concretizing itself in the mansion in the style of *Resident Evil*. This occurs to such an extent that in *NieR*, the genre, with its codes, its limitations and its own methods, does not constrain the game, but rather opens it up and allows it to breathe, offering it another dimension. Paradoxically, this densification is also achieved by the player's loss of control. Indeed, in video games, changing the genre usually means changing the rules, or the camera: top-down perspective for the shoot them up, side-view perspective for platformers, etc. As a result, the complete freedom offered by the movements and the 360-degree camera from the RPG section is often challenged.

Thus, rather than increasing the player's room for maneuver, *NieR* regularly reduces it and imposes the constraint of the viewpoint it has chosen. It thereby succeeds in bringing together, in its core, several fields of vision, several views of itself, each expressing a different aspect of its universe, atmosphere or purpose. It is as if, deep down, the game had drawn from the color chart of video game genres to produce a patchwork, seeking out the right texture and pattern for each of its pieces.

Metamorphoses

Emil's mansion is undoubtedly the most illustrative part of this process. The vision here which had to prevail, the point of view which had to be expressed, was therefore the gloomy sordid one. Especially in order to set the scene for the encounter with the cursed character that is Emil. To capture this atmosphere, the entire segment follows the survival-horror codes and more specifically those of the first *Resident Evil* game. The player enters a large black and white residence, in which he can no longer use the camera as he pleases, as it has been replaced by still frames. He is therefore stripped of one of his key abilities, which allows him to check his surroundings and watch out for enemies. This causes a slight feeling of fear, or at least affects the sense of confidence and control normally provided by an action game. The rest of the sequence also copies survival-horror codes, with its narrow corridors, comings and goings, and hidden keys. It is no coincidence that this trio has defined the genre. It is used to generate a fear dynamic.

Solving riddles to collect the keys is the player's goal and it sends him all over the building. The resulting comings and goings assist with becoming acclimatized to the environment, taming it in a way, and thus building more confidence. And it is precisely at this moment that the monsters appear, right in the middle of a narrow corridor which allows little room for maneuver and, therefore, strengthens the feeling of panic. *NieR* thus imitates the basic old-school survival-horror gameplay loop: riddles, exploration, confidence building, and then anxiety caused by lack of space (the player is less likely to jump if the monster appears on an open plain). However, the effect is somewhat mitigated in this case as the controls are not as cumbersome as in a game of this genre. But this hardly undermines the original ambition: transforming the game's design to reflect the tone of the moment.

Façade also features one of these metamorphoses which is worth a closer look. The kingdom city, with its masked subjects and its thousands of absurd rules, is a satire of the Japanese society plagued by bureaucracy and the importance of appearances. This also applies to the scene in which the commonplace soldiers do not know how to help their young prince who has vanished into the Lost Shrine: should they find him and defile the sanctuary by their presence, or save face by obeying the law? Façade's methods clearly reflect the shortcomings of the Japanese class-based society, governed by the legibility of social labels and paralyzed by compliance with norms and traditions. Is Fyra's social ascension, in the center of the second arc, not depicted as totally pointless due to her hasty death? And is the king's mask, the symbol of a people hiding behind labels, not ironically portrayed as the embodiment of his power?

In Façade's dungeon, *NieR* therefore uses the puzzle-game framework to reverse the trend. The kingdom's rules, so tedious and restrictive, paradoxically result in the emergence of the game, since it is necessary to successfully pass through a series of rooms while following arbitrary rules. *Drakengard*'s desire to create a dialog between the game's rules and social norms is reflected here. Indeed, *NieR* literally correlates the limitations of the traditional puzzle-game rules (pushing this block, dodging that beam, complying with such a condition) and the social restrictions dictated by Façade's tradition. This parallel is not insignificant, since traditional Japanese game design, focused on controlling the experience, seems to be anthropologically mirrored in the important role played by customs and usages on the archipelago. "In Japan, everything is tailored," explained Jordan Amaro, a French developer in Japan who worked for Konami, Capcom and Nintendo, in an interview with *Rolling Stone*[117]. "You've probably heard Sheena Iyengar's[118] TED talk, in which she went to a restaurant in Japan and tried to order sugar in her green tea. The people at the café said, 'One does not put sugar in green tea,' and then, 'We don't have sugar.' But when she ordered coffee instead, it came with sugar! In Japan, there's a sense of, 'We're making this thing for you, and this is how we think this thing is best enjoyed.' "

Thus, just as Japanese life is determined by the barriers dictated by appearances and customs, the Japanese game is born from the control exerted by the developer over the player's actions. Taro Yoko's intuition that games could be used as harmless replicas of reality, as virtual stages where everyday social behaviors can be safely repeated, is reflected in this association of ideas. The transition between Façade and its dungeon thus conveys—in-game—the real link between social norm and video game rules. Incidentally, Weiss highlights with a certain exasperation this connection between the game and reality, when he breaks the fourth wall[119] by becoming irritated, in unambiguous terms, with the strangely entertaining nature of the trial.

---

117. http://www.rollingstone.com/glixel/features/splatoon-2-hideo-kojima-nintendo-japanese-games-w501322
118. Psycho-economist whose studies focused on choices.
119. The virtual wall separating the work (game, book, play, movie) from the audience and guaranteeing the accepted suspension of disbelief, namely the consistency and credibility of the fiction.

The purpose of this puzzle-game inspiration, which has the advantage of better emphasizing the rules of the game, therefore also naturally involved making light of the arbitrary nature of video games, and by extension of life in society.

Perception and genre are inextricably linked in the Forest of Myth. The transition from the role-playing game to the text adventure game takes on its full meaning when combined with the dream world that the game tries to elude to at this moment in the game. Dreams are made up of the intangible and elusive matter known as imagination. They tolerate confinement in a physical space with difficulty and are not suited to overly precise graphical representation. The use of the text adventure genre therefore helps render their evanescent texture. During the sequence, the progressive merging of the backgrounds into the dialog box which bit by bit devours the game space, conveys this renouncing of any literal and terrestrial meaning. Right up until the screen goes completely black and the world is replaced by words. The game's style then changes before our eyes and gives rise to a new oneiric sensitivity, inherited from an entire tradition of text-based games which consecrated the imaginary, from *Zork* (Infocom, 1980) to *A Mind Forever Voyaging* (Infocom, 1985). Once again, this metamorphosis occurs through the player's loss of control, as they can only scroll through the text. In short, the change in appearance comes with a different take on the game's universe.

Affordance

As Shigeru Miyamoto, the creator of *Super Mario*, claimed, the video game's form influences the way the player interacts with the product. This ergonomic design lesson entirely applies to *NieR*, which juggles between genre affordances[120] to convey the desired intonation to the player. Then, in a secondary move, the game seeks to question the form it adopted by examining the rules it induces. It doubles back on itself and cross-examines itself to discover a flaw in its own engineering, as if to question its foundations. The objective, as always, involves casting doubt and breaking the monoliths of truth, of which video game genres are perfect examples. This however does not always work out. *NieR*'s platform and shoot them up phases say very little about the genres from which they are derived. But the effect works in the case of the puzzle-game, oft berated for the absurdity of its arbitrary mechanics. Similarly, the omniscient narrator of the Forest of Myth's Deathdream, when he plays with the stage directions and incisions describing the characters' attitudes, reveals the artificiality and

---

120. The ability of an object to suggest its own use.

irreversibility of the text adventure narrative, entirely circumscribed by the writer: the player is not exactly playing, or in any case has no freedom, since he is forced to follow the path imposed upon him.

It is obvious that the diffracting perception effect produced by the prism of genres could not have worked if, instead of borrowing from other genres, *NieR* had invented an arsenal of new gameplay. Because players were already familiar with the genres–given that they are already formatted and standardized–and because these already convey an entire corpus of sensations and references, they thus immediately add their ethos to the segment in which they are employed. Their idiosyncrasy simplifies the process of putting things into perspective and also the dialog between the game mechanics, each questioning the other about its validity and purpose. Is the 360-degree camera relevant to arouse anxiety? Are the puzzle-game's limitations not undermined by the action game's possibilities? Is it really possible to resist the narrator in the interactive fiction? It would have been much more difficult for new gameplay, devoid of history and tradition, to impose its interpretation on the game.

In a nutshell, genre after genre, *NieR* builds a dynamic around its inspirations, which allows it to approach the game as a protean experience, which can be sampled in several ways. Thus, the question arises as to whether or not this patchwork is actually greater than the sum of its parts.

The whole equals something other than the sum of its parts

Let's take a break and try to recap. *NieR*'s aim is to cast doubt on the player in order to sweep away his dangerous and potentially lethal certainties. To do so, it seeks to confront him with several perspectives. In concrete terms, this is played out by adopting a profusion of forms drawn from other video game genres. It then uses this transformist act to question the validity of these genres' postulates, to examine their certainty. Through these successive metamorphoses, a dialog opens up based on a key question: what is the appropriate form? In other words, which form gives meaning to the game?

This questioning could be compared to an early twentieth century psycho-philosophical theory: Gestaltism or Gestalt psychology. According to this discipline, *Gestalt*, meaning form in German, is a structured form with its main characteristic being that it represents a whole that is something other than the sum of its parts. A T-shirt is something other than cotton threads, a video game console is something other than just computer components, a desk is something other than planks of wood. The human mind, according to Gestaltism, perceives its environment in such a way that it first identifies structured forms before discerning details. In other words, it is first and foremost sensitive to a whole loaded with a meaning.

This theory, when applied to *NieR*, helps to better understand the composition effect that characterizes it, and what emerges from it. Thus, when viewed in detail, *NieR* resembles a collage of game prototypes. Its parts, taken separately, have little meaning. Together, they look like an inconsistent exhibition gallery: a text adventure game, a *Resident Evil* ersatz, a few platformer and *danmaku* sections... Thus only with hindsight can *NieR* be viewed as a coherent whole, a structured form: a *Gestalt. NieR*'s *Gestalt*, the whole being something other than the sum of its parts, is paradoxically formless. Formless because *NieR* is elusive. Thanks to its multiple genres, it is able to build and structure itself so as to never suggest that it only exists as one form, one dimension. It is perpetually transformed and thus eternally deformed. Of course, dominant features can be identified: action, role-playing and boss fights. But *NieR* cannot be limited to the few bricks of its foundations—moreover it does not even excel in these areas. It flickers too much and is too elusive to even be assigned a definitive form. Does not *NieR* look more than ever like its true self during its unexpected mutations?

The structuring formless nature of the game reflects another theme that haunts *NieR*: disappearance. The world's disappearance, which collapses onto itself, the disappearance of life, which fades away with the Shadowlord, and ultimately the disappearance of the game and player, when the save file of ending D is erased, which sends *NieR* back to nothingness, the ultimate negation of form. In its outcome, the game thus refuses to be saved, to be materialized in a file. It transmutes itself one last time, into nothingness, thus closing the loop of its immaterial journey, eternally intangible, like a passing dream. In *Gestalt* theory, this return to nothingness, when the form disappears, is called "fertile void." It describes a new dawn, a calm state, a kind of retreat from which form can be reborn. But it could also rhyme with vacuity. *NieR*'s formless nature constantly places the game in this fertile void interval, from which spring a profusion of forms—platform games, adventure games, puzzle games and so forth—but also in which nothing clearly stands out: the multiplicity conveys the lack of a clear line and prevents the form from establishing itself. It is from this constant tension between creation (genres) and disappearance (ephemeral transformation, the ineluctable return to nothingness) that *NieR* draws its ambiguity. Since it is undefined, or rather constantly redefined, it can allow itself to glean from perspective to perspective, to overthrow the models considered as established, and thus cast doubt on the true nature of our perception. Inevitably, without the continuum of a silhouette to interpret them, our certainties collapse.

Gestalt versus Replicant: a philosophical battle

In addition to its mechanics, *NieR* uses its dense narrative web to strengthen the climate of uncertainty that it seeks to install. Except that here, instead of adding perspectives, the game's storyline opposes them, to better extract the violence that arises from their encounter. This is the case with the rivalry between Tyrann and Kaïné, which results in the death of the heroine in ending C. Between Gideon and Kalil, one driven mad and the other killed. Between the pack of wolves and the king of Façade, the former exterminated and the latter deprived of his wife. *Et cetera*. However, the aim here is to examine the wider confrontation between the Gestalts (humanity) and the Replicants (its "replacements"). Their struggle could easily be described as civilizational. Each one is defending the survival of its species, a way of life and a territory (that of the game). In a nutshell, they both have valid reasons to fight and kill. *NieR* cautiously puts both parties on an equal footing. Despite the second run and the discovery of the Shades' point of view, the Gestalts do not, in general, gain the moral authority over the Replicants. As illustrated by the long sequence which divides the game in two, they are in open war against the Replicants and do not hesitate to attack the defenseless villagers. And it is precisely this ethical stalemate that makes the confrontation interesting, with *NieR* showcasing it in such a way that it can be depicted as a fundamental philosophical conflict.

Let's examine the situation and the arguments of the first side. The Gestalts, namely humanity, found a way to survive a terrible epidemic. But they had to make a huge sacrifice: abandon their world for a thousand years in the hope that, upon their return, they would find it in a decent state. However, when they wake, the situation has drastically changed. The Replicants, the disease purification agents and the vessels enabling them to return to human life, have acquired a conscience and built a civilization. The Gestalts face a double threat: their inevitable relapse following the awakening of the Replicants, and the animosity of the latter towards them. In the Replicants' view, they are monsters and are fittingly referred to as Shades. The Gestalts' main concern is therefore their survival. This drives them to wage war against the Replicants. But on what grounds is their legitimacy based?

The Gestalts have two major arguments in favor of their return to life, and therefore in favor of war. Firstly, they were, in a way, the first to inhabit this world, which gives them a strong reason to claim control over it.

Secondly (and this was the principle idea), their future resurrection was part of the natural order of things in a broad system designed for this purpose, the Project Gestalt. They are, in other words, merely fulfilling a greater will, which preceded them and was expressed through them. One might thus argue that their claim for life is based on a certain coherence, a certain logic that is imposed upon them, determined by a superior model. In other words, the command to conquer the Replicants is instigated by a superior machinery which they obey. If an analogy can be made, one might say that in the same way as the mailman does his job to preserve the postal institution, the Gestalts play their role in accordance with their place in the overall ecosystem of Project Gestalt.

The Gestalt's vision of the world is thus organized around institutions, roles and functions: "Replicantization" and "Gestaltization," the supervising androids, the Original Gestalt, the Grimoires, etc. All these elements stemming from Project Gestalt are involved in the creation of a hyperstructured environment, which must achieve a single goal: to bring humanity back to life. In short, from the Gestalt point of view, the world's progression is driven by the macro level, by the ascendancy of a greater order over a weaker order. In the human sciences, this approach is referred to as holistic (from the Greek *holos:* "whole"). Human systems are not explained by units, i.e. individuals, but by a superior organization that leaves its mark on them. Through this prism, our societies are divided into a series of structures and systems which influence each other, but do not depend on individual behaviors. While this paradigm does not make individuals invisible, it does treat them as undifferentiated agents, recipients of a purpose that dominates over them. Similar to the waves of anonymous Shades that throw themselves at the player, always (or almost always) in groups, as if they are all driven by a collective and superior individual principle, which they cannot resist. The war between the two factions, in this case, is interpreted as the result of Project Gestalt's failure, the collapse of the organization overlooking the fate of humans. The Replicants' point of view is based on holism's opposite theory: individualism.

Unlike the Gestalts, the Replicants' struggle is not governed by an entire series of systems and institutions. In fact, this struggle becomes essential in each character's quest. Kainé seeks to avenge her grandmother. Gideon wants the Shades to pay for his brother's death. Emil (who is not a Replicant, but shares their struggle) wants to help his friends. Sechs, Façade's king, is burning with rage against those who killed Fyra, his wife. And finally, Nier is planning to rescue Yonah from the Shades' clutches. All these actions, combined, justify the conflict. In other words, to understand war from the Replicant point of view, one must understand the motivations of its actors, of the units that are involved in it. This is individualism's postulate in social sciences: communities and social reality are developed on the basis of individuals' intentions and objectives. Here, the system is based on the elementary properties of its parts. But let's be clear:

the Replicants' struggle is not imposed on them by an ascending diktat, but is instead determined by their respective motivations[121] [122]. The most striking illustration of this reductionist approach can be found at the end of the game and focused on the dilemma opposing holism against individualism.

Humanity's demise, confirmed by the death of the Shadowlord, begins with the selfish quest of the Replicant Nier, in his unshakable and personal certainty that the Shades embody evil; simply put, within individual-based rationality. The individual, Nier, thus triumphs over the personification of the Gestalt system, the Original Gestalt. In any Japanese RPG, this epilogue in which the hero defeats the system would be a happy ending, but not in *NieR*. In this case, there is no winning side, everyone loses, since this event marks the end of both species. Not quite yet, but eventually in a few hundred years. As though the victory of one perspective over the other, of the individual over the structure, of the unit over the whole, had upset a balance and condemned the world to perish. And it is in fact the case, as a balance had been upset: the symmetrical opposition between holism and individualism. When Nier strikes the Shadowlord with his sword, he buries the holistic vision of the world and imposes his individualistic vision. This is a crucial moment, for what is at stake here concerns nothing less than the nature of reality. And the player's subsequent choice of ending C or D either validates or rejects that nature. Siding with holism or individualism means choosing a standpoint in an unsolvable metaphysical debate. Depending on whether one believes that the whole accounts for the many or that the many account for the whole, we position ourselves on either side of diametrically opposed ontologies. The disagreement is fundamental, and actually divides the entire field of science, like a demarcation line. Sociology versus psychology, ecology versus biology, dialectical materialism versus atomism, communists versus liberals and so on. On one hand, the object of study is the global form, and on the other its parts. Thus, is truth contained in the whole or in the units, in the system or its rules, in the organism or the organs, in the multidimensional universe or the dimensions, in the Gestalts' or the Replicants' struggle? In other words, is the nature of reality embedded in its indivisible groups or in the essence of its elements? Nier, by killing the Shadowlord, shares his point of view, which

121. It is worth noting that this questioning of individual will and how it may influence people in the face of adversity is not dissimilar to the existential themes addressed by Ridley Scott's movie, *Blade Runner*, from which *NieR* borrowed the term Replicant.

122. It is also interesting to mention that this individualistic interpretation, given that it places the individual at the center of its reasoning, results in the humanization of Replicants, whereas in reality, they are basically nothing more than mass-produced bodies, lacking the ability to procreate. Thus, the emerging question, which of the Replicants or Gestalts are the most human, is only vaguely examined in *NieR*. It nevertheless reappears, though on entirely separate terms, as one of the common themes of *NieR: Automata*.

is also the Replicants' position: the individual takes precedence. The truth of Nier's world is therefore limited to the one he administers, it is subsumed and reduced to his own truth. But the player can then decide whether to accept this universe subjected to Nier's perception, or to erase it.

Either he lets Kainé die, while keeping the protagonist alive, who can therefore be reunited with Yonah, and in doing so endorses the reductionist foundations of the Replicant vision. Or he can resurrect Kainé, obliterate Nier, physically and in the minds of all those he has known, and thereby express his disapproval. This logically results in the erasure of his save file. Since it is no longer perceived by the annihilated Gestalts, or by the repudiated Replicant perspective, the game's world, stripped of the points of view which shaped it and henceforth devoid of form or future, fades away. Then, in a symbolic last stand, the system (that of the console game) takes its revenge on Nier and deletes him along with the file containing him. The gamepad in hand, the player falls prey to doubt faced with the looming ruin in one case (ending C), and the absolute void in the other (ending D): is the struggle worth it?

DRAKENGARD 3: LOOMING DEATH

Erasing the world

Drakengard 3 starts as *NieR* ended, sucked into the void by its violence. In the prologue, Zero has reached Cathedral City to eliminate her sisters, but only manages to get her dragon, Michael, killed and succeeds in losing an arm. This brutal beginning *in medias res* foreshadows the rest of the game: an endless nihilistic vendetta that will only end with the death of all the characters, including Zero. Even more so than in the first opus, in which violence primarily emanates from the circumstances, *Drakengard 3* is shrouded in an atmosphere of desolation and decay. Once again, the successive non-linear storylines aggravate the situation, as if the player is falling further down into hell with each ending. As the Flower corrupts the sisters' minds and makes them sink into madness, the world becomes vile and falls to ruin, driven to obliteration. The same is true of the second confrontation sequence against Five, one of the climaxes of this slow agony. The air of the forest reeks of rotting carcasses, Dito's disturbing sadism and Five's terrifying return to life: this part is evidence of the deadly attraction that leads *Drakengard 3* towards the precipice. The entire game is haunted by a suctioning vacuum-like force, like an overhanging premonition of the extinction and disappearance that plagues it. Every step forward is a step towards this extinction, every enemy killed a promise to soon reach it. The Flower forms the matrix of this race to destruction, constantly present in the background, leading the protagonists to their demise. But the game's main antagonist is nothing more than an allegory of *memento mori*, a simple materialization of the death principle: one day, we will all disappear. Thus *Drakengard 3* tries to explore and reproduce that indescribable feeling which sometimes strikes us, that anxiety conveyed by a lump in the throat when our mind is wandering and considering its own eclipse. In an interview[123], Taro Yoko expressed his opinion on the issue, and how it had influenced the game: "Suppose you were sentenced to death and would be executed the following day. You're just lying there in bed. At that moment, how would you feel? What would it feel like to die? I think it would be different from simple fear. Like feeling, 'Tomorrow, I will not exist anymore.' More than fear, though, is the sense of space while thinking, 'this is the end' and a sense of loss while thinking, 'I will disappear'—all of that mixed together to form one feeling. I didn't want to display a one-sided emotional view of fear and death with *Drakengard 3*. Actually, I don't believe people are so straightforward as to simply scream at scary things. It's much more complicated than that. For example, to create contrast when the enemies shout, 'No! I don't want to die!', we also included vulgar conversations between Zero and her companions to formulate an absolutely abnormal scene." Thus *Drakengard 3*, unlike its boisterous predecessor, takes the form of a meditation exercise on death. It is fundamentally more nuanced and therefore more realistic. Hence the fact that this time, the main character can speak. Unlike Caim, Zero does not passively endure the madness of her actions. She is perfectly aware of her quest's trajectory and its future outcome. She knows the stakes, and understands the Flower's and her sisters' nature. She is aware of every perspective, including that of the android Accord, who informs her early on about the time branches. In a way, unlike Nier, Zero is omniscient: she understands the world and what threatens her. And this makes her demise all the more unavoidable. Trapped in the tunnel of death, she cannot escape from this forced progression towards nothingness. Therefore, *Drakengard 3* primarily addresses the erasure of its protagonist, which is reflected in the depopulation of the world surrounding her. The depopulation of men, savagely annihilated by Zero. The depopulation of the entourage, with the successive sacrifices of the disciples who accompany the heroine, and Mikhail's deaths. And finally, the depopulation of the family. The sisters, whose on-screen time is in reality relatively short, only serve to further Zero's emotional arc, like electrons gravitating around a nucleus: with

---

123. http://nier2.com/blog/2014/02/28/an-interview-with-yoko-taro-by-4gamer/ Translated from Japanese into English by Rekka Alexiel.

each eliminated Intoner, it is essentially a part of Zero that disappears, as if she is gradually being erased from the world. Her hatred against One and the others is thus actually directed against her irrevocable sentence, which she must carry out herself.

The curse

To understand *Drakengard 3*'s nihilistic aspirations and its heroine's self-flagellation, it is necessary to examine the production aspect and its impact on Taro Yoko. As previously explained, the game was calibrated by Square Enix to resemble the first *Drakengard* and take advantage of the license. Thus, Yoko could only benefit from a relatively restrictive creative license. In an opinion column published in *Famitsu* magazine sometime after the release of the game, the director had been driven to despair by this situation: "Even though I was bristling with excitement at the thought of creating something new, I was also struck by despair. This is what it's like now for someone who entered the industry 20 years ago. If I may speak bluntly, there is no challenge, no invention or surprise. However, that's when I noticed something for the first time. The rule that I had set for myself to 'always do something different or strange' is what actually bound and condemned me to this role, like a curse. I was afflicted with a kind of 'repetition sickness' that overwhelmed me, and despite my aversion to repetition, I did it anyway. That's why I ended up producing the exact same ending as in *Drakengard*. It's not really new or surprising. And I feel a dark and cynical sense of disappointment for not having managed to change anything." Nevertheless, he added, this was a fitting conclusion for someone like him, who continued to "bare his teeth to the world to create his cursed games." He had failed to change the world with *NieR*, and therefore chose to end *Drakengard 3* in the same way as *Drakengard*, with the collapse of the world. In short, Yoko, the man who sought to break down barriers, had allowed himself to become trapped in the mental image of a barrier breaker. And that depressed him. In the exact same way, Zero suffers from the determinism of her condition, from this "curse" that leads her towards the inevitable. Through *Drakengard 3*, it is impossible not to see the expression of Yoko's constrained renunciation, forced to follow a path that he has not chosen, both a victim and an executioner, much like his character. It is clear that *Drakengard*'s universe burdens him, that it holds him back in terms of creation. He therefore precipitates its downfall, staging its lengthy disappearance through Zero's suicidal quest, all the way to the ultimate boss at the end of branch D, an even more complex version of the end boss in *Drakengard*. The principle is similar: align the dragon's circle with the enemy's circle, with the risk of having to start an eight-minute confrontation all over again. The changes of camera angle, which sometimes causes the player to disappear from the screen, greatly increases the battle's difficulty. It is no longer a simple challenge as before, but is now an insurmountable obstacle: the last command to enter in order to defeat the enemy appears in the middle of a dialog on a black background, without any visual clues. In this case, the arbitrary level has been replaced by the bitterness stemming from Yoko's helplessness in the face of his conditioning. In short, the director is exorcising his demons. The death at the end is his creative death, which haunts him beyond all else, he who loathes boredom and routine. Thus the never-ending shift of the game into nothingness is quite different from that of *Drakengard* in that it is not based on devastation and transgression, but rather seeks to summon a vacillating feeling of distress and loneliness. A disturbing melancholy, before falling into the void.

The search for meaning

Nevertheless, *Drakengard 3* does not just paint everything in black. As Yoko suggests, the feeling of death is not reduced to a simple fear, to the distress of the afflicted individual. The Egyptian winner of the Nobel Prize in Literature, Naguib Mahfouz, wrote in his novel *Palace Walk* that "suffering brings its share of joy, despair is pleasant and death has meaning." *Drakengard 3*'s ambivalence could not be better illustrated. Undoubtedly Yoko's most desperate game, it is also the most sincere and gentle. Pearls of life and fragments of beauty are buried in the putrid mass of its vengeful and bloody universe. In the depths of its death setting lies a jewel of raw emotions. As if the premeditated disappearance of its world has precipitated the emergence of a desire to fully exist, one last time. Its most striking moments arise from this contrast. It is the second death of the buxom Five, personifying the carnal desire to live in a zombified state, who succumbs when her love for Zero is sincerely revealed for the first time. It is the gentle and amusing farewell slap given by the heroine to the masochist Decadus before his sacrifice. It is the disciples and Zero debriefing around the campfire about their last sexual experiences before throwing themselves into their final battle, the ultimate ribaldries before extinction. It is Zero's terrible and repeated distress when Mikhail passes away in endings A, B, and C, and the touching dignity of the latter when he must finally resolve to achieve the impossible in ending D: killing his partner. On their marked path towards the guillotine, all the characters, as sadistic and crazy as they may be, are entitled to a surge of humanity in order to claim their own demise. Zero's entire quest is based on this idea. Her forced renunciation of life triggers her pilgrimage towards death, during which she attempts to find something, a meaning or an answer to her fate. Her omniscience reaches its limit here: exhaustive knowledge of the facts proves to be useless in answering such existential questions. On the contrary, because it nips all of Zero's rational attempts to understand the world in the bud, it fuels her despair and the character's sense of being trapped in her relentless and irrational violence. The outcome can thus only be revealed at the end of a reflective dynamic, directed inward. Thus the game's intermittent tempo, slowed down by the numerous camp phases, provides the necessary space for the progressive deployment of Zero's introspection, notably through dialogs with the disciples and Mikhail. Before throwing in the towel, Zero, perhaps a little like Yoko who sees his career coming to an end, thus tries to give meaning to her forced disappearance. So that everything has not been in vain; to find a way to embrace what the circumstances have dictated. Thus, from the withering life forces arises a powerful will to understand the underlying reasons for existence.

NIER: AUTOMATA: EXISTENCE'S AUTOPSY

Our aspirations and our nature

In many ways, *NieR: Automata* follows the reasoning initiated in *Drakengard 3*. From the prologue, the heroine 2B outlines, in a short monologue, the ideological framework of the game: "Everything that lives is designed to end. We are perpetually trapped in a never-ending spiral of life and death. Is this a curse? Or some kind of punishment? I often think about the god who blessed us with this cryptic puzzle... and wonder if we'll ever get the chance to kill him." Like Zero, 2B realizes that everything that lives is doomed to disappear sooner or later. She is well aware of this, she who has had to accompany and then kill 9S dozens of times. And like Zero, she has asked herself the question: what is the "mystery" of life? It is the game's first pillar, inherited from *Drakengard 3*: the awareness of death raises questions about the meaning of existence. As for the second pillar, it is rooted in *NieR*'s obsessions: the certainty of our beliefs and the determinism of our nature. To such an extent that with *NieR: Automata*, Yoko establishes a thematic connection between his early works, between beliefs and meaning, and between determinism and existence. He describes it as such in an interview: "I often think about how you can't find the reason to live if there's nothing that you can believe in. We currently find ourselves in the same situation, in which our 'self' is dependent on science, numbers, religion, politics, money, work, country, family and those that we love. Just as the androids blindly believe in human kind, I believe that we are also blind to what we believe in[124]." Thus *NieR: Automata* focuses on how meaning traps us in an identity and influences our behavior and mindset, but also describes, as a second step, the tragedy of lost meaning. This is where Yoko's brilliant simplicity in narrating and exploring this philosophical dilemma must be recognized.

Namely two opposite species, androids (and *a fortiori* the YoRHa units) on one side and machines on the other. Both are, in essence, determined by a command dictated by their respective creators. Androids have no choice but to love and protect mankind as revealed by 9S in his final battle against A2. Whereas machines only obey a single instruction: destroy the enemy, namely the androids. However, as Nietzsche wrote in *Human, All Too Human*, "Whoever lives for the sake of combating an enemy has an interest in the enemy's staying alive." In other words, a species whose very purpose is based on the annihilation of another can neither accept total victory nor peace, as it risks losing all meaning. Noting this paradox, the machines decide to sabotage their own network in order to diversify the "evolution vectors," and consequently detach part of their forces from the mission assigned to them. In a nutshell, the woodland machines and Pascal have simply acquired a form of independence–of freedom. The YoRHa units' emancipation process is quite similar. Shortly after ending B, their base is destroyed and the android hierarchy along with it. The Council of Humanity still exists, but the YoRHa units lose their home, their superiors and no longer receive orders. 9S, since he is actually the only more or less healthy one remaining, ends up disconnected from the network like the machines: left to face himself. Death, for 9S as for the machines outside the network, becomes tangible, since devoid of the base on the one hand, and the network on the other, they can no longer regenerate themselves. Thus, with death looming, begins the struggle to conquer their identity, the famous *agaku*[125] at the center of the game. *NieR: Automata* uses this backdrop to ask a simple question, equally explored by machines and androids: does the meaning of life stem from who we are, or what we want? Can we escape from the determinism of circumstances to attain freedom? Basically, to use Jean-Paul Sartre's famous proposition quoted by one of the characters: does existence precede essence[126] ?

124. https://waypoint.vice.com/en_us/article/xw8xzd/does-the-designer-behind-nier-automata-be-lieve-in-god
125. The fight to get out of a bad situation. The Japanese equivalent of "struggling."
126. It is important to clarify what this maxim implies. For Sartre, existence is defined in opposition to the essence, and therefore in contradiction with essentialists. The latter argue that man is endowed with an essence, a nature, which is defined by God in some cases, and by the material conditions of his

Or is it the opposite? To explore the ramifications of this complex issue directly stemming from existentialist philosophy, Yoko plays about going back and forth with his narrative, alternating between the determinism and the emancipation or his characters, constantly comparing perspectives. The same applies to the exchange between Adam and 9S when the latter is trapped in the machine network. Adam, cut off from his fellow machines so as to become mortal and give meaning to his life, criticizes the puppet 9S, a tool of humanity with no desire or will of his own, incapable of freeing himself from the chains of his condition. Facing his own helplessness, 9S then begins to realize the ambivalence of his feelings, the conflict between what he wants and what he is. Yoko happily fuels his game with this tension: "My characters curse their own circumstances, but also believe in their own choices and continue to fight against their life sentence even if they fail. This reflects their commitment to their own beliefs, but at the same time, they are fools that can't change the way they think. I love that kind of foolishness in human nature." Tragedy, in *NieR: Automata*, often emanates from this feeling of helplessness generated by a return to the essence and the determinants of its universe. Thus, while the machines of Pascal's village have succeeded, in complete freedom, in building a haven of peace far from violence, their initial injunction—to destroy the enemy—is nonetheless reactivated as the android camp begins to excessively gain the upper hand in the war, and their voracious primitive nature precipitates the destruction of the hamlet. The whole emancipation initiative is destroyed by a brutal wake-up call: the machines are originally weapons designed by aliens.

A little later, towards the end of the game, Devola and Popola's story is revealed to us in detail. We learn that the two androids are scorned by their fellow androids due to the doings of another pair of Devola and Popola, the pair in contact with *NieR*, who virtually condemned humanity to disappear. A classic case of discrimination, but the sisters' reaction is interesting. Rather than take offense, they accept denigration as their punishment, in the name of the identity they share with the culprits, and constantly try to atone for a sin they did not commit. Even though it becomes known that this attitude is determined by a feeling of guilt inserted in their software, the question raised by this episode is

---

existence in others (social background, economic capital, etc.). Sartre refutes this thesis, because he believes that this vision turns man into an object, since like an ashtray with its predefined essence, his role in life would be predetermined. In short, he would not be the actor, and therefore would not be capable of acting freely. Yet, for Sartre, man is condemned to be free and accountable for his actions. Only then does he define himself by exercising this freedom. Therefore, existence precedes essence. "Man first of all exists, encounters himself, surges up in the world—and defines himself afterwards [...] He will not be anything until later, and then he will be what he makes of himself. Thus, there is no human nature, because there is no God to have conceived it."—extract from Jean-Paul Sartre's lecture *Existentialism Is a Humanism* (1945).

nonetheless related to the broader theme of identity which is a part of the game: if we are primarily the product of our roots, our nature and our determinism, is it not logical to share responsibility for actions carried out by individuals defined by the same roots, nature and determinism? Implicitly, the issue here revolves around a conflict between essentialists and existentialists over human nature, with or without a communitarian approach to the world as a corollary. Before further exploring the topic, let's take another example from the game.

When A2 first meets Pascal and saves him before considering killing him, the village chief readily agrees to die to appease the android's anger. His reasoning is the following: machines caused harm to A2's friends, he is a machine, therefore he deserves to die. Absurd? Not if we recognize that an individual's identity is primarily built in the community, and belongs to the "we," and that collective responsibility is equitably shared among all the members of that "we."

Pascal is aware of the machines' misdeeds, and carefully distances himself from them with his pacifism. But the "we" of his village is a subset of the larger machine species, as the destruction episode described above tragically reminds. Pascal never denies or totally dissociates himself from what he is, where he belongs and what his fellow machines do ("We Machines can be rather unpredictable. Even me," he tells 2B). His affiliation is all the more obvious because he is opposed to it. The character claims to be an antithesis of the image conveyed by machines, thus a variant of a "we" which he declares to belong to, but which he hopes to change from within. It is this that causes part of his vendetta against his fellow machines to become tragic, or even leads him to offer his life to A2. Because his existence, his "self," only becomes meaningful within the whole to which he belongs.

It is therefore, indeed, difficult to see the point of such a logic when it equates a pacifist android with angry machines that have committed crimes. It might seem fairer that Pascal, who has nothing to feel personally guilty about, should not have to suffer reprimands based on his background. But it is nevertheless on this very logic that our societies are built. One does not choose to be born French, Indian or Canadian, just as Pascal did not choose to be a machine. Yet, by virtue of their nationality, which is an arbitrary identity, citizens acquire rights, social welfare and access to services, as well as duties. So many elements which are the expression of a common heritage that binds together individuals, of which war is unfortunately also a part, and which catches up with Pascal during his first confrontation with A2. But although Pascal shares a heavy burden and suffers prejudices because he belongs to the machines' "we," the collective identity is also what allows the machines from his village to come together around a common ideal. This philosophical conception, which can be described as communitarian, is radically opposed to the assertion that existence precedes essence, and that therefore man is free to choose his nature, another of the game's leitmotifs. One of *NieR: Automata*'s main themes emerges here: out of the expression of our identity and from the way we understand the being, results a series of consequences, including the path that leads to the meaning of life. For existentialists, exercising their freedom to choose what they believe in is what defines them. Whereas for communitarian philosophers, although what defines them is not completely determined, it is at least derived from the being's position concerning collective allegiances and determinism.

Before ending E, *NieR: Automata* does not really settle this theoretical quarrel. It prefers to facetiously juggle between the two points of view, or even blend them, to see what emerges—and it is not reluctant to a certain amount of name dropping when it comes to philosophers to support its point. Some examples are given below.

The Woodland Kingdom perfectly illustrates the idea of communitarianism. The woodland machines do not attack 2B and 9S through a deliberate choice, but rather due to an instinctive allegiance of the subjects towards their king, and through him, loyalty to the kingdom, the collective entity they all form together. Since all the woodland machines share a common origin, namely that of having acquired a conscience thanks to the king's parts, a powerful bond unites them, which they seek to preserve. By transferring the memory of their late sovereign into a baby machine, expecting it to grow up and become their new regent, they reflect their shared hopes and intend to ensure the continuity of the "we" without which their existence would be stripped of its original meaning. Since man is nothing without the community points of reference which account for his existence, he is constantly striving to create and replicate the structures that stabilize his identity, primarily society. Here, the machines only reproduce what they have learned from mankind. The irony being, of course, that unlike human children, the baby machine Immanuel did not grow one iota in the space of one hundred and twenty-eight years.

Thus begins another interpretation of the woodland machines' turpitude, which derides the humanist philosophy of Immanuel Kant, to whom the baby's name refers. In a nutshell, Kant proposed an axiom that allows people to know when an action is indeed ethical or not. "An action done from duty has its moral worth, not in the purpose to be attained by it, but in the maxim according with which it is decided upon." In other words, the intention underlying an action outweighs the final outcome, and the intention is deemed to be good when the guiding principle can be universalized. The moral action is therefore the one that obeys a law that can be established as a universal value[127]. Thus the first woodland king, by literally sacrificing himself, is driven by the purest of intentions: helping others. Similarly, the knight machines of the kingdom, by transferring their legacy into a baby machine, act with noble motives: to honor their savior and preserve his memory. But *NieR: Automata* kindly makes fun of the moral law by emphasizing the importance of purpose. For ultimately, what is the nobility of intent worth here? After all, the woodland machines are a monarchless, disorganized and lost people who have been waiting for more than a century for a baby to lead them. The king's sacrifice is therefore of little use. The conclusion of this demonstration occurs with A2's sudden arrival, appearing out of nowhere. Her reasons are unknown, but the tragic result of her actions is clear: Immanuel dies, and the woodland machines are left with no hope for the future and no reason to live.

A few scenes later, during the encounter with the factory sect, *NieR: Automata* uses the same trick to overthrow the theory of one of the first existentialist philosophers: Søren Kierkegaard. Kierkegaard, also the name of the cult leader that 2B faces, dedicated his work to questioning human existence. The main element of his approach must be taken into account when interpreting the factory segment. Man's balance, the meaning of life, lies in a strong faith in God, an inner faith that transcends reason. However, he does not deny the latter, nor the freedom of choice and the quest for truth it allows. He instead identifies different stages of existence, including the ultimate stage—the religious stage—which remains the only one capable of curing the despair that takes hold of men, torn apart by their fundamental contradictions, defined both in their necessity and in their potentiality. Thus: "The believer possesses the ever-sure antidote to despair: possibility, since for God everything is possible at every moment. This is the health of faith which resolves contradictions." For him, the capacity to believe, the "leap of faith" which allows existence to be reconciled with itself, consists in losing one's mind—abandoning reason—in order to find God. The extent to which this reasoning is applied with fierce irony to the religious machines is clear: when 2B arrives at the factory, they suddenly lose their minds and proclaim in unison: "We shall become gods," while they begin a massacre around her, in the hope of also being slain. Some simply commit suicide by throwing themselves into the lava.

Naturally, Kierkegaard never states that to find God, one must die, nor even that man can become God. Nevertheless, neither does *NieR: Automata* seek to completely adhere to the existentialist theories of the authors it draws

---

127. It is worth noting here that Kant's humanism inspired the existentialist movement, since his philosophy, which aims to free us from our desires through moral law, is partly a philosophy of emancipation.

its inspiration from. It takes stock, tackles a part and then plays with it, simultaneously trying to subvert it and consider its implications on the game's characters.

Kierkegaard is an action theory philosopher, in the sense that he rejects pure speculative philosophy and dedicates himself to developing a theory that can result in transformations in human life. In this case, *NieR: Automata* seems to ask itself: if he abandons reason for a spiritual faith entirely devoted to God, can the transformed man truly avoid fanaticism? In other words, this is *NieR*'s point in question: solving contradictions, erasing doubt, through faith, God, or anything else, does this not open the way to dangerous certainties that lead to extreme behaviors?

What is also interesting in this factory sequence, and which, in the same dialectical dynamic between existence and essence, this time refers to both the identity and the group, is that the sect is split in two: the machines that have lost their minds, and those that have remained sane. The former seeks to kill the latter, but not only–"Machines! Living beings! Androids! All shall become gods!" one shouted. The latter, obeying a pacifist principle ("May hardship and conflict be forever banned from this world," one of them says), not only fear their fellow machines, but also the android 2B who is slaying them. Thus, through the complex division of the various "we" it depicts–the universal "we" of the death of fanatics, the pacifist "we" of sane religious machines, the "we" of androids opposed to machines–this section provides a good illustration of how ideals segment identities and create conflicting relationships according to group affiliation. The confrontation at the heart of the tower between A2 and the red girls, called N2, extends this reasoning about division and conflict a little further, and attempts to combine it with existentialist intuitions about the self.

"Self-consciousness is the only mode of existence which is possible for a consciousness of something," wrote Sartre in *Being and Nothingness*. But what happens when consciousness becomes aware of its existence more than once? During the confrontation against N2, Pod 042 realizes that the enemy's multiplication of self will fracture its ego and open the way to victory. Thus, A2 puts away her sword and lets her enemy endlessly duplicate itself.

When its consciousness is eventually divided, two opposed groups emerge: those who want to kill A2 to preserve the survival of the species, and those who prefer to leave her alive so that she will complicate the machines' lives and promote their evolutionary process. This antagonism reflects the existentialist intuition according to which man is a synthesis, a dialectic, or even a tension between two poles: death and possibility, or annihilation and eternity. At the same time, the proliferation of N2 has made it "aware of the diversity of life." Since N2 is a synthetic concept born from a vast network of machines and human data, it actually becomes aware of the universe of possibilities contained within it and expressed through it. In short, N2 has become aware of the diversity within itself. Consequently, its division highlights the fact that between the poles of death and possibility, the ego manifests itself in a multiplicity of "I." These "I" are actually just as many "we" here, since N2 encompasses all the machine communities that the game has disseminated throughout the adventure. It is indeed known that in order to avoid extinction and ensure their evolution, machines tried to replicate human social structures and patterns. The N2 concept thus incorporates this collective diversity, which is none other than that of human societies reproduced by machines. It thus embodies an ultimate "meta-we," an existential "I" of the community "we." The N2s' fight to death against themselves thus reveals, as A2 suggests by observing that they "act like humans," the propensity of the "we," of our collective identities, to enter into conflict with each other. And since N2 exists on two levels, the "I" and the "we," the individual and the community, it is clear that the internal discord generated external conflicts. This is the link that *NieR: Automata* seems to want to establish, the one connecting our personal identity conflicts, our struggle to give meaning to our "I" and to the perpetual wars. Because it always seems necessary to justify our identity against something—against machines, against androids, but also against circumstances—we are thus doomed to fight to legitimize our lives. Even Pascal, a fierce pacifist, must take up arms to preserve his purpose in life. In short, human quarrels are nothing more than disagreements about the meaning of life. But when meaning completely vanishes, absurdity takes over.

The loss of meaning and the awakening of absurdity

NieR: Automata focuses successively on two main axes. On one hand, that which has just been described, which examines the meaning of existence through its positivity, its presence, whether it is innate or acquired for the characters, defined either by contingencies or freely chosen beliefs. This is the identity axis, which tries to determine what defines us. And on the other hand, there is the one we will now further develop, which is symmetrically opposed to its neighbor, since it focuses on the negation of meaning, or at least the absence of it due to the loss of identity. This is the absurdity axis, which scrutinizes our inability to find a purpose in this world, to give meaning to existence. The disappearance of meaning leads to the awakening of absurdity.

The leap from the identity axis to the absurdity axis manifests itself very clearly in the outcome of Pascal's story. To defend the village children who have taken refuge in the factory, namely to preserve his purpose, Pascal abandons his non-violence ideal and takes control of a Goliath to fight an armada of violent machines. When he returns to the room where the children are hidden, he is no longer the same. Part of the principles he fought to defend died on the battlefield. Nevertheless, it is the children's suicide that truly destroys him[128]. The meaning of his existence disappears at the same time as the last survivors of his pacifist utopia. Pascal lived through others, and therefore no longer lives at that moment, or more precisely "could no longer live." In his opinion, the children's death has no meaning, no logic with respect to what he intended to accomplish by teaching them emotions: preparing them for their future. The result is the exact opposite. At that very moment, he becomes aware of the absurdity, as defined by Albert Camus in *The Myth of Sisyphus*: the encounter between the human aspiration for clarity and rationality and a profoundly irrational world ("unfair and illogical" Yoko explained when he spoke of his game), "This divorce between man and his life, the actor and his setting." Thus absurdity, Camus argues, raises the only truly serious philosophical issue: suicide. Aware of the certainty of death and of the meaninglessness of existence as such, since man cannot use his reason[129] to draw meaning from a world which is impervious to reasoning, should we not irremediably come to the conclusion of suicide? "Suicide is a solution to the absurd," Camus wrote. Pascal makes this choice and asks A2 to either erase his memory or kill him, two equivalent methods which amount to assisted suicide. The symbolic here is powerful: the most rational and intelligent character in the game has been defeated by the world's madness. Nevertheless, there is a third option, which is not suggested. To condemn Pascal to an eternity of absurdity by leaving the room, without fulfilling his request.

This seemingly anecdotal ploy actually underlines the player's dominant influence in exposing or imposing absurdity. The more he uses his free will to deviate from the path, the more absurdity will spread and surround him like quicksand. Mentioning the "joke endings" is enough to be convinced, these unorthodox endings are the result of an action of the player which is considered unconventional (leaving an area at a given moment, using a certain object, etc.). By blocking the player with these arbitrary and incongruous barriers, *NieR: Automata* breaks the coherence of its world, placing it beyond the reach of any

---

128. "I taught them fear," he says. It is worth noting that the philosopher Blaise Pascal, after whom Pascal is named, is known for his *Thoughts*, the aim of which is to persuade the reader to turn to God by convincing him of the failings of human life: "The greatness of man is great in that he knows himself to be wretched." By teaching them fear, Pascal had not foreseen that the children would succumb to it.
129. "To an absurd mind reason is useless and there is nothing beyond reason," Camus wrote.

reason. Thus, with a delirious total of twenty-one, these endings (which for the most part lack substance or logic) lose the player and entrap him in a cage of incomprehension. How many were indeed surprised by the credits which were reached too quickly and which brought them back to their last save, two hours earlier? How many have asked themselves: "Why?" Why: because of absurdity. Because the game world much like ours does not make any sense and the player's as well as man's logic are both pointless. We believe we have a goal: reaching the end of the adventure; but the game slips away, refusing to be captured and labeled. It pushes us back to absurdity, to our helplessness. It is during these moments that all the reflexive genius of *NieR: Automata* unfolds: it is not only spouting its intention in its narrative, but is also illustrating it with a variation of its mechanics which directly appeal to the player. As with the previous opus, Yoko blends the entertaining with the thematic in the game, through a clever ironic discourse about video games. So let's continue the demonstration with yet another example: the side quests.

By definition, side quests are optional and not the main focus of video games. To accomplish them, the player must deviate from the main path, and exercise his freedom as an actor within an entertaining life. Traditionally, side quests are therefore emancipatory for the player, who is rewarded for his curiosity and the exercise of his autonomy. They also give meaning to the explored world by enriching its background. In short, side quests, in theory, create foundations and encourage, but also reward, in a sense, the player's inclination to use his independence in order to understand the world in which he finds himself[130]. There is none of this in *NieR: Automata*, since the player's desire to apprehend his environment through quests is most of the time welcomed by a torrent of absurdity. A small anthology of these fables without any other moral than nonsense:

- The young recluse machine which repeatedly double-locks itself in its house, because it fails to exist in the outside world, and thus seeks to create the strongest lock in the world—which 9S keeps breaking.

- An amnesic android gradually remembers her dead friend, but finally discovers through 2B and 9S that it is she who had killed him under her hierarchy's orders, and that she had erased her memory in order to expurgate this crime and this break.

- A fugitive android couple tries to escape from the members of the resistance who are hunting them down to punish them for treason. After several adventures that opened their eyes to the dangers of life as exiles, they choose

---

130. A vision truly embodied by the *Mass Effect* or *The Elder Scrolls* series in the West, or to a lesser extent by *Xenoblade Chronicles* in Japan.

to sacrifice their love and reset their consciousness to become normal members of the resistance again. Once the male android's memories have been destroyed, the female android refuses to follow the same process, and admits that the whole story was in fact a ploy she had devised to try and shape her partner's personality according to her personal tastes. He is by then on his sixth reset.

• And finally, the one that unambiguously conveys the concept of absurdity: three machines silently contemplating the emptiness of existence. Why were they born? How does one exist? They are suffering because they cannot find any meaning in their own lives–their reason is useless. Later, once they have realized that their nature has trapped them in a cursed cycle of birth and resurrection, they decide that they do not need this world and leap to their death.

It is obvious: almost all of the player's optional attempts to probe the world culminate in a dead end, a meaningless story. Worse still, sometimes the player himself imposes absurdity on the NPCs by depriving them of their purpose–and condemns them to suicide. Servo's quest comes to mind, the karateka machine who lives only to become more powerful, but whom 2B and 9S constantly defeat. But also the super-fast machine, which only aspires to be... the fastest, and which 2B surpasses three times. In both cases, the player's obstinacy to dominate his opponent–although he is not obliged to–deprives the machines of the meaning of their existence. Which, overwhelmed by absurdity, then choose to die.

A last illustration of the absurdist trajectory is evidently found in 9S's journey. Again, the player is mechanically facing absurdity, but let's first try to figure out how 9S sinks into absurdity on the narrative level. Two main elements characterize 9S in the first part of the game: as a YoRHa unit, his passion for humanity, and as an individual, his attachment to 2B, which are expressed both through love and hate. 9S loses these two things in quick succession, first by discovering the truth about the YoRHa units, then by witnessing 2B being–permanently–killed by A2. From then on, the motives which animate his existence are stripped of their substance, of the reality they depicted. Yet 9S does not abandon his feelings, as his altercation with the false 2Bs in the tower demonstrates. But his reason is unable to connect them to the world in which he now finds himself. He is in the heart of absurdity, incapable of reconciling the world's irrationality with his ability to think. Thus what appears to be a vendetta against the machines and A2 quickly turns into a purely suicidal spiral of violence. It therefore quite fittingly ends during the final battle with his accidental suicide as he stumbles and impales himself on his opponent's blade. This concludes the storyline. But, from the player's perspective, what naturally most characterizes 9S is his hacking ability. It proves to be fundamental in 9S's absurdist career, since it conveys the world's irrational nature and allows the player to experience it.

Hacking is a special feature of *NieR: Automata*. It can infiltrate everything, objects, androids, machines, computer networks, and so forth. Most importantly, it possesses a transformative value: it takes something and changes our point of view on it by modifying its existence, on a different level, by transferring it to its own very particular and different world. "A world that can be explained even with bad reasons is a familiar world. But, on the other hand, in a universe suddenly divested of illusions and lights, man feels an alien, a stranger," argued Camus. In other words, it is only once it has rid itself of its common artifices and its illusory romanticism that the world reveals itself as it is: strange and inhuman. "At the heart of all beauty lies something inhuman, and these hills, the softness of the sky, the outline of these trees at this very minute lose the illusory meaning with which we had clothed them, henceforth more remote than a lost paradise. [...] The world evades us because it becomes itself again. That stage scenery masked by habit becomes again what it is. It withdraws at a distance from us." While *NieR: Automata*'s "normal" world represents this familiar world, that of the "softness of the sky" and the "outline of trees," the hacking environment symbolizes this strange and distant world. The minimalist aesthetics, with little texture and based on simple shapes (circles, squares, triangles) give the impression of a bare world, reduced to a primary state of truth, almost conceptual. Its roads, branches and blocks have no meaning, and do not provide any insight into existence. This world cannot be humanely apprehended and interpreted—there is no sense of belonging. Naturally, the player gives it a function, that of hacking, but it only creates the necessary distance for the world to become itself again, impervious to our beliefs. Indeed, it is through hacking that the whole truth about Project YoRHa is discovered, through hacking that the unsuspected consciousness of machines is gradually revealed (Simone, Eve, suicidal machines, etc.), through hacking again that 2B's real name is unveiled, and finally through hacking that the player can become someone else by controlling a machine and thus experiencing the strangeness of alterity. In short, it is through hacking that the world collapses, reconfigures itself and distances itself, that it once again becomes such as it is, empty, true and indifferent to reason, that it gains that "density and strangeness" called absurdity.

Rebellion

But absurdity is not necessarily a bad thing. So far, the main focus has been on how *NieR: Automata* links it with despair and suicide. However, it is also turned into a fertile tool, literally. This is in reference to the desert machines which, recognizing the absurdity of their attempts at procreation, experience a surge of pride ("This cannot continue") and give birth to Adam. Absurdity does not only entail death, but also life. Camus's theses are once again alluded to. The writer rejected suicide as a valid solution to absurdity, since it removes one of the parts composing the equation: man. For the philosopher, absurdity must in reality be perceived and experienced as a passion, "the most harrowing of all." Since knowing that there is no eternity, no greater sense beyond reason, frees the man who no longer believes in fake futures and illusions. He is therefore free to experience the world in all its irrationality, without remorse. Moreover, the life of the man who acknowledged the limits of his understanding would no longer be anything more than excitement and rage, for he knows that he cannot have a better life, but only a longer life. "It was previously a question of finding out whether or not life had to have meaning to be lived. It now becomes clear, on the contrary, that it will be lived all the better if it has no meaning." wrote Camus.

So even if, like humans, the machines and androids constantly reiterate their mistakes and perpetually repeat the same cycle of life and death, without ever reaching a clear goal, is their life not worth living for what it is, to its fullest? Taro Yoko has explained: "To me, even if you fail every single time but you still repeat yourself... I don't think there needs to be a kind of 'final answer' to everything we do. Just to give an example, if someone were to climb a mountain, and they were to fail—along the way, they're still having the experience of climbing that particular mountain, and I think there is some meaning from that experience[131]." This is a nod, perhaps unintentional, from the director to The Myth of Sisyphus used by Camus to illustrate the bliss of the absurd man.

Condemned by the gods to eternally push a boulder up a mountain only to see it roll down again each time, Sisyphus embodied the archetype of the absurd man. But Camus does not regard him as a man afflicted by his meaningless task, since "The struggle itself towards the heights is enough to fill a man's heart. One must imagine Sisyphus happy." In the same way, must we not regard the machines and androids as being happy? Must we not, like 2B who repeatedly killed 9S,

---

131. http://wegotthiscovered.com/gaming/interview-yoko-taro-nier-automata/3/

yet felt joy in his company despite the inevitable, turn towards absurdity so that the struggle may fill our hearts? According to *NieR: Automata*, we must–because rebellion is the only way to give real meaning to our existence.

The player is once again transformed into a small white triangle. This is ending E. A2, 2B, 9S and all YoRHa units are dead. Yet the pods survived. They contest their objective which consists in permanently erasing the data from Project YoRHa. Throughout this adventure, they had become attached to their comrades and were reluctant to see them disappear. Their purpose no longer makes any sense to them. The situation is absurd. What to do? *Act.* But how? Man, *the player*, must act. He must initiate the movement, rebel, overthrow the system, and break the chains to seek hope. The player's rebellion against the game symbolizes man's insurrection against the criteria of his fake existence. He annihilates Square Enix, PlatinumGames and their developers as he escapes from all the gods, progenitors and creators who deluded him with their illusions of the absolute, as 2B desired in the introduction. In ending E, it is the player, mankind (as one) who say no. No, I will not give up. No, I do not accept defeat. No, not everything is insignificant. No, games are not trivial little things. No. Man is not tantamount to renouncement, but is made for action and undertaking. It is therefore, at the same time, mankind asserting himself, saying yes to the uprising, fully declaring his existence, because "In order to exist, man must rebel," theorized Camus in *The Rebel*. Rebellion is the only way to live absurdity, the one thing that gives meaning to the world and to existence, the one thing that creates man in the present moment, the one that gives birth to "that strange joy which helps one live and die." We are aware of our destiny, but we have to face it to become its master. The player thus makes his way through the hellish rain of bullets, shoots, pulverizes, dies and restarts. And restarts again and again. Until the obvious saves him and paves the way to his freedom: "I rebel– therefore we exist." Players' ships scattered all over the world join our own, and their combined power tears the game system apart. Rebellion is a collective aspiration, "the adventure of all." It extracts man from his solitude and unites him with his fellow men, caught up in the same existential torment, struck by the same sense of absurdity. The player-men who awaken to the absurdity of the world and the game rise together in a vibrant and entertaining wave to rebel against death, against illusions, against nihilism, for both hope and freedom. Thus with the erasure of the save following ending E, *NieR: Automata* does not end in disappearance like *NieR*, but with sacrifice in the name of rebellion, an emancipatory movement which epitomizes the promise of a fanatical humanism. Finally, the game invites us to write a message for our anonymous comrades, a message in a bottle that they will see during their fight against the credits. The player is perfectly free to write a nasty remark. But in reality, virtually all of these missives are encouragements or expressions of solidarity. Stunned by emotion, glad to have been guided by a light shining in the darkness of absurdity, the players also choose to light a beacon in the night. *NieR: Automata* is not a blind advocate of humanity. It allows free men and women to demonstrate that they can rise above the fray.

"They kept fighting because they believed they could overcome someday! Even if it's pointless, you still have to do it! Because this is the world my friend tried to save!"
– Emil

CONCLUSION

Alterity of video games

Through the rebellion caused by *NieR: Automata*'s ending E, Taro Yoko finally develops an exit strategy for the stalemates of his obsessions. It helps to overcome *Drakengard*'s atrocious violence by redirecting it against the system. It resolves the conflicts generated by the division of points of view in *NieR*, since it imposes itself as the only valid certainty, as the first truth of the being, the one that unites men within a universal movement. And finally, it cancels out the nihilism caused by mortality in *Drakengard 3*, since it recognizes the ineluctable end of life and challenges it in the same impulse—in this way actually giving meaning to existence. Furthermore, for Yoko, ending E symbolizes a form of achievement, his "Rosebud[132] " in a way, since it confirms his lifelong intuition that some things can only exist in video games. Since *Drakengard*, the director has never stopped harnessing this feeling which led him to become a developer, the one that convinced him from an early age that video games were a unique and different medium. Like an explorer, he had to embark on an adventure to unveil this alterity and show it to the world. It could be said that this has been achieved through *NieR: Automata*, and with great panache given that the entire game prepares us for this unique conclusion that is unlike anything else. One could also say that the game fulfills the rescue mission that Yoko had assigned to himself: the world seldom never appeared so close to its salvation than when the choir of the final song *The Weight of the World* joins our collective and ardent progress towards a new hope. One might therefore think that there is nothing more to say, given that this ending E, in fifteen minutes of suffering, doubt, despair, bravery, solidarity and beauty, seems

---

132. The famous word pronounced by media mogul Charles Foster Kane just before his death in Orson Welles's movie *Citizen Kane* (1941), and which triggered a broad investigation to discover its meaning. The movie's ending reveals that it was Kane's childhood sled. By analogy, the word is used to indicate the key element of a person's life, or that person's most precious possession.

to exhaust the subject of what video games can achieve. However, this would be an abrupt conclusion to the story after this first victorious battle.

Taro Yoko is clearly nearing his fifties, but we get the feeling that he still has more to say, that he has only just begun unleashing the full potential of his strokes of entertainment genius, finally entrusted to high quality creators such as PlatinumGames. And with the successful game designer reputation he has recently acquired thanks to *NieR: Automata*'s sales, it is very likely that, if politely asked, Square Enix' executives would agree to provide him once again with the means to achieve his ambitions, and maybe a little more. The only obstacle on Yoko's path actually seems to be... himself.

After *NieR: Automata*'s release, he explained in an interview with *Rolling Stone* magazine: "When I was young, I had one wish from the bottom of my heart: 'I wish all the useless and controlling elders of the gaming industry would die so I can create a game that I like!' Now that I have fulfilled my dream to 'create a game that I like,' there's not much left for me to do. However, because I don't have much else to do now, I am clinging onto my job as a game director. In a way, I'm just living out of habit now. And now, I have become that troublesome elder that I hated when I was young. Like a demon king in an RPG, I feel like I'm clinging to my castle of authority all alone and waiting for a new hero to come slay me." And thus continues the eternal cycle of life and death. Hopefully, Taro Yoko will fight a little longer in the industry before passing the baton, and sacrificing his save.

ƎƧ⩜ѹѹƧ⌇

BIBLIOGRAPHY

Video Games

YOKO Taro. (director), Cavia, *Drakengard* [PlayStation 2], Square Enix, 2004.

YOKO Taro. (director), Cavia, *NieR* [PlayStation 3, Xbox 360], Square Enix, 2010.

YOKO Taro. (director), Access Games, *Drakengard 3* [PlayStation 3], Square Enix, 2014.

YOKO Taro. (director), PlatinumGames, *NieR: Automata* [PlayStation 4], Square Enix, 2017.

Online articles and websites

ALEXIEL Rekka. (*Fire Sanctuary*), ''An Interview with Yoko Taro by 4Gamer'', February 28 2014: http://nier2.com/blog/2014/02/28/an-interview-with-yoko-taro-by-4gamer/.

ALEXIEL Rekka. (*Fire Sanctuary*), ''Yoko Taro's 'Bad Thought Process' '' (1 of 4), January 10 2014: http://nier2.com/blog/2014/01/10/yoko-taros-bad-thought-process-1-of-4/.

GIFFORD Kevin. (*Polygon*), ''*Drakengard 3* will not'feel much like a Square Enix' release, if music department has its way'', July 17 2013: https://www.polygon.com/2013/7/17/4530966/abot-drakengard-3-and-making-the-music-for-a-very-strange-game.

GIRARD-MELI Jowi. (*We Got This Covered*), "Yoko Taro On Machine Empathy And Butts In *Nier: Automata*", March 2017: http://wegotthiscovered. com/gaming/interview-yoko-taro-nier-automata/3/.

IGN STAFF (IGN), Square and Enix Merge, November 25 2002: https://web.archive.org/web/20120517102726/http://ps2.ign.com/ articles/378/378635p1.html.

J.F. (*Dixiemeart*), "Emi Evans, la voix de *NieR*", June 8 2010: https://web.archive.org/web/20100709014743/http://www.dixieme-art. com:80/2010/06/08/emi-evans-la-voix-de-nier/.

DEFADE, DABUBBA, GISAELLE, RAIZINMONK, SUNZI (*Google Docs*), "traduction du *Grimoire NieR*", 2010-2017: https://docs.google.com/ document/d/1vEP2iZ52P-DWhQBQ2Is6R8Wjao99AGi0YuWShTvA-tA/ mobilebasic?viewopt=127#h.10b541c47d56.

KLEPEK Patrick. (*Waypoint*), "Does the Designer Behind *NieR: Automata* Believe in God?", June 5 2017: https://waypoint.vice.com/en_us/article/ xw8xzd/does-the-designer-behind-nier-automata-believe-in-god.

LEO John. (*Gamespot*), "Sound Byte: Meet the Composer – *NieR*", August 24 2012: https://www.gamespot.com/articles/sound-byte-meet-the-composer- NieR/1100-6393188/.

NAPOLITANO Jayson. (*Original Sound Version*), "Deep into *NieR*: Interview With Vocalist and Lyricist Emi Evans", May 4 2010: http://www.originalsoundversion.com/deep-into-NieR-interview-with-vocalist- and-lyricist-emi-evans/.

NIIZUMI Hirohiko. (*Gamespot*), "Sammy reveals new logo, changes at SEGA", June 1 2004: https://www.gamespot.com/articles/sammy-reveals- new-logo-changes-at-sega/1100-6099624/.

RAY CORRIEA Alexa. (*Gamespot*), "New *NieR* Will Stay Weird, But This Time With Platinum's Combat", June 16 2015: https://www.gamespot.com/ articles/new-nier-will-stay-weird-but-this-time-with-platin/1100-6428262/.

SCHWEITZER Ben. (*Square Enix Music*), "*Drag-on Dragoon* Original Soundtrack : Liner Notes Translated by Ben Schweitzer", February 2013: https://web.archive.org/web/20140222144620/http://www.squareenixmusic.com/features/liners/Drakengard.shtml.

SHIBA Takamasa. (*YouTube*), "Interview with Producer Takamasa Shiba | *Drakengard 3*", March 4 2014: https://www.youtube.com/watch?v=D5Q7J7rHts0.

SUELLENTROP Chris. (*Rolling Stone*), "Nintendo Dev On Working With Kojima, '*Splatoon 2*', Rise of Japanese Games," September 2017: http://www.rollingstone.com/glixel/features/splatoon-2-hideo-kojima-nintendo-japanese-games-w501322.

SUMMERS Nick. (*Engadget*), "How '*NieR*' was brought back from the dead", February 13 2017: https://www.engadget.com/2017/02/13/how-nier-was-brought-back-from-the-dead/.

UEDA Masami. (*PlatinumGames Official Blog*), "Happy Hacking : Music implementation in *NieR : Automata*", July 31 2017: https://www.platinumgames.com/official-blog/article/9581.

VANORD Kevin. (*Gamespot*), *NieR* Review, May 3 2010: https://www.gamespot.com/reviews/nier-review/1900-6260971/.

WALDEN Matthew. (*Rolling Stone*), "*NieR: Automata* Director Taro Yoko Doesn't Envision a Happy Ending for Humanity", March 17 2017: http://www.rollingstone.com/glixel/interviews/qa-nier-automata-director-taro-yoko-w472664.

WELSH Oli. (*Gamesindustry.biz*), Square Dance, June 15 2008: http://www.gamesindustry.biz/articles/square-dance.

YOON Andrew. (*Shacknews*), "*Drakengard 3* trying to avoid 'formulaic' J-RPG tropes with its dark setting", October 14 2013: http://www.shacknews.com/article/81558/drakengard-3-trying-to-avoid-formulaic-jrpg-tropes-with-its.

Books

CAMUS Albert, *The Rebel*, Paris, Harmondsworth, "Penguin Modern Classics", 1971, 269 p.

CAMUS Albert, *The Myth of Sisyphus*, New York, Vintage Books, "A Vintage book", 1955, 151 p.

FREUD Sigmund, *Beyond the Pleasure Principle*, New York, Norton, "The Norton library", 1959, 68 p.

FREUD Singmund, *Civilization and Its Discontents*, London, Penguin, "Penguin Modern Classics", 2002, 144 p.

JUN Eishima. *Drag-On Dragoon 3 Story Side*, Japon, Square Enix, 2014, 255 p.

JUN Eishima. *NieR:Automata Novel*, Japon, Square Enix, 2017, 318 p.

KANT Immanuel. *Critique of Pure Reason*, United States, Cambridge University Press, "The Cambridge Edition of the Works of Immanuel Kant", 1999, 796 p.

KIERKEGAARD Søren. *The Essential Kierkegaard*, United States, Princeton University Press, "Kierkegaard's Writings", 2000, 536 p.

SARTRE Jean-Paul. *Being and Nothingness*, United States, Washington Square Press, 1993, 864 p.

SARTRE Jean-Paul. *Existentialism Is a Humanism*, United States, Yale University Press, 2007, 108 p.

SQUARE ENIX, *Drag-on Dragoon Official Guide Book*, Japon, Square Enix, 190p.

SQUARE ENIX, *Drag-on Dragoon 10th Anniversary – World Inside – Book*, Japon, Square Enix, 2013.

SQUARE ENIX, *Drag-on Dragoon 3 Official Complete Guide Book*, Japon, Kadokawa, April 2014, 255 p.

SQUARE ENIX, *Grimoire NieR*, Japon, ASCII Media Works, 2010, 224 p.

SQUARE ENIX, *NieR:Automata Strategy Guide*, Japon, Kadokawa, 2017, 304 p.

SQUARE ENIX, *NieR:Automata World Guide*, Japon, Square Enix, 2017, 190 p.

Magazines

ANONYME (2017), ''Machine Learning», *Edge*, January, pp. 56-67.

TURCEV Nicolas. (2015), ''Le maître des marionnettes : interview de Taro Yoko", *Games*, Septembre-Novembre, pp. 45-47.

ᑌᒣᐃᒣᒣ

AUTHOR'S ACKNOWLEDGMENTS

❀ To Mehdi and Damien for their kindness.

❀ To Taro Yoko for his availability and for writing the foreword.

❀ To the incredible community of Taro Yoko's game fans for their countless translations and thoughts: Rekka Alexiel, but also all those who contributed to the various wikis.

❀ To those who gave me a chance: Mateo, Martin, Jérôme, Thomas...

❀ And above all, to my friends, from the bottom of my heart: Anthony, Marie, Noémie, Marie-Caroline, Thomas, Rémi, Mathilde, Aurore, Alix...

ｉＡＤ Ｙ